THE GERMANS
IN
COLONIAL TIMES

BY LUCY FORNEY BITTINGER

AUTHOR OF "MEMORIALS OF THE REV. J. B.
BITTINGER" AND OF "THE FORNEY
FAMILY OF HANOVER, PA."

PHILADELPHIA AND LONDON
J. B. LIPPINCOTT COMPANY
1901

Lucy Forney Bittinger
1901

Facsimile Reprint
Published 1986, 1993, 1998

HERITAGE BOOKS, INC.
1540E Pointer Ridge Place
Bowie, Maryland 20716
1-800-398-7709

ISBN 0-917890-90-6

A HERITAGE CLASSIC

FOREWORD

SINGULARLY little is known of the magnitude of the German emigration to America in colonial times. The very fact of such a movement is commonly unknown to the American at the present day; and even the descendants of these Teutonic pioneers are often ignorant or—more inexcusably—ashamed of their progenitors, and have sought by anglicizing their names and lightly passing over the fact of their descent from "Dutchmen" to conceal the wide and deep traces which this movement has left on American life. Yet this Völkerwanderung (for it merits the name) brought to our shores in the century before the Revolution one hundred and fifty thousand people, one-half of the population of the great province of Pennsylvania, besides large settlements in the provinces of New York, the Carolinas, Virginia, Maryland, Georgia, not to mention the small and ill-fated colonies of Law on the Mississippi and those in the State of Maine. Nor is their history lacking in interest, containing as it does the peaceful picture which Whittier has immortalized in his "Pennsylvania Pilgrim;" the self-sacrifice of the Moravian missionaries among the Indians; the dramatic fire of Muhlenberg throwing off his pastor's gown for a Continental uniform and calling to his flock that "the time to fight had come;" and the tragic resolution with which the embattled farmers of Oriskany held back, with the sacrifice of their own lives, the English rifle and Indian scalping-knife from their Mohawk Valley homes. Or we may turn to the quaint Rosicrucians, the hermits of the Wissahickon, or the cloisters of Ephrata for a life almost unknown among the more practical English colonists.

If we would sup full of the horrors of war, pestilence and famine, or religious persecution with stake and fire and noisome prison, with midnight flight for conscience' sake, we can find these told in simple pathos in the stories of the Palatines of the Rhine, the Mennonites of Switzerland, the Moravians, or the tiny sect of the Schwenkfelders. If we would meet with good men or great, we may see here the gentle Pastorius, first protestant against American slavery, or Conrad Weiser, whose adventurous life was largely filled with embassies to mighty Indian chiefs and nations, whom he held back from war from the white men's frontier, or, last but not least, William Penn, whose mighty figure dominates the history as its counterfeit presentment does the city he has builded beside the Delaware. And indeed "time would fail us to tell" of the many people and incidents, interesting, pathetic, humorous, or containing in them the germs of our present American development, which fill the annals of those "Pennsylvania Germans" and their kin in many States, whom the New England historian, Parkman, slurred over with the description, "dull and ignorant boors, which character their descendants for the most part retain."

How many even of these same descendants know that to this people belong, by ancestry more · or less remote, some of the first scientific men of America, such as the Muhlenbergs, Melsheimer, the "father of

Foreword

American entomology," Leidy, and Gross, the great surgeon ; Herkimer, the hero of Oriskany ; " Moll Pitcher," the heroine of Monmouth ; Post, the Indian missionary, to whom Parkman himself pays a noble tribute ; Heckewelder, the Moravian lexicographer of the speech of the Delawares ; Armistead, the defender of Fort McHenry in the war of 1812, whose flag, "still there," inspired the "Star-Spangled Banner ;" Barbara Frietchie ; and General Custer? Surely this people merit that some slight account be drawn from the mostly unknown books and documents where they have for years reposed, known only to antiquarians and often veiled from English readers by the German language in which many of the best and most valuable are written, and be given to the English-speaking world of America. Such is the purpose of the present work.

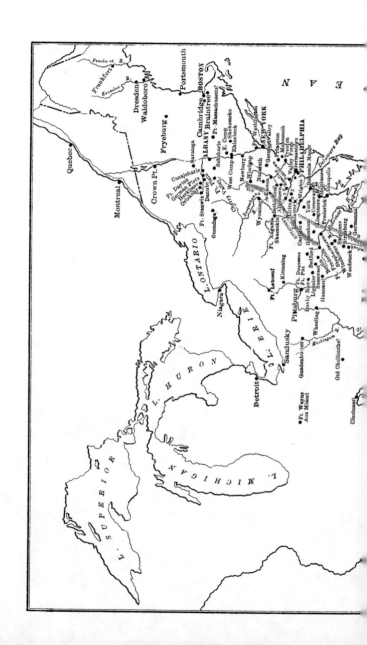

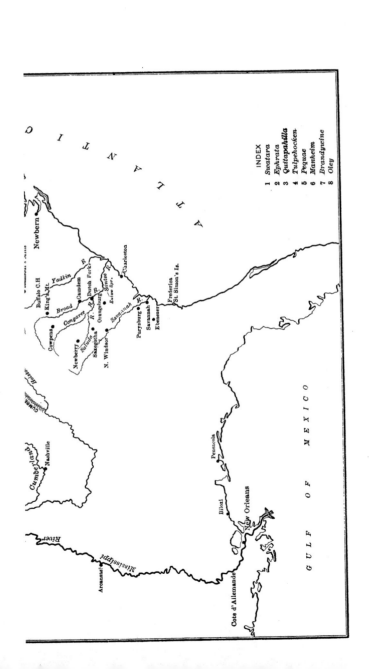

CONTENTS

THE GERMANS IN COLONIAL TIMES

❧❧

CHAPTER I

CONDITIONS IN GERMANY WHICH LED TO EMIGRATION

THE large emigration of Germans to America and especially to Pennsylvania in colonial times seems on first examination a mysterious phenomenon. The Germans were aliens in language among the mainly English-speaking colonists; were obliged to undertake a long and toilsome journey before reaching the ocean over which they must sail for weeks and months, amidst the greatest hardships and dangers, before they could even attain to their desired haven; their own government, so soon as the size of the movement attracted attention, did all in its power to restrain it, and the English provincial authorities received the foreigners by no means with open arms; yet the cry was still "They come." The well-known energy, resolution, and fondness for emigration characterizing the Germans of earlier times—the merchants of the Hansa, whose flag was on every sea and whose warehouses and trading-posts dotted every land and strand—had been crushed out of the seventeenth-century Germans by the fearful *peine forte et dure* of the Thirty Years' War. So the Americans who saw this tide of strangers rising on their shore were naturally surprised, and the few of their descendants who know the proportions of the early German emigration to America are still astonished at it. But a slight knowledge of the condition of Germany at the time that the emigration took its rise and for some generations previous will explain it.

This movement had a twofold cause : first in point of time as of importance, a religious motive ; and secondly, a social or material one. That the religious was predominant may be seen by the character of the emigration, which at first and for two generations consisted entirely of the sectaries who were persecuted in Germany by state and church. And it may also be proved by the rise and course of the emigration which was begun and fostered by such men as Penn the Quaker and his Mennonite and Pietist friends and religious acquaintances.

The Rhine country, from which such an overwhelming proportion of the colonial German emigrants came that it may be almost exclusively considered, was the home of Mysticism and Pietism, two most elastic designations, which include phenomena as various as the wild and immoral fanaticism of the prophets of Münster and the peaceful purity of Tersteegen and his little circle of pious friends. Mysticism had had its home on the Rhine ever since " Master Eckart" taught a strange mystical pantheism among the Brethren of the Free Spirit, and Tauler and the author of the "Theologia Germanica" preached a self-surrender as complete as that which Loyola exacted from his "Company of Jesus." This mysticism flowered later into the practical endeavors of

Conditions in Germany which led to Emigration

Gerhard Groot and the "Brethren of the Common Life" to instruct youth in their schools, and one of their scholars was that Thomas of Kempen who wrote the "Imitation of Christ," still beloved among us. The final result of this movement was the Reformation.

But the Reformation did not go far enough to satisfy many of the pious souls looking for more or different light than Luther and Zwingli found to break forth from God's word. Nor did it content the longings of many among the Swiss compatriots of Zwingli who felt the danger of his union between church and state or the coldness of his somewhat rationalistic views of the sacraments. So among the many scattered circles who fed their spirits upon the mystical writings of Boehme, Tauler, and Swedenborg, or the hidden people who proudly retained in secret the pure, early Christianity of the Waldenses, lived, amid continual suspicion and persecution, the beliefs which crystallized here and there into "the Sects." These flourished mainly among the lower classes, those who had wished during the Reformation to abolish nobles and kings along with priesthood, and these social and socialistic views naturally made them obnoxious to the authorities. "The persecuted Sects" they were designated, and persecuted they were indeed : unto death by fire and sword and drowning in earlier times; then, as civilization advanced, through imprisonment, harassments by the authorities, and forcible conversions ; and, finally, by all sorts of worrying attacks, such as spared life and limb but left little else. No wonder that as soon as an asylum was provided them, they flocked to it, one little company after another of the sectarians braving the dangers of

the long, trying voyage and the hardships of the unknown wilderness to find the precious jewel of religious
freedom.

In the midst of the religious intolerance and persecutions of the century after the Reformation fell upon
Germany the unimaginable and indescribable horrors of
the Thirty Years' War. It is difficult to call up to one's
mind what this event was. Many portions of Germany
became uninhabited wildernesses ; many of the miserable
people became in the extremity of their distress robbers,
murderers, and even cannibals. The free peasants were
degraded to serfs, the rich and energetic burghers became
narrow-minded shopkeepers, the noblemen servile courtiers, the princes shameless oppressors. Of the rich,
blooming land, full of trade and learning and refinement,
was left a wrecked country, the sites of burnt villages
overgrown by the forests, tiny towns amid the ruin of
their former greatness, and a handful of broken-spirited
people creeping fearfully about the work of earning a
bare existence. It was a full generation after the war
before the exhausted and demoralized nation could stir
itself to an interest in those spiritual things which were
seemingly all that were left to it.

From desolation and barbarism, persecution and oppression on earth, the Germans looked to heaven. The
churches,—and by this I mean the three "tolerated
confessions" (Lutheran, Reformed, and Catholic),—at
least the Protestant churches, had fallen into a state
of formalism and indifference to religious things, while
retaining a vivid and often virulent interest in orthodoxy
and the stiffest scholastic theology. The use of the
sacraments had become in many places a magical cere-

mony. The youth were not instructed, the openly scandalous in life neither admonished nor excluded from the church. Men with none of that preparation of heart which our forefathers quaintly called "experimental religion" were ordained and ministered to congregations, famished for plain teaching of duty, scholastic treatises, or furious polemics against the sins of sectarianism, the dangers of good works, and the wickedness of prayer-meetings. It is not strange that many simple and godly people went off into the extravagances of the various mystical coteries where the Bible was at least studied, and, after a most singular fashion, expounded. The Rhine country was full of little circles of devout, if ignorant, people, who listened to some self-constituted minister,—perhaps a pious and sensible mystic like Tersteegen, perhaps a wild dreamer like the " Inspired Saddler" Rock, a learned lady like Eleanora von Merlau, or an immoral fanatic such as Eva von Buttlar.

But, fortunately for these ofttimes deluded good people, there arose the movement called or nicknamed Pietism, given a direction by the devout, learned, and lovable Spener, whose principle was "that Christianity was first of all life, and that the strongest proof of the truth of its doctrine was to be found in the religious experience of the believing." It embraced among its leaders—along with the fanatical cranks who are the curse of any movement which stirs men's enthusiasm—men like Gottfried Arnold, the church historian, the equally learned Professor Thomasius, the noble and benevolent Francke, the founder of the Orphan House of Halle, and his son, the benefactor and guide of the neglected Lutherans of Pennsylvania. The Pietists struggled not only against the dry and dead theology of the time, but for the purity and simplicity of the German language against the barbarous scholastic German of the time. The whole Pietistic movement was earnestly directed to the betterment of mankind, materially as well as spiritually. It found its field, in contradistinction to the mysticism of the "plain people," among the upper and cultivated classes, and many names of those rich and noble and mighty according to this world adorn its roll. The Pietists stood like the Deists for freedom of thought in religious matters and against the mental oppression which everywhere existed ; both appealed to the New Testament from the decisions of councils which in every case the authorities desired to maintain. The Collegia or conventicles of the Pietists were nothing but simple assemblies as harmless as a Methodist class-meeting, where the members appealed to the Scriptures in the original from the pedantic systems of the theologians. This new school was strong and pure so long as it preached free investigation, liberty of thought and conscience, and rectitude of life. The leaders were noble men and did a noble work, and not the least of their services to humanity was the part which they took in the colonization of the New World, where freedom of conscience existed. It is to the Pietists and their unknown and often unacknowledged brethren, the mystical and persecuted sectaries, that we owe the inception of the early colonial emigration of Germans to Pennsylvania.

The second cause of the colonial German emigration was the social and political condition of Germany, and this may be summed up as deterioration in every way.

Conditions in Germany which led to Emigration

The Rhineland recovered more rapidly from the ravages of the Thirty Years' War than other parts of Germany, but misgovernment and religious intolerance were more severely felt there than in other sections of the country. To the reader of its depressing history it finally becomes a wonder, not that so many of its inhabitants emigrated, but that any one had the courage and the truly German perseverance to remain behind in the miserable land. The rulers sought only their own advantage and pleasure, the prosperity of their subjects was not at all in their thoughts. Wars were almost unceasing : French devastations and "reunions" along the Rhine, wars with the Swedes and Turks, the two dynastic wars named of the Spanish and Austrian successions, the Seven Years' War, and unceasing feuds among the little principalities. "The peasant did not conceive of a time in which there was not war." They must have prayed with a special feeling the pathetic petition of the litany : "Give peace in our time, O Lord : because there is none other that fighteth for us but only Thou, O God." All Southwest Germany was as full of misgovernment as of sectarianism, "filled with tiny principalities, old religious foundations,—secularized or still remaining,—free cities of the moribund empire and even free villages ; counts, princes, and lords of all kinds, who caricatured Louis XIV. sometimes by dozens to the square mile and kept the fruitful land in an artificial condition of perpetual exhaustior.."

This unhappy section of Germany included first in an unfortunate pre-eminence the Rheinpfalz or Rhenish Palatinate ; Swabia, Würtemberg, Silesia, and the many little principalities between Bavaria and Austria. The Rhenish Palatinate was a model of these badly ruled and plundered principalities, and so many of its inhabitants fled that in America all German immigrants were called Palatines, and we even encounter in colonial records that nondescript "A Palatine from Holsteyn." When, after the Thirty Years' War, the elector Karl Ludwig returned to his desolated dominions, he found but a fiftieth part of the inhabitants remaining, and all his efforts (for he was a good ruler taught in the hard school of personal adversity) to restore prosperity were frustrated by the continual wars of his time. In 1668 was war with the neighboring Duke of Lorraine; in 1673 the invasions of the Most Christian King, Louis XIV., began without declaration of war or any excuse save that he desired a desert made to protect his frontier. In the intervals of peace were carried on the shameless reunions by which territory was taken for France on the flimsiest pretexts of law. During the various campaigns, Mannheim and Heidelberg were burnt; two separate efforts, four years apart, were necessary to destroy the strong and beautiful castle, to-day "majestic though in ruin;" at Speyer the graves of the old Kaisers were broken open and their dust scattered by the French soldiers. Worms was burnt "on Whit-Tuesday," the French military bands playing dance-music while the city and its old cathedral were reduced to ashes. From this destruction Worms and Speyer have never recovered, and traces of the work of Louis's robber bands are still apparent; all the villages and towns between Heilbronn and the Lower Rhine are new, with no remains left of their historic past.

To these outward afflictions of the Palatinate was now added religious intolerance. The succeeding elector, Johann Wilhelm, was a Catholic, and endeavored by taking advantage of the differences between the Lutherans and the Reformed to make the whole land of his own faith. Under his orders children were taken from their parents to be brought up Catholics. In some cases his Protestant subjects were driven away, sometimes their churches taken from them by force, or they were forcibly converted under pain of fines impossible to pay. In some places they were hunted into church by soldiers and the host crammed into their mouths. The Huguenots and Waldenses who had been invited by Karl Ludwig to take asylum in the Palatinate after the revocation of the Edict of Nantes were turned out and went with other Palatines to America. The Reformed were made incapable of holding civil office, the stipends were withdrawn from preachers and teachers, and, following the illustrious example of Louis XIV., they were subjected to the dragonnade. But the Protestants stood firm and almost none became Catholics. The elector meanwhile lived away from his country and spent his subjects' money gayly in private theatricals, buildings, and art collections.

His successor, Karl Philip, was one of the worst rulers that the Palatinate ever had, though he showed some little consideration for his subjects ; some of the feudal services were remitted in 1735 in order that the peasants might till their fields, but the despairing people refused to accept this, because they knew that all their crops would be taken from them by the invading French. The elector received an indemnity from the invaders, but retained it in his own pocket. The court was inconceivably costly—the master of horse, for instance, had one hundred and eighty persons under his orders alone, while other officials whose titles and rank are alike untranslatable and incomprehensible to us had as many or more. There were mounted life-guards, falconers, court musicians, and court architects besides.

It might have been supposed that this was the high-water mark of extravagance, but Karl Theodor, whose long reign filled out the eighteenth century, was the worst of all under whom the miserable Palatinate suffered. The elector was shamelessly in the pay of France, and under the influence of the Jesuits, like most of the Simmern branch of the Palatinate house ; bribery was open in the government ; in the court, avarice, extravagance, and immorality. He forbade his loving subjects to leave his well-governed land, where he destroyed the peasants' crops and fields with his magnificent hunts. His court far exceeded in expense and extravagance that of his predecessor. This magnificent court, with innumerable fine rooms, stables with hundreds of horses, gardens, and orangeries, was the resort of countless adventurers who were fed by scores at the monarch's table. Meanwhile, every nineteenth inhabitant was a beggar ; and the result of the census was concealed, for it showed a progressive diminution of population.

Würtemberg, which, next to the Palatinate, sent most emigrants to America, offers a replica of these conditions. In Würtemberg the French robbers came twice, in 1688 and 1693 ; the Spanish Succession War brought desolation to the country and a three days' plundering to the city of Stuttgart ; but from the beginning of the eighteenth century to its end Würtemberg had the advantage over its neighboring country, that no foreign

army entered it. Its dukes for a hundred years, however, were merely bad imitations of a wretched model in
their endeavors to equal the oppressions, extravagance,
and wickedness of the French sovereigns. Karl Eugen
of Würtemberg, whose treatment of Schiller and the
poet Schubart has made him notorious, had two thousand courtiers, the finest ballet and opera out of Paris,
increased the taxes of his subjects threefold, and drove
them by thousands to America. In Baden reigned
another imitator of Le Grand Monarque, Karl Wilhelm,
the builder of Karlsruhe ; his people emigrated to New
York and also to Pennsylvania in goodly numbers.

Truly an unpleasant and disheartening picture to
contemplate,—these gilded princelings, these crushed
people solacing themselves in their misery with wild religious dreams or subdued into the dumb non-resistance
of sheep. One wonders that so feeble a folk ever had
the spirit to leave their homes, embittered as their existence there was, to go across the sea to the New
World.

This portrayal of the social conditions of Germany
has brought us rather in advance chronologically of our
subject, for the first emigration of Germans to America
in 1683 was influenced by purely religious motives and
not at all by any social conditions. Many causes, as is
usual in any large movement, combined to influence this :
mysticism with a Rosicrucian coloring, Pietism and the
unfavorable aspect towards it of German church life, the
Mennonite movement, and last, but not least, the personal influence and presence of a man great enough to
lead events,—William Penn, Founder of Pennsylvania.

CHAPTER II

PENN made, it is probable, three visits to Germany and Holland. The first, to Labadie, had probably no influence on subsequent emigration ; the second, in 1674, to Embden and Crefeld, led only to the writing of several religious pamphlets ; but the last, in 1677, more extensive in its scope, set in motion the tiny rivulet of sectarian emigration, which grew presently to a mighty river.

The journal of this religious visit was subsequently published, but we take from it only notices of those portions of the journey which influenced subsequent emigration. The Mennonites in Holland and Germany offered prepared ground for Quaker missionary endeavors ; the two sects held many principles in common, as the wrongfulness of war, of judicial oaths, of a paid ministry, of ornament in dress, and of infant baptism. Early Quaker missionaries had set up meetings at Krisheim and Crefeld. The Pietists also sympathized with many of the Quaker views, in particular that of the Inner Light ; but Spener, the leader of these believers in Frankfort, avoided a meeting with Penn. The Philadelphian societies, of English origin, were tolerably numerous both in Holland and Germany ; the Labadists and the mystics generally also formed strategic points, of which Penn, like the able man he was, took advantage.

At Frankfort he became much interested in the young

and nobly born mystic, Fraülein von Merlau, who, after her marriage to the learned Chiliast professor, Petersen, wrote apocalyptic books "hard to be understood." Penn made from Frankfort a short visit to Worms and Krisheim ; at the latter place he edified the plain folk of the village in a barn ; the magistrate of the little town hid behind a door to spy upon the conventicle, but afterwards reported that "he heard nothing but what was good, and as to heresy he had not discovered any."

After Penn returned to England and obtained the grant of his province, four years later, he thought of the distressed "Friends" of Germany, and wrote to Benjamin Furly to recommend him Pennsylvania as an asylum for all oppressed sects. A number of pamphlets were prepared, setting forth the advantages of the new province beyond the seas : such as "Some Account of the Province of Pennsylvania," which was translated into German under the title "Eine Nachricht wegen der Landschaft Pennsilvania in America" and went through several editions, also Dutch and French translations. The "Frame of Government" of the new province was also published, as was a little tract giving "Information and direction to such persons as are inclined to America," which was translated into German and Dutch. "A Brief Account of the Province of Pennsylvania" was immediately translated by Furly into Dutch, French, and German. There soon began a flood of books, broadsides, and pamphlets, some setting forth the advantages of the Quaker province, others attacking or defending the Quakers or their doctrine. But enough had been disseminated to show what a haven of refuge

had been opened for the troubled sectaries of the Rhineland, and into it flocked all manner of persecuted,
plundered, and down-trodden people.

Furly established two companies, one (not formally
associated) at Crefeld, the other, the Frankfort Company,
at that city on the Main. Of this Eleanora von Merlau
and her husband, Dr. Petersen, were among the original
stockholders, as also the merchant, Van de Walle, at
whose house Penn held his first meeting in Frankfort.
None of the Frankfort Company ever came to America ;
but the weavers of Crefeld and the simple Mennonites
of Krisheim did emigrate and were the pioneers of the
immense emigration of later time.

Dr. Seidensticker, the first and fullest investigator of
the German roots of the emigration, says, "To complete
the proof that the project of buying land and founding
a settlement in Pennsylvania originated in the very circles that had been in contact with Penn, we have the
statement of Pastorius, contained in an autobiographical
memoir, to this effect; 'Upon my return to Frankfort
in 1682, I was glad to enjoy the company of my former
acquaintances and Christian friends assembled together
in a house called the Saalhof, viz. : Dr. Spener . . .
Jacobus von de Walle . . . Eleanora von Merlau . . .
etc., who sometimes made mention of William Penn, of
Pennsylvania, and showed me letters from Benjamin
Furley, also printed relations concerning said province
[probably the "Account"]; finally the whole secret could
not be withheld from me that they had purchased
twenty-five thousand acres of land in this remote part of
the world. Some of them entirely resolved to transport
themselves, families and all. This begat such a desire

in my soul to continue in their society and with them to
lead a quiet, godly, and honest life in a howling wilderness, that by several letters I requested my father's consent, besides two hundred and fifty reichsthalers ; whereupon I went to Krisheim and immediately prepared for.
the journey.'" So at last we are face to face with a body
of sectaries who really intend to emigrate, and with the
man who is to be their leader. The era of journeying,
of preparation, of pamphleteering, is passed, and that
of action, of emigration, of pioneering, has begun.

The German emigration to America has been com-
pared to a mighty river ; the simile is a good one. And
as a river is made up of the waters of many streams and
these in turn flow from numberless tiny springs rising in
obscure places, so many things and people little accounted
of by the great world went to feed the tide. The cen-
tury-long suffering of Mennonite in Switzerland and
Protestant in the Palatinate ; Penn's apostolic journeyings along the Rhine from one little group of " Friends"
or Mystics or Pietists to another ; Furly's industrious
pamphlet-writing ; the mystical dreamings of "the fair
von Merlau" and her Pietist friends of the Saalhof concerning the possibility of better serving God in the vir-
gin wilderness of Pennsylvania, which fired the noble,
simple, courageous heart of Pastorius ; all went to
prepare the way—may we not reverently say ?—for Him
who led His humble people by a way they knew not,
through the sea to a promised land of peace and freedom and brotherly love.

CHAPTER III

As we enter upon the history of the settlement of Germans in the New World, we feel that nothing in that history, no homely trait nor trifling detail, can be uninteresting. It has the freshness and importance that inhere in all beginnings. Yet the story is largely but "the short and simple annals of the poor."

The colonists were Mennonites, weavers from Crefeld on the Rhine. They belonged to that persecuted sect of "defenceless Christians," as they often entitled themselves, who trace their spiritual descent back to the pure doctrines of the early Waldenses. But it is likely that they represent only one of the streams of tendency of Reformation or indeed pre-Reformation times; one which arose among the common people and represented obscurely, and sometimes faultily, their blind and passionate desire for a pure, simple church in which all believers should be equal, in which no importance should be attached to forms and ceremonies, in which there should be no strife between brethren, neither wars nor judicial oaths; and an equal desire for such a reform in the state as should make their burdens and oppressions a little lighter and by which the state should not persecute any man for doing or believing what he thought to be right. These Swiss and German peasants of the time of Columbus were inarticulately desiring what the great Italian statesman of our own day phrased in his in-

mortal watchword of "a free church in a free state."
But the idea was too great and free for the time. The
unlearned men who taught it and tried to practise it,
though they sometimes enjoyed the leadership of men
like Felix Mantz, learned and wise and good, yet fell for
the most part under the guidance of leaders so maddened by their wrongs that they could but strike blindly
at the whole existing order of things or who reacted from
churchly formalism into a fanatical freedom which broke
all laws, human and divine. The excesses of the Peasants' War turned Luther's mighty influence against
them. John of Leyden and the other mad "prophets"
of Münster gave the Anabaptists a name and a fame
which centuries of pious and peaceful life could not
clear.

But in this lowest point of the life of the sect—if a
body so formless and heterogeneous could be called a
sect—there arose their Luther, their Calvin: Menno
Simon, from whom they take their present name. He
was a Frieslander, formerly a Catholic priest, converted
by witnessing the martyrdom of an Anabaptist ; and his
first writing was a protest against the party of violence
in the Anabaptist body. He succeeded in discrediting
this party, and henceforth the Mennonites were men of
peace.

But church and state, alike exasperated against them,
gave them no rest. Their martyr-roll is a long and
piteous one. For three centuries they found no toleration save in Holland, where William of Orange protected them. In Germany and Switzerland their property was confiscated, they were exiled, imprisoned,
burnt, broken on the wheel, drowned, according to the

disposition of the reigning princes or existing govern-
ments. So it is not strange that the little band of Mennonite weavers had the courage to leave their Crefeld
homes and try the new place of refuge, even beyond
seas, which was opened to them by their friend, Penn.
They had little to lose and might gain much.

Certainly in looking into the history of the tiny company who first dared the dangers of the ocean and the
wilderness for freedom of worship, we must recognize,
as they would most gratefully have done, the good hand
of their God upon them; and not the least of their
blessings was the character of their leader, Pastorius.
He was an educated man, as to religious opinion a
Pietist; he had travelled and studied widely for those
days. His family were people of position in the Fatherland; he had many wealthy and learned friends there,
and his noble character, his learning and culture, made
many more in "the forest court of William Penn." He
was a bit of a pedant, it is true. The construction of
his Rusca Apium, which

> "with bees began
> And through the gamut of creation ran—"

a compendium in all the many languages he knew, of
all human knowledge, was the occupation of years, but
it was the harmless diversion of a scholar almost alone
in the wilderness, and we do not know that he neglected
his colony or his school for the entrancing amusement
of writing it. He went delightedly to an exile in the
strange New World from all that makes life precious to
the cultivated and refined, and for the rest of his
earthly pilgrimage he led and cared for and instructed
wisely and patiently the simple weavers of Crefeld who

formed his colony, condescending to men of low estate, although enjoying to the full the society of cultivated people such as the President of the Provincial Council, Thomas Lloyd, or Lloyd's greater master, William Penn.

Pastorius's arrival preceded that of his colonists by six weeks. His first impressions of the City of Brotherly Love were not very favorable ; a few huts, "the rest woods and thickets in which I several times lost myself," so he describes it. His earliest residence there was a cave or rather such a "dug-out" as is still the primitive shelter on our Western frontier.

It was the 6th of October, 1683, when the first German colonists landed in Pennsylvania from the ship "Concord"—auspicious name ! They had had a prosperous voyage. "The blessing of the Lord did attend us," writes an English fellow-traveller, "so that we had a very comfortable passage and had our health all the way." There were thirteen families of emigrants, but the number of people is uncertain ; " 33 freights," they are counted, but as a child was called a half-freight, we cannot know of just how many men, women, and children the party consisted. They proceeded immediately to settle themselves. On the 12th of October a warrant was issued to Pastorius for six thousand acres of land "on behalf of the German and Dutch purchasers ;" on the 24th it was surveyed and divided into lots, and the next day the Germans met in the " cave" of Pastorius to draw lots for the choice of location.

And it was then, at the beginning of the records of this pioneer settlement of Germans in America, that Pastorius, seeing as in a vision the long train of Teutonic emigrants which should follow the little "Concord" and her " 33 freights" across the seas, greeted them in the stately Latin which Whittier has translated into English rhythm of touching beauty :

> " Hail to posterity !
> Hail, future men of Germanopolis !
>> Let the young generations yet to be
>> Look kindly upon this.
> Think how your fathers left their native land,—
>> Dear German-land !   O sacred hearths and homes !—
>> And, where the wild beast roams,
>>> In patience planned
> New forest-homes beyond the mighty sea,
>> There undisturbed and free
> To live as brothers of one family.
>> What pains and cares befell,
>>> What trials and what fears,
> Remember, and wherein we have done well
>> Follow our footsteps, men of coming years !
>> Where we have failed to do
>>> Aright, or wisely live,
> Be warned by us, the better way pursue,
> And, knowing we were human, even as you,
>>> Pity us and forgive !
>> Farewell, Posterity !
>> Farewell, dear Germany !
>> Forevermore, farewell !"

The colonists of Germantown built small huts, dug cellars, and passed the winter in much discomfort. "It could not be described," wrote Pastorius, "nor would it be believed by coming generations in what want and need and with what Christian contentment and persistent industry this Germantownship started."   But by the next year one of the settlers could write his brother, "I have been busy and made a brave dwelling-house and under it a cellar fit to live in and have so much grain such as

Indian Corn and Buckwheat that this winter I shall be better off than what I was last year."

Each summer brought them new accessions of prosperity and of fellow-countrymen to swell their numbers. Among the men of the "Concord" or those who afterwards cast in their lots with them, were Jacob Telner, a merchant, one of the original purchasers of land while yet in Crefeld, the leader, next to Pastorius, of the little community; Willem Rittinghuys, who built the first paper-mill in the colonies, but is more widely known as the progenitor of David Rittenhouse, self-taught genius, surveyor, orrery-maker, philosopher, astronomer, and patriot; Reynier Jansen, an early Pennsylvanian printer and a very bad one; and the two Op Den Graeffs, men of mark in the little community of their day, but known now because their names with those of Gerrit Hendricks and "Francis Daniell Pastorius" are signed to that simple petition against slavery which the Germantown Friends sent to "the monthly meeting held at Richard Worrell's" in 1688.

Let us hear a few of its simple words : "Is there any that would be done or handled at this manner? viz. to be sold or made a slave for all the time of his life? How fearfull and fainthearted are many at sea when they see a strange vessel being afraid it should be a Turck and they should be tacken and sold for Slaves in Turckey. Now what is this better done than Turcks doe? yea, rather is it worse for them which say they are Christians. . . . Now tho' they be black, we cannot conceive there is more liberty to have them slaves as it is to have other white men. . . . To bring men hither or to robb or sell them against their will, we stand

31

against. . . . Pray, what thing in the world can be done worse toward us than if men should robb or steal us away and sell us for slaves to strange countries, separating husband from their wife and children. Being now this is not done at that manner we will be done at, therefor we contradict and are against this traffic of menbody." It was promptly decided "not to be proper for this meeting to give a positive judgement in the case," and stifled into silence. Yet, as Pennypacker says, "A little rill there started which further on became an immense torrent, and whenever hereafter men trace the causes which led to Shiloh, Gettysburg, and Appomattox, they will begin with the tender consciences of the linen-weavers and husbandmen of Germantown."

There are few incidents to record in the life of the colony. In 1691 the town was incorporated, but no one wished to hold office and the government perished through lack of political ambition in its intended burghers. A few years after there tarried briefly at Germantown the strange community of "The Woman in the Wilderness."

In the same year there was another arrival which awakened pity rather than curiosity, and yet it was the end of a strange story which came before their eyes. Twenty years previous to the landing of Penn, the Mennonites of Amsterdam had endeavored to plant a colony in the New Netherlands under the leadership of one Cornelis Plockhoy; but the English fell upon the settlement of "defenceless Christians" and destroyed it, as their governor proudly boasted, "even to a naile." The waters of oblivion closed over the luckless colony.

Germantown

Thirty years after there came to Germantown a blind old man led by his aged wife. The pity of the benevolent Mennonites was excited for him, the more that he was a brother in the faith. They built him a little house and gave him a tiny garden for so long as he and his wife should live ; they planted a tree in front of it, under which he might sit to feel and hear the peaceful happiness about him. Rittinghuys and another were appointed to take up for the poor old people "a free-will offering." This blind old wanderer was the leader of that hapless colony, Cornelis Plockhoy.

The little community grew and prospered ; they had a paper-mill ; they made "very fine German Linen such no Person of Quality need be ashamed to wear ;" they built a prison and a church, and a school-house in which Pastorius "kept school." In 1702 they colonized, when Matthias Van Bebber chose to take up his land "on the Skippack" and established there what was often called Van Bebberstown, to the great confusion of later historians. Another fertile source of perplexity and mistake was the Dutch custom of adding the father's name instead of the surname, so that Dirck Op Den Graeff appears as Dirck Isaacs, and Matthias Jacobs is really Matthias Van Bebber.

At the opening of the new century the Germantown colonists passed through a period of great alarm, lest their little properties, which they had won from the wilderness twenty years before, should be taken from them. The Frankfort Company, perhaps dissatisfied with Pastorius's stewardship or yielding to his request to be relieved from the burden of the business, appointed new agents,— Daniel Falkner, Kelpius the hermit, and a certain Jawert.

3

Falkner seems to have been the only one who acted. He sold a large tract of the Montgomery County land to an unprincipled speculator, Sprögel, who attempted also to eject many of the Germantown colonists. They hurried in their extremity to Pastorius, who was able, by following the advice given him by his friend James Logan, to save the Germantown people's land ; but the twenty thousand acres in Montgomery County, much the larger portion of their original possessions, were lost to the Frankfort Company, though German colonists settled upon it and peopled "Falkner's Swamp," New Hanover, and Pottstown with the Teutonic stock.

Pastorius's life was now drawing to a close. It had been a busy one ; as school-teacher, land-agent, member of the Provincial Assembly, justice of the peace, notary, and, in short, guide, philosopher, and friend to the whole little community, his hands and heart and head must have been filled. His later years were embittered by the quarrels and accusations of those who supplanted him in the agency for the Frankfort Company. He complains :

> "Nun in meinen alten Jahren
> Muss ich noch viel Leids erfahren,
> Und in meinen schwachsten Tagen
> Die allerschwersten Lasten tragen."

And later:

> "Mein Gott und Heiland, welcher hat,
> Mich an bisher erhalten,
> Wird hoffentlich mit seiner Gnad
> Auch ob der Meinen walten."

It was for these, his two sons, and only children, that he wrote the great MS. folio, the compend of knowledge and good advice, which is still possessed by his descendants.

The very day of his death is unknown, though it took place probably in the last weeks of the year 1719. Of this Moses of the German exodus must be said, as of him of old, "no man knoweth of his sepulchre unto this day." But though he lies in an unmarked and unknown grave, he is not without a monument in the esteem and affectionate reverence with which all who have studied the history of the early German emigration to America have contemplated this figure which William Penn, his friend, fitly characterized as "sober, upright, wise and pious—a man everywhere esteemed and of unspotted name !"

CHAPTER IV

ANOTHER body of emigrants who came over about the same time as the Germantown colonists merit at least mention, for although emigrating from Friesland, their leader Sluyter was a German from Wesel, and there were among the sect, if not among the colonists, many Germans. They came, like the Crefelders, from the border land between the " High and Low Dutch," as the two peoples were called by our forefathers ; they represented the sectarian tendencies of the time in Europe, and they came here seeking, like the Mennonites of Pastorius' colony, " freedom to worship God ;" but they were different people from the simple and sensible weavers of Crefeld, and they had leaders very different from Menno and Pastorius.

The sect of Labadists, as they were commonly called, took its name and rise from the fervent preaching of Jean de la Badie, a Frenchman of noble birth, son of the Governor of Guyenne ; a pupil of the Jesuits, who, seeing his superior talents, persuaded him to enter their order, much against the wishes of his family. He became what in our day would have been called a popular revivalist, a preacher of rare eloquence and marvellous power over his hearers. The study of the "Institutes" of his fellow-countryman Calvin taught him that he had more in common with the Reformed than the Roman Church, and he left the Catholic communion. In the

The Labadists in Maryland

Reformed Church he evidenced his singular power over men's minds by gathering about him a company of believers, noblemen and gentlewomen, many learned and of wide reputation and spotless character. Of these were Yvon, his successor, the nobleman Du Lignon, and the most learned woman of her time, Anna von Schurmann, as well as the three ladies van Sommelsdyk, sisters of the Governor of Surinam, in whose ancestral castle of Wiewaert in Friesland the wandering sect found its last and longest home.

The doctrines which he taught resembled those of many mystics of the times—such as the insistence that the church should consist exclusively of those who could convince Labadie of their personal regeneration; the baptism of adult believers only; the indwelling of the Holy Spirit in all believers, so that the gifts of prophecy were still continued to the church (an article held vehemently by the so-called "Inspiriten" of Germany); together with some beliefs peculiar to Labadie, such as the duty of holding all possessions in common and the holiness of marriage between believers, their children being born sinless, but the invalidity of a marriage between a "believer"—in this case a Labadist—and one outside the church. The founder frequently separated husband and wife when not convinced of the regeneration of either party, and it may readily be seen that interference in domestic concerns of such delicacy would result in hatred, malice, and all uncharitableness on the part of the outside world, together with many accusations which seem to have been ignorant or wicked slanders. But with all its extravagance and Labadie's lack of "common discretion," the influence of his preaching of

37

personal righteousness still blesses the Reformed church on both sides of the sea, as does that of the Pietist Spener, the Lutheran.

William Penn says that the Labadists were "a plain, serious people and came near to Friends as to silence in meeting, women speaking, preaching by the Spirit, and plainness in garb and furniture." Whether Penn's visits had that influence in directing the Labadists towards the New World which we know they had upon the emigrants to Germantown does not appear. Probably they rather sought an asylum in some Dutch colony, being mainly of that race ; for their first attempt was in the direction of Surinam, where, as I have said, the brother of their patroness was the governor ; but this tropical country proved most ill adapted to their purpose ; the deadly climate and the rampant vegetation conquered the pious laborers, and the assassination of Governor van Sommelsdyk, with the seizure and plundering by pirates of the second shipload of colonists, forced them to abandon the enterprise.

Accordingly, they sent two of their number, Sluyter and Dankers, to spy out the land in the New World. The journal of these forerunners was preserved by some strange chance out of the general wreck of the Labadist community in Holland, and finally coming into the hands of an American antiquary was published, and affords us a detailed picture of the colonies as they appeared to rather prejudiced and splenetic travellers of the time. Sluyter and Dankers came over under assumed names, and seemed to have been in considerable fear lest their connection with the "Bush-people" (as the Labadists were called in Wiewaert) should be discovered.

The Labadists in Maryland

They explored the shores of the Delaware and the Chesapeake, and finally selected a tract called Bohemia Manor, on Chesapeake Bay, at the junction of the Bohemia and Elk Rivers.

A patent for this land, expressed with the convenient indefiniteness of those early grants, had been issued to Augustine Heerman, a Bohemian by birth, a surveyor by profession, and a man of position and distinction in the colony of New York. His eldest son, Ephraim, had been converted by the Labadists, who met him on a journey from New York to New Castle to bring home his young bride, and he had promised them part of the manor which his father intended to leave to him, making him lord of the manor, for the aged surveyor in his old age and feebleness was pathetically anxious to found a family and to perpetuate his name in the new country. Ephraim Heerman, however, promised that the tract should never be given to any but his new religious friends with his consent, and so provided the two investigators returned to Holland and brought over a little colony of about one hundred persons, landing in New York July 27, 1683.

They found on their arrival that old Augustine Heerman by no means assented to the project of his eldest son and heir to dower these strange religionists with part of the manor which he had hoped to make hereditary in his family. It was only after legal proceedings that Heerman was forced to execute the deed which gave the Labadists nearly four thousand acres of land, afterwards known as the "Labadie Tract."

Sluyter took the position of head of the community, which was regarded as a daughter church of the sect at

The Germans in Colonial Times

Wiewaert. All credentials of persons desiring to join the community must be passed upon in Holland. Sluyter's wife assumed the place of abbess, having oversight of the women in the settlement. Their rule was reported to be strict, if not tyrannical and arbitrary ; they separated husband and wife, mother and child, assigned the refined and educated of the community to any, even the most menial, tasks, and exacted much simplicity of living from the members of the sect, but were said to have accumulated considerable property themselves, and to be notoriously cruel to the slaves whom they held.

Sluyter was once ordered back to Holland by the head of the church there, but replied that it was evident to him that it was not the will of God that he should obey the summons, and remained in Bohemia Manor. They made some converts from among the colonists, but their most notable one, Ephraim Heerman, had a short and tragic history. His old father, incensed at his conduct and his desertion of his young and lovely wife to unite himself with the Labadists, pronounced upon him the curse that he should not survive two years after joining his new-found friends. Ephraim left the community after a brief residence with them, and returned to his wife, but in less than the prescribed two years fell ill and died a raving maniac.

Two descriptions of the little sect have been preserved, one by Dittlebach, a temporary adherent, who soon left them and naturally paints everything as to the hardships of the life and the tyranny of Sluyter in the darkest colors ; another by a Quaker preacher, Samuel Bownas, who visited the community about twenty years after their

The Labadists in Maryland

foundation and saw but the outside of the life which he portrays as a quiet, industrious, and religious one.

The Labadists as a sect were not of long continuance, either in their Friesland home or in the Maryland one. After the death of the last of the van Sommelsdyk ladies, there were no more Labadists left to shelter in the old castle of Wiewaert. In America Sluyter died in 1722, leaving his property to his nephews and his son-in-law, for the sect abandoned the principle of community of goods about fifteen years after coming to Maryland.

What finally became of the "daughter church" of Bohemia Manor we cannot tell. We know that when Sluyter died there were several of "his brethren and sisters in Christ Jesus" still expecting, in the so-called "Great House" of the community, that final consummation of all things which Jean de la Badie had announced as imminent seventy years before. In an old map published at the end of the eighteenth century there is marked a tree notable by its size or position as the "Labadie poplar." This seems all that then remained to mark the fact that at Bohemia Manor there had once labored and prayed and waited the followers of the eloquent "prophet of Bordeaux," Jean de la Badie.

CHAPTER V

THE WOMAN IN THE WILDERNESS

ABOUT ten years after the Labadists had settled on their tract at Bohemia Manor, another band of strange mystics arrived at Bohemia Landing, and, kneeling to thank God for having carried them " as on eagle's wings such an immense distance through all the gates of death," they set out on their way towards Philadelphia, the Mecca of many such pious pilgrims in those days. There were forty of them,—men, women, and children,—the number of perfection in the Rosicrucian philosophy ; and a mixture of this strange mystification from the Kabala, with Jakob Boehme's visions of the Morning Redness, the Philadelphian doctrines of Jane Leade, and the first ascetic enthusiasm of the most mystical of the earlier Pietists, made up the composite creed which they had come into the American wilderness to propagate and to practise.

The little community, which came later to be nick-named " Das Weib in der Wüste," or " The Woman in the Wilderness," from an allusion to Rev. XII : 14, was the result of the strange Chiliasm and the prophecies of a Lutheran pastor of Würtemberg, Zimmermann, who had reached the conclusion, from the study of Boehme's writings, that the Lutheran church was the Babylon denounced in the Apocalypse, and having published these views extensively under various pseudonyms, was, not unnaturally, deposed from the Lutheran ministry and expelled from the country by the government, the head of church as well as state. Zimmermann retaliated by informing his ruler that the cruel invasion of Würtemberg by the French was a punishment sent by heaven upon the wicked country which had cast him out. After a sojourn in Hamburg among the "host of mystics, millenarians, and dreamers with which the tolerant city was blessed," he led the little congregation which he had gathered towards Pennsylvania, doubtless influenced, like Pastorius, by a desire to live a purer life in the wilderness far from European vanities. But the Moses of this new exodus, like him of old, died in sight of his promised land. On the eve of their sailing from Rotterdam, Zimmermann passed away; his widow and children, helped by "good hearts," went on with the little band to Pennsylvania.

The headship of the community passed to Magister Johann Kelpius, a man alike of learning, lovely character, and the strangest mystical views. He was the son of a pastor in Siebenbürgen, and had been a student, and an especial favorite, of the learned Dr. Fabricius at the University of Altorf. Where and through whom he became attached to the peculiar mystical and separatistic doctrines which he afterwards professed and practised in the wilds of Pennsylvania, we cannot tell. Boehme attracted him as he did others of the Pietists and mystics. Dr. Petersen, who, with his wife, was a member of the Frankfort Company, seems to have indoctrinated Kelpius with his own belief that the end of all things, and their restoration to the perfection of Paradise, was at hand; and the delusion of Rosicrucianism, fostered, as it seems, by the pious fraud of a

The Germans in Colonial Times

Lutheran clergyman of pietistic Würtemberg, possessed Kelpius and his community of forty in the fullest measure.

We may find in Kelpius's diary of their voyage what it was in those days to leave "dear Germany," as Pastorius touchingly calls it, to find rest for one's conscience in the New World. The pilgrims went to London, stayed there six months, received both spiritual and financial help from the Philadelphian Society and other devout people of their way of thinking, and then took passage in the ship "Sarah Maria," whose prosaic name they wondrously allegorized. After narrowly escaping shipwreck on the Goodwin Sands, they arrived at Deal, where ensued another tedious waiting, this time for a convoy, since the war between the European powers and Louis XIV. made the seas unsafe. No convoy came, so they went to Plymouth, hoping there to find protection for their voyage. None being obtainable, they made an arrangement to be escorted "200 Holland Miles" on their route by some war-ships which were on their way to Spain. When they and their little consort had been left to their own devices, three French vessels attacked them. The Brotherhood of the Rosy Cross would not take up carnal weapons, but fortunately there were other passengers not so conscientious, and the ships were beaten off—one even taken as a prize.

So they went on their way, not further molested, to the "Capes of Delaware," which they sighted on the day of a solar eclipse, and finally, on the 24th of June, 1694, they safely arrived at Philadelphia. This was St. John's Day, a date peculiarly sacred to the Rosicrucians, and there is a strange tradition that after nightfall the forty faithful went to "Fair Mount" and heaped together wood and pine boughs to make the Baal-fire, which yet blazes on Irish headlands and in German villages. The brands of "St. John's fire" scattered, and their ceremonies over, the pilgrims returned to the little city, and the next morning took their way to Germantown, the head-quarters of all newly arrived Germans.

But they remained here only a few months. It was never their intention to settle among other men, however kindly they were welcomed, but to live a hermit life somewhere in the wilderness, supporting themselves by their labor while they watched the signs of the times, and "expected that blessed hope, the bright appearing of the Lord." A friend in Philadelphia—probably Thomas Fairman, surveyor of the province—gave them a tract of woodland on "the Ridge," near the lovely Wissahickon. In this *Waldeinsamkeit* they built themselves a log-house forty feet square, its sides true to the cardinal points, and containing one large room for meeting, having an iron cross fixed against its wall. Besides this room were cells for the brethren, and a school-room for the children whom they gathered and instructed. Upon the top of the building was an observatory, whence some of the brethren kept watch all night for the signs in heaven and the coming of the Bridegroom. Surmounting the log-house was the Rosicrucian symbol, the cross within the wheel of eternity ; this was so placed that the rising sun should flood it with rosy light, the "morning redness" which the shoemaker of Görlitz had seen in his vision, the herald of the end of this world. Kelpius himself built a little cave near by, and there in a tiny room he lived out his short life, expectant of the final consummation of all things. A dark, cool spring, still called the Hermit's Spring, and the beautiful dell in which religious meetings were held in the open air, remain to testify of the Hermits of the Wissahickon.

The hermit life was not passed in useless contemplation. The people of the neighboring Germantown loved and revered these gentle enthusiasts, sympathized with their millenarian ideas to some extent, gladly sent their children to be instructed free of charge by these learned men, or thronged the services conducted after the Lutheran forms by the Falkner brothers or Köster in the hermitage or the near-by city. The mystics also possessed some medical skill; particularly were they believed to have a magical knowledge of the properties of herbs, to be able to use the divining-rod for the discovery of springs and precious metals, to cast horoscopes, and to prepare amulets, which, hung about the neck, were of marvellous efficacy in sickness.

More useful and less recondite crafts were followed by the Brethren of the Rosy Cross. When Jansen brought his press into the province and perpetrated those misprinted incunabula which were among the first fruits of the Pennsylvania press, the hermits gave him much-needed help as compositors and correctors; and Johann Selig, one of their leaders, practised for Jansen and for others his craft as a bookbinder. They held public religious services daily, to which all were welcomed, and tried to bring about a union of sects in the province where, contrary to Whittier's line, "the many-creeded men" dwelt often the reverse of peacefully. They investigated the Indian beliefs and religious or mystical practices. Kelpius kept up an extensive theo-

The Woman in the Wilderness

logical correspondence with friends of his own way of thinking both in Europe and the colonies, and seems to have been a sort of general religious adviser. The Seventh-Day Baptists of New England sent an embassy to consult him ; a good woman in Virginia wrote to know his opinion of the Quaker beliefs and practices. Kelpius also composed hymns, which those persevering persons who have read them pronounce stiff, unpoetic, verbose paraphrases of the Song of Solomon ; besides religious letters, in which " the universal restitution," the millennium, the "Metempsosis," the "Heavenly Sophia," and other wonders figure to the confusion of the modern student, who would rather learn something of the daily life and actions of the pure, noble, gentle dreamer,— " maddest of good men," as even the congenial Hermit of Amesbury was forced to call him.

The magical practices of the community must not condemn them with the modern reader when we remember that the saintly Tersteegen had to warn his followers against the time-wasting search for the elixir, that medicines given by his holy hand were thought to have a supernatural efficacy, and that Sir Isaac Newton copied out long extracts from Boehme for his own use. The mystics of the Wissahickon were neither in advance of their time nor behind it.

This quaint, ascetic, mystical life in the American wilderness lasted with little change until the death of Kelpius in 1708. The life in this case, though at first it strengthened his health, later proved prejudicial. A succession of heavy colds gave rise to consumption. When he was very feeble, a good tailor in Germantown, Christian Warmer by name, took him to his own house to nurse him, and there he wrote, " at Christian Warmer's house, very weak, in a small bed not unlike a coffin," one of his last hymns :

> " Therefore kiss or correct, come to me or go,
> Give presents or take them ; bring joy or bring woe,
> If I can have Thee, Thy will may be so !"

When Kelpius felt his death approaching, he at first prayed to be exempted from the fate of "the children of Adam ;" but feeling that his prayer was not to be answered, he directed his *famulus* or attendant, Daniel Geissler, to take a casket which he gave him and throw it into the Schuylkill. Daniel was unwilling to destroy something which was of unknown value, so he hid it on the bank and returned to his master, who immediately told him that he had hidden the casket. The *famulus*, terrified by this supernatural knowledge, went back and did as he was told. But when the casket touched the water it exploded, peals of thunder and lightning welcomed it, and the mysterious Arcanum disappeared forever from human eyes. Daniel told this, a generation afterwards, to the patriarch Muhlenberg. So a noble, if deluded, dreamer passed from earth to where his strange visions are lost in sight. With him passed the flourishing period of the Hermitage upon the Ridge.

He was buried at sunset ; his brethren stood about the grave in a circle, chanting the De Profundis, until the sun touched the rim of the horizon ; then Selig gave a signal, the coffin was lowered into the grave, and, at the same moment, a white dove was set free and winged its way towards heaven, an emblem of the ascent of the master's soul, while the remaining brethren, lifting their hands, cried thrice, "God grant him a blessed resurrection !"

The Woman in the Wilderness

The society made an attempt to continue its life after the loss of Kelpius; but it was in vain. Selig, the especial friend of the dead master, and the one most resembling him in his sweet and lovable disposition, was chosen head of the community; but he soon renounced the office, feeling unfit for it, and took up the life of a hermit, dwelling alone in his little cell, supporting himself by cultivating a small herb-garden and by occasionally working at his trade of bookbinding. Köster, another early member of the community, quarrelled with them, set up a rival hermitage, called the Irenia or House of Peace, engaged in religious controversies with Pastorius, and has the distinction of having produced the first Latin work written in Pennsylvania,—a rhapsodical religious production with a tremendous title,—which he was obliged to have printed in Europe, as no one here could read the proof. He returned to Germany after a few years' sojourn here, and died there, a very old man. The two Falkner brothers became ordained clergymen of the Lutheran Church, ministering to the wants of the scattered Lutherans of New York, New Jersey, and Pennsylvania, and died useful and beloved. Geissler, the attendant of Kelpius, went with Dr. Witt to Germantown, where the latter (who was, by the way, of English birth, the only exception in the German community) practised medicine, and was believed to have knowledge not only of the innocent "white magic," but also of the black art. He was a botanical friend of Bartram's, and supplied the latter with rare specimens. In his later years, Bartram mentions a visit from him to his gardens, when "the poor old man" was grown so blind that he could not distinguish a leaf from a flower.

The Germans in Colonial Times

The last of the Hermits of the Ridge was Conrad Matthäi, a Swiss, who succeeded to the headship of the community after Selig's withdrawal to his hermitage. He, with the few brethren who were left,—each in his own cell, for community life had now been abandoned,—formed a sort of nucleus around which gathered various mystical religionists ; thus, he was the counsellor of the Eckerlins, who were afterwards so prominent in the Ephrata community. Zinzendorf visited him, and Matthäi joined with him in signing the call for a meeting which was to unite all the Christian sects of Pennsylvania in a new Philadelphian brotherhood, like that of which the London friends of the hermits had had visions more than fifty years before ; but it was destined to no more success than the dream of Jane Leade. When at last " Father Conrad" became old and helpless, a Moravian brother was sent to minister to him. The teacher of the Moravian school in Germantown took the children to sing hymns in their childish voices to the dying man,—an act which gave him great pleasure. When the old mystic felt that his last hour was near, he sent for the children, asked them to sing for him a favorite Moravian hymn describing the joy of the released soul when it flies away from this earthly tabernacle, then turned to the east whence he had hoped through his long life to see his Saviour come,

> " When in glory eastward burning
> Our redemption draweth near,
> And we see the sign in heaven
> Of our Judge and Saviour dear."

He prayed fervently, then turning to the awe-struck children, he blessed them after the manner of the mystic brotherhood. Two days afterwards he died. He was buried by his own request near his master Kelpius's grave. The old disciple had asked in his humility to be interred at his master's feet, as he felt himself unworthy to lie by his side. Some of the brethren of Ephrata were present, as well as the last survivor of the community, Dr. Witt, and the services were conducted after the Moravian order: a biographical sketch of the deceased was read, and the body was laid in the grave during the singing of the hymn familiar to us through Wesley's translation:

> "Jesus, Thy blood and righteousness
> My beauty are, my glorious dress."

When, in 1765, Dr. Witt died, old and blind, in the house of his kind friends the Wüsters, the last survivor of the brotherhood passed from earth. Their relics are scattered abroad; their Latin books, their chief wealth, have, some of them, been preserved in the library of Christ Church, Philadelphia; the domain where they lived and watched for the "Aurora"—the new heavens and the new earth—is partly covered by a gentleman's country-seat, partly taken into Fairmount Park. As to Kelpius and Selig and the humble disciple, Matthäi, no man knoweth of their sepulchre, only the God whom they so devotedly if mistakenly served, who will raise them up at the last day. We echo the prayer of the burial ritual of the brotherhood, which the white dove bore upward on its wings from the grave of Kelpius,—
"God grant them a blessed resurrection!"

CHAPTER VI

GERMAN VALLEY, NEW JERSEY

NEXT in chronological order apparently belongs the settlement of German Valley, New Jersey, if we are to accept the statement given by Löher from the oral tradition of descendants of the first settlers. He says, " In 1705 a number of German Reformed, residing between Wolfenbüttel and Halberstadt, fled to Neuwied, a town of Rhenish Prussia, where they remained some time, and then went to Holland, where they embarked, in 1707, for New York. Their frail ship was, by reason of adverse winds, carried into the Delaware Bay. Determined, however, to reach the place for which they were destined, and to have a home among the Dutch, they took the overland route from Philadelphia to New York. On entering the fertile charming valley of New Jersey which is drained by the meandering Musconetung, the Passaic and their tributaries, and having reached a goodly land, they resolved to remain in what is now known as the German Valley of Morris County."

This statement is so circumstantial that we must give it some consideration; yet the Rev. T. F. Chambers, the fullest investigator of the early German settlements of New Jersey, asserts that "this early date receives no support from any records of land transfers or from family history." This being so, their historian is inclined to think that the early Germans of New Jersey were of the " poor Palatines" who came to New York in the large emigration of 1710 and the years following. Perhaps the truth lies between the two, and some Germans of the Reformed faith did really arrive so early as stated, while the bulk of the settlers came in the large emigration of later years. Be this as it may, we find by 1713 Dominie Justus Falkner and, after his death, his brother Daniel ministering to the wants of the scattered Lutherans.

The two Falkner brothers were, in succession, the chief ministrants to the Lutheran portion of these emigrants, and as they were originally connected with the community of Kelpius, of which I have just spoken, it may not be uninteresting to regard them for a moment. Justus Falkner, the younger of the brothers, came to this country a student of theology, and in deacon's orders in the Lutheran Church, but with the intention of joining the mystic community on the Wissahickon. Fortunately both for himself and others, he was so appalled by the religious destitution among the Germans that he devoted himself and his life to the service of the church, and, ordained in the half-finished church of Gloria Dei in Wicacoa, he went to New York to be the pastor of the oldest church of his faith in this continent, Holy Trinity, of New York. The Latin prayer which he entered on the church register shows in what a spirit of humility he began his work : " God, the Father of all mercy, and Lord of great majesty, who has thrust me into this harvest, be with me His lowly and ever-feeble laborer with His special grace, without which I should perish under the burden of temptations which often powerfully assail me. Make me fit for my calling. I have not run, but Thou hast sent me, yea, thrust me into my office. Free me from whatever taint my lost nature—always without my consent—may mingle with my service, and pardon me, I humbly beseech through our, yea, *my* Lord Jesus Christ. Amen."

He was in labors abundant for more than a score of years, ministering to the German Lutherans from Albany to New York in the winter, and in the summer months itinerating through New Jersey. Amidst these strenuous efforts he found time to compose several hymns, which are still in use, both in German and in English translation ; among them, the best known is the spirited and courageous lyric, " Auf, ihr Christen, Christi Glieder," translated as " Rise, ye children of salvation." It breathes the humble yet trustful courage of the pioneer evangelist, whose sweet, strong, arduous life closed, it seems prematurely, in his fifty-first year. His fittest epitaph would be the conclusion of his own hymn of the Church Militant :

> " Da Gott seinen treuen Knechten
> Geben wird den Gnaden-lohn,
> In die Hütten der Gerechten
> Stimmen an den Sieges-Ton ;
> Da fürwahr Gottes Schaar
> Ihn wird loben immerdar.''

The elder brother, Daniel, though he so far followed in the footsteps of his younger brother that he left the Wissahickon community, married, was ordained, and ministered to his brother's congregation, was of a very different spirit. He was appointed by Benjamin Furly the successor of Pastorius as agent of the Frankfort Company, and so became involved in a lengthy and acrimonious controversy with the latter. Apparently Pastorius had allowed the company's affairs to fall into a state unsatisfactory to the members of the society in Europe (none of whom, as will be remembered, ever carried out their expressed intention of emigrating to Pennsylvania), and the Falkner brothers and a man named Sprögel were appointed agents. Sprögel, who seems to have been an unscrupulous speculator, finally succeeded in getting into his hands, and away from both the Falkners and the Frankforters, the entire property of the company.

Daniel Falkner followed his brother Justus in the charge of the New Jersey congregations on the latter's death in 1723, and labored there for nearly a score of years. We have a last glimpse of the old Theosophist in the diary of Pastor Berkenmeyer, of New York, who went in 1731 to compose the differences which had arisen between Daniel Falkner and his congregations. The eccentricities of the former mystic had made the congregation desirous of a new pastor, and Berkenmeyer with two of his elders went to deal with Pastor Falkner, who had gone to the woods to gather medicinal herbs, and was with difficulty found and recalled from this characteristic occupation to discuss the affairs of his church. After the ensuing resignation of his pastorate, Falkner is reported as living in retirement with his daughter near New Germantown. This was in 1741, but the year of his death is not known ; this ends the history of " Daniel Falckner, Bürger und Pilgrim in Pennsylvanien in Norden America."

The German settlement of New Jersey extended from the Delaware to Hackensack, German Valley and New

Germantown being perhaps the centre. "The bulk of the German population," says their annalist, "was perhaps to be found between Lambertville and Newton, and the Delaware and Bound Brook." There were about a dozen German churches and congregations here, over which Muhlenberg and Schlatter exercised their missionary supervision, composing differences, settling and removing ministers,—for the Jerseys had, in early times, their share of those "vagabond shepherds" who tried the souls of both the patriarchs,—and occasionally ministering there in person.

The early settlers, though poor in this world's goods, bore a good reputation for industry, piety, and a pathetic desire for the ministrations of some one who could speak to them in their own tongue; for this they made great sacrifices in their poverty, and showed a patience truly marvellous with the disappointments in the character of their early ministers which they were often called upon to endure.

Among other German settlements of later times was the Moravian village of Greenland or Hope, which existed from 1769 to 1808, and was then given up by the Brethren's Unity.

These pioneers were so pre-eminently a religious people that their story is largely a history of their churches; yet they were not neglectful of the school. In 1760 the sum of a thousand pounds—large for the time—was left to New Germantown for the support of their church and school. The people willingly bore the trouble and expense of importing ministers from Germany that they might thereby secure men of learning and regular ordination; the recommendation of Muhlenberg, that the ministers sent out should be able to speak Latin, so as to communicate with their English fellow-clergymen, shows what the Jersey pioneers demanded of their pastors. The first settlers of German Valley, in particular, were said to have been distinguished for their intelligence.

And to anticipate a little, we find in Revolutionary times a sense of honor in the New Germantown vestry which may be recommended for imitation at the present day ; for, having borrowed the church funds, they refused to repay in the depreciated Continental currency, but offered a remuneration in something of real value. Pastor Nevelling of the Amwell Church mortgaged his whole property, loaned the money to Congress, and, having lost his certificate, never recovered any of the sum. The British set a price upon his head, as upon that of several other German patriot pastors.

CHAPTER VII

KOCHERTHAL'S COLONY

THE brief and unfortunate history of the colony led by their pastor Kocherthal to Newburg on the Hudson is of slight importance, save as they were the forerunners of a much larger emigration,—"the first low wash of waves where soon shall roll a human sea,"—for they were the precursors, in point of time, of the great emigration of the years 1709 and 1710. It is probable, too, that the news of their favorable reception had something to do with that immense movement.

The little colony, sixty-one souls strong when it started upon its wanderings, consisted of some poor Lutherans from Landau in the Palatinate. Most of them were vine-dressers, as might have been expected from their nativity, but other occupations were also represented. They had been impoverished and driven from their homes by the severities of the war called of the "Spanish Succession," which had run but half of its course of desolation in their home-land, when they started out under the leadership of their pastor, the Rev. Josua von Kocherthal, and, taking refuge at Frankfort, besought Davenant, the English representative there, to send them to England; they did not ask to be sent farther. Davenant, applying to his home government, was directed to tell the Palatines that they must first secure the consent of their elector to their expatriation.

But, not waiting for this formality, the Palatines, in

Kocherthal's Colony

March, 1708, came to England, by whose help does not appear, and excited the compassion of "good Queen Anne," who gave them a shilling a day for their maintenance, and took steps to send them to some of the British colonies. New York was finally selected, and having been naturalized without fee, the Lutherans were given free transportation to New York, tools, and a promise of support for the first year until they could maintain themselves. Pastor Kocherthal had a donation of a hundred pounds and a grant of five hundred acres for himself and the church he was to build. Thus furnished, the little colony, now reduced to fifty-two persons, sailed in the same ship with the newly appointed governor, Lord Lovelace, for New York, where they arrived on the last day of the year 1708. Land was assigned them upon the west side of the Hudson, and they named their town Neuburg, after the place in the Palatinate, which was the *Stammsitz* of the then reigning house of Pfalz-Neuburg.

But they met with continual misfortunes. Their protector, Lord Lovelace, died a few months after his and their arrival. He had paid the cost of their passage out of his own purse,—a purse not too well furnished, for on his recent accession to his title he is said to have inherited little or nothing but creditors' claims. His widow, "a penniless lass wi' a lang pedigree," was only reimbursed after many years.

And now religious dissensions broke out among them ; they complained to the new governor that nineteen of their number had turned Pietists, and their English ruler, unversed in German theological squabbles, had to send a committee of English and German Reformed clergy to see what manner of thing a Pietist might be. Reassured as to their harmlessness, he continued to them the same ration as to their more orthodox brethren. Kocherthal, discouraged by the condition of his flock, asked permission to go again to Europe to beg some help for them; this was granted, and the support promised the colonists for the first year of their settlement was continued them through the second.

Still the colony did not thrive. Kocherthal did not reside among the poor people of Neuburg, but on the other side of the Hudson. After his death, about 1718, they were left to the occasional ministrations of the apostolic Justus Falkner, and afterwards of other New York clergymen. They seem never to have had a settled pastor; not until near the middle of the century was their long-promised church built, a simple log-house. The bell given them for it had meanwhile been lent to a Lutheran congregation in New York. Many of the earlier settlers, and those who from time to time reinforced the colony, tarried only briefly, and then went to Pennsylvania, where the German pioneers were in a more flourishing state. At length their very church was taken from them by a piece of chicanery on the part of the English Episcopalians. The precious bell was saved from the wreck and for a time was hidden in a swamp.

The loss of their church was a fatal blow; in losing it they lost their bond of union, their language, their customs,—all that marked them as a German colony. Though descendants of the "Kocherthalern" remain, there is nothing left of the first German colony of New York but the changed name of the city which they baptized in honor of the town in the Palatinate.

CHAPTER VIII

THE GREAT EXODUS OF THE PALATINES

WE come now to a movement almost unexampled in its extent,—the so-called "Massen-auswanderung der Pfälzer," the great exodus of the Palatines. With all allowance for the exaggeration of their numbers which the frightened authorities of Rotterdam and London may have made, it was an immense movement, by far the largest emigration of colonial times from any continental country to America. So amazing was it that modern historians have sought out all sorts of recondite reasons why so many of the home-loving Germans should have expatriated themselves; but, like most large movements, it is probable that many causes—some great, some trifling—contributed to the result.

First in point of time was the desolation of the war of the Spanish Succession, lasting from 1701 to 1713, and devastating Würtemberg in its long-drawn-out miseries; Stuttgart, in particular, experienced a three-days' plundering in this invasion. The Palatinate fortunately escaped this war, in large measure. But its exemption from war was more than made up in the misgovernment which prevailed in that unhappy country.

In Würtemberg, which next to the Pfalz furnished the largest contingent to the exodus, conditions were painfully similar; the reader is oppressed by the repeated accounts of the unhindered French devastations, the injuries of the succeeding war of 1701–13, the exactions of Villars, who pressed from the miserable people the incredible sum of nine million gulden, and the tyranny and extravagance of their petty potentate.

Eberhard Ludwig, ruler of Würtemberg for fifty-six unhappy years, was a fine type of the German caricature of Louis XIV. "L'état c'est moi" is echoed by Eberhard Ludwig's declaration, "I am the pope in this land." Of his mistress, the Grävenitz, it was said, "Würtemberg was destroyed more by a woman than by war." She ruled everything through her favorites for twenty-five years; her royal lover built a little Versailles to please her, and after his death she left the country laden with spoil. The grand duke's Ludwigsburg is said to be no bad imitation of Louis's Versailles, but it was built from the resources of a tiny war-scourged country no larger than many an American county.

In the contemporary accounts of the distressed Palatines and their coming over to England, religious persecution is constantly alleged as a motive for their emigration. This touched the electoral government, anxious to stand well with its Protestant relatives of the English court, and the Protestant consistory, "by direction from the Elector Palatine," issued a declaration that "it is not known to any of the consistory that those withdrawn subjects have complained that they suffered any persecution on account of religion." The fact has been doubted also by some recent writers, chiefly because there were some Catholics among the emigrants, who could not have been persecuted by the Elector Palatine. But no one asserts that all the people of the exodus left for religious reasons; and we know that most of the Catholics returned to Germany, where they could not have found life unbearable. The fact seems to be that there were plenty of the petty persecutions previously mentioned, frequently—to their shame be it spoken—inflicted by the Reformed Protestants upon the Lutherans, after the former were somewhat protected from molestation by the Religions-Declaration of 1705, when England stirred up Prussia to energetic reprisals upon her own Catholic subjects for Protestant persecutions by the elector's government.

England was at that time warmly interested in the cause of any distressed Continental Protestants. As a generation before she had given refuge to the fleeing Huguenots, so now she was prepared to take in other Protestants who alleged the same reasons for their coming. Queen Anne, a woman of most benevolent and kindly private character, was distantly related to the Palatinate electors,—Karl Ludwig, the last of the Protestant line of Simmern, being her cousin, though with the Catholic line (Pfalz-Neuburg) she was more distantly connected in blood as in religion. The assertion, "currently reported," that Queen Anne had *invited* the distressed Palatines to come to England, though it was "certainly believed," is proven unfounded. Perhaps the circulation of a book on America, with its title printed in golden letters, and thence called the "Golden Book," may have given rise to it, for this contained a portrait of Queen Anne. The favor which she showed to Kocherthal's colony of the year before had evidently been reported in Germany, for we find that the Board of Trade in one of the many meetings in which they considered what was to be done with "the Palatines" were told that "Many of them were from the same county as those who had gone to New York and were anxious to go there.''

One of the last, yet probably a determining, factors in the emigration was the fearful ''Cold Winter'' of 1708–1709. This was felt throughout Europe ; but in the desolated Rhineland it completed the devastations of war. The wild animals froze to death in the woods ; the very birds also. Wine froze in casks ; the vineyards and fruit-trees were destroyed ; and, worst of all, hundreds of the wretched inhabitants perished of cold and starvation, while their rulers, in their splendid little courts, amused themselves after the fashion set by the Grand Monarch.

So, as soon as the fearful winter was over, in May, 1709, bands of ragged, miserable Germans began their painful way down the Rhine towards the Low Countries, Rotterdam, and England. At first they were received with kindness by the benevolent people of Rotterdam, but as the summer wore on, and the emigration of ''destitute families'' continued, finally reaching the immense figure of fifteen thousand persons, the Lords Burgomasters became not unnaturally alarmed. ''The poor pence of the city is exhausted,'' they wrote. Their High Mightinesses sent word to the Palatinate that England would transport no more to her shores ; two of the Rotterdam merchants were sent up the arms of the Rhine to intercept ''those poor people,'' and a thousand of them were turned back. Messages were sent to the ministers of Holland at Cologne and Frankfort to ''warn the people over there not to come this way ;'' but all produced little apparent effect.

The mass of misery, poverty, and distress kept on its

road, seemingly impelled by its own weight of woe, and irresistible as a force of nature. Dayrolles, the English minister, offered transportation for five thousand of them, but by June of 1709 ten thousand were said to be in Rotterdam awaiting a passage to England. Dayrolles sent over three thousand more, and tried the same repeated orders and advertisements which the Dutch government had used to stop the emigration, but with little result. By the end of October, 1709, about fifteen thousand of these "poor miserable Germans" had reached London, and the problem was, what to do with them.

The number given above seems to be about the correct one, but the statements of all who have written upon this little-known movement vary widely. An anonymous writer who published a now rare little book with the quaint title " Das Verlangte nicht Erlangte Canaan," gives us, in Chapter VI. of his work, a professedly exhaustive account of the arrival and numbers of the "poor Palatines." There were, he says, in all, thirty-two thousand four hundred and sixty-eight of them, and this colossal number, copied by Löher and accompanied by the remark that it furnishes a measure of Germany's misery, has been repeated by every writer since. But it is manifest, when we come to read of the provision made for the refugees, and the number sent to various colonies, that not more than one-half or one-third of this number are "accounted for." The author of the "unreached Canaan" makes his numbers mete up by the simple expedient of subtracting those provided for from this thirty thousand odd, and remarking that "these seventeen thousand all died in England." This mortality is perfectly incredible, especially as he has already spoken of three thousand and sixty who died there. Surely twenty thousand Palatines, whose coming and condition excited such interest, did not die and "make no sign" on the history or records of the time. Another equally loose statement begins his apparently careful and detailed enumeration of the ten or more distinct ship-loads which he mentions. The first arrival, he says, consisted of eighteen thousand and six persons on eleven ships, which would give an average of more than sixteen hundred passengers on each of the little ships of the time ; packed like herrings though they may have been, this exceeds probability. Everything *known*, not conjectured or imagined, about the emigration points to fifteen thousand or less as the true figure.*

And surely this is imposing enough when one considers what perils and difficulties these poor souls had to come through in order even to reach England, and that then they were still separated by months of journeyings and leagues of ocean from their goal ; for all, it seems, had set their faces towards the "verlangten Canaan" of America.

There was much perplexity as to where and how this host of utterly destitute people was to be kept. Camps

---

* Diffenderffer counts up the various colonists,—those who died, returned, and so on,—and makes the total eleven thousand five hundred, with a confessed discrepancy of three thousand, which would make the number fourteen thousand five hundred. The author of "Canaan" makes his detailed account sum up in round numbers fourteen thousand four hundred. Another apparently very careful list, with the various little principalities from which each contingent came, amounts to fifteen thousand three hundred and thirteen. As will be seen, the variation is slight, and the number given in the text may be regarded as approximately correct.

were finally established at several points in the neighborhood of London, notably at Blackheath, where tents from
the English military stores in the tower were erected,
and the multitude was lodged after a fashion. Blackheath had seen many strange gatherings since the Dan-
ish invaders of Britain had encamped there centuries
before. The miserable hordes of Wat Tyler and Jack
Cade had lain there ; the people welcomed back Henry
J. from Agincourt on Blackheath ; regiments often encamped there, and highwaymen found it a good place to
ply their trade ; but surely never did the waste heath
support more poverty and misery or attract greater
crowds to gaze upon the encampment. Thither streamed
the English folk to gaze upon the strange concourse of
refugees, and wonder or sneer or pity, according to
their inclinations, but often, to their honor be it said, to
help.

The Queen, "gracious Anna whom three realms
obey" of Pope, showed herself both good and gracious
to the distressed, as was her kindly wont. She gave
them several liberal donations, provided subsistence for
them, and presented them with "one thousand High
Dutch Bibles." A collection was taken up for them
throughout the kingdom. Bishop Burnet, the kindly,
meddlesome, impulsive ecclesiastic and historian, who has
been ridiculed as "P. P. Clerk of this parish," worked
nobly for the distressed Palatines, having collections
made in his diocese for them, and opposing the High
Church projects of the Bishop of London, who would
have had them all converted to the Church of England.

These various charitable schemes yielded the sum
of two thousand pounds ; many appropriations were

made by Parliament for subsistence, transportation, etc., amounting altogether to more than half a million dollars (£135,000), while charitable people gave them clothing, and shoes, the Queen distributed coal at Christmas, and the commissioners, besides the gift, on the refugees' first reaching England, of "a loaf of a bread as white as snow and a Reichsgulden in money," issued to them every fortnight straw to lie upon. Some Indian chiefs of the Mohawks, then in London upon an embassy to the Queen, visited the camp, and, touched by what they saw, told the Palatines that in their own country was land enough and to spare, and promised them a grant of this land if they chose to come and make their home among them. This promise had important and un-dreamt-of consequence, as we shall see. For all this most of the refugees displayed a touching gratitude.

The Lutheran and Reformed clergymen of the German Chapel of St. Mary in Savoy ministered to their spiritual wants and interested themselves for their temporal settlement. About one-half of the number were married couples, and two-fifths children under fourteen years of age. Nearly all the men were "husbandmen and vine-dressers," as might have been expected of emigrants from the vine-draped Rhenish hills ; there were plenty of mechanics and artisans among them, however, representing the commoner trades. Several churches came over, led by their pastors, and there were noted among the emigrants, school-masters, students, and engravers ; people of a condition in life usually removed from the necessity of emigration were forced among the others in those calamitous times, and we hear that overseers were appointed among them from those of noble birth in the company. But, taking them altogether, it is probable that most were as ignorant and lowly as they were desolate and oppressed.

A contemporary publication gives the nationality of a portion of the emigrants; from this we can see what countries were most untenable to their wretched inhabitants. The Palatinate has the bad eminence of yielding more than one-half of those enumerated; next comes, in the order given, Darmstadt, Hanau—those tiny lands supply a surprising quota of the remainder; then comes "Frankenland," probably a portion of Franconia, the free cities of Worms and Speyer, Alsace, and Baden, with a few little groups from other localities.

A contemporary description of the life in the Palatine camp gives a very favorable picture : " They spend their time very religiously and industriously, having prayers morning and evening, with singing of psalms and preaching every Sunday, where both old and young appear very serious and devout. Some employ themselves in making toys of small value, which they sell to the multitudes that come daily to see them. They are contented with very ordinary food, their bread being brown and their meat of the coarsest and cheapest sort, which, with a few roots and herbs, they eat with much cheerfulness and thankfulness. Great numbers of them go every Sunday to their church in the Savoy, and receive the Sacrament of their own ministers. . . . On the whole, they appear to be an innocent, laborious, peaceable, healthy, and ingenious people, and may be rather reckoned a blessing than a burden to any nation where they shall be settled."

But all Englishmen did not regard the refugees with

equal friendliness. Dean Swift, who was in London at this time trying to induce the Whigs to make him a colonial bishop, spattered some of the venom of his pen upon the "foreigners of all religions, under the name of Palatines, who understood no trade nor handicraft, yet rather chose to beg than labor, who besides infesting our streets, bred contagious diseases by which we lost in natives thrice the number of population gained in for-eigners," all of which was as untrue as it was bitter; and certain fellows of the baser sort, following the lead of the great dean, showed their hostility to the beggars who had come to take the bread out of their mouths, by attacking the camp, one dark night, to the number of two thousand, armed with scythes, hammers, and axes, and were with difficulty beaten off. One of the reasons for this animosity was that the Palatines were suspected by the ignorant English of being Catholics, and against this religion the most rabid anti-Popery feeling still existed.

It must have been in consequence of this feeling of hatred that the "poor distressed Palatines" issued a pathetic "Address." "We humbly entreat," Its words ran, "all tradesmen not to repine at the good disposi-tion of her sacred Majesty and of the Quality and Gen-try. We Intreat you to lay aside all Reflections and Imprecations and ill language against us for that is contrary to a Christian Spirit and we do assure you it shall be our endeavors to act with great humility and gratitude and to render our prayers for you which is all the returns that can be made by

"your distressed brethren

" the Palatines."

The Great Exodus of the Palatines

But what was to be done with them? Here they were, fifteen thousand strong, utterly destitute and help-less. The Board of Trade wrestled with the problem all through the summer of 1709, while one ship-load after another of the refugees accumulated upon their hands. They listened to propositions from various persons and companies who wished to secure some of these people, commonly, it is to be feared, only for the profit which was to be made out of their labor.

The Queen offered five pounds a head to any one who would take Palatinate refugees and settle them anywhere in England, but this measure had but a modi-fied success. Most of the people thus disposed of soon returned to London, complaining of the hostility of the English people and the avarice of their new masters ; although a certain, or rather uncertain, number did eventually remain in England, the majority of these settlers finally returned in despair to Germany. Several hundred young men enlisted in the British army. A large number—probably about three thousand—died in England.

At length it was resolved to select from among the refugees those who were Catholics, and offer them the alternative of becoming Protestants or being sent back at the Queen's expense, and with ten Reichsgulden each for consolation, to Germany. About five hundred Catholics changed their religion, and so remained in England. It is said that most of these converts were people of Protestant descent who had become Catholics, and their first conversion may have been more from force than from conviction. But three thousand five hundred of the German Catholics stood firm, and were deported. The author of "Canaan" says that "they could not be allowed to remain under the laws of the realm," but probably the suspicious hostility which had issued in the mob's attack upon the camp was what made their retention impossible.

A British naval officer conceived the plan of settling a colony on the Scilly Islands, off the coast of Cornwall. Some six hundred, or, according to another account, sixteen hundred, Palatines were loaded upon ships bound for the islands. But "when the Inhabitants of that place received news of their coming they sent a woefully worded petition to parliament, stating they could not support themselves, much less the Germans who did not understand fishing and could not ward off hunger." After six weeks had passed, they were again set on land, and went to Germany, accompanied by their Lutheran pastor.

But the Mecca towards which their prayers were turned was America, and an opportunity was now afforded a few of them to go thither. Some time previous to the Palatine exodus the Swiss canton of Berne, or, according to some authorities, the persecuted Mennonites in that canton, had cherished a plan of forming a colony in America, and had sent two commissioners, Christopher de Graffenried and Louis Michel, to spy out the land. The project, so far as it was an exclusively Bernese one, seems to have been abandoned. But the commissioners, being in London at the time of the refugees' arrival, were inspired by the brilliant idea of securing some of these people, who were literally going begging, for their projected settlement. Some of the commissioners charged with the settlement of the Palatines arranged for six hundred and fifty of their people being transported to North Carolina ; de Graffenried and Michel secured from the proprietors of the colony ten thousand acres of land, with an option upon one hundred thousand acres more when the settlement should be fairly started. They were to give their colonists free transportation, some clothing, support for a year, and the stock and agricultural implements necessary to work the land. The Palatines were ultimately to be given two hundred and fifty acres of land apiece. For this colonizing enterprise de Graffenried, to whom alone the land was granted, was made a baron ; according to one account, he received the title of " Landgrave," one of those which decorated the curious frame of government thought out by the English philosopher Locke for his friend the Earl of Shaftesbury, one of the proprietors of North Carolina.

De Graffenried transported his colonists safely to their new home ; they landed in December, 1710, at the confluence of the Neuse and Trent Rivers, where they formed the settlement, to which they gave, in compliment to their Swiss leaders, the name of New Berne, now contracted into Newbern. All went well with the little colony for a time ; in two years they had made a prosperous beginning, and had a good outlook towards paying for their lands.

But a storm was gathering of which the Germans suspected nothing. The Tuscarora Indians, the most warlike of the tribes in that part of the country, had been exasperated against the English, partly by the encroachment of the settlers under the direction of the Surveyor-General of the Province, Lawson. There were many of their race living among the whites as domestic servants, and with them their savage brethren formed a plot to fall upon and exterminate all white men ; the distinction between harmless Germans and hostile English was of course unknown to the Indians.

Meanwhile, de Graffenried with his negro servant and Surveyor-General Lawson had gone to explore the country, threading the swampy forests of the Carolinian lowlands in a canoe. So, they came suddenly upon a body of professedly friendly Indians, who, nevertheless, detained them, upon some pretext, overnight in their camp. It was, though the baron and his companions did not suspect it, the time which had been chosen for the onslaught upon the white settlements. At dawn the Indian servants were to give the signal, their wild tribesmen were to fall upon the half-aroused palefaces, and they were to be killed with all the horrible and fantastic cruelty of which the red men are capable. This terrible plot was carried out while Baron de Graffenried and his companions were held prisoners ; sixty of the settlers of Newbern were killed and as many more dangerously wounded.

In the forest, meanwhile, their leader was tried for his life ; Lawson, the chief enemy, and the luckless negro servant were slaughtered, probably with all the tortures of Indian barbarity, and the Swiss nobleman only saved himself at the last moment by a lucky inspiration. He told the Indian chief that he was the King of the Palatines, and the Indians had no right to put to death a person of such exalted rank. After cogitation on this point of international law, the chief gave way. If the King of the Palatines would sign a paper promising not to take from the red men any more of their land, and also to hold his subjects neutral in the war between the races, he might be permitted to go back to his subjects to make known to them these terms and to insure their neutrality. We may be certain that de Graffenried gladly made these or any other required promises, and he went his way, out of the very jaws of a horrible death, back to his crushed and half-destroyed colony.

During the war which ensued the baron did, indeed, observe the promised neutrality, though he privately gave information to the English governor of such of the savages' plans as came to his knowledge. "His neutrality," wrote the governor, "is of great benefit to the province, as he can expose the designs of the Indians, though he runs the risk of paying dear for it, if they ever come to know of it." Some time elapsed before the Tuscaroras were finally subdued, but it was so thoroughly done that most of the tribe left the South, went to the province of New York, and there joined the confederacy of the "Five Nations," which by this accession became the familiar "Six Nations" of our colonial history.

But before this happened, Baron de Graffenried, perhaps discouraged by his experiences, left his colony and returned to Europe. The title to the land had been given to him alone, and he mortgaged it to an Englishman in payment of a debt. The unfortunate colonists petitioned the Colonial Assembly some years afterwards for relief, and their lands were, it seems, secured to them. Michel, the other commissioner, remained in Newbern, where his descendants have anglicized themselves into Mitchell. Descendants of Baron de Graffenried are also found in the "Old North State."

The Germans in Colonial Times

Some of de Graffenried's deserted colonists, terrified and disheartened, quitted North Carolina and took ship for the North. Misfortune followed them ; they were wrecked at the mouth of the Rappahannock River in Virginia. But this mischance was a blessing in disguise, for it cast them into the strong and capable arms of Governor Alexander Spotswood, of the colony of Virginia. This energetic Scotchman—born at Tangier, a soldier of the great Marlborough, wounded at Blenheim— was now finishing his stirring career, in the New World, by exploring tramontane Virginia, founding the order of the Knights of the Golden Horseshoe among his adventurous comrades, and establishing the first iron furnace in North America at his plantation up the Rappahannock. The "Tubal-Cain of Virginia," as he was called, received this flotsam of Germans with delight. "I have placed here a number of Protestant Germans," he writes the Lord Commissioners of Trade, "built them a Fort, and finished it with two pieces of Cannons and some Ammunition, which will awe the Stragling parties of Northern Indians and be a good Barrier for all that part of the country. . . . They are generally such as have been employed in their own country as Miners and say they are satisfyed there are divers kinds of minerals in those upper parts of the Country where they are settled and even a good appearance of Silver Oar."

The governor named his plantation, in honor of his new settlers, "Germanna." Three years after, the colony received an accession of eighty persons, who had suffered a variety of misfortunes which throw light on what emigration was, or might be, in those days. Held in an English port for the captain's debt, their provision failed before the long voyage ended ; many starved to death ; they were wrecked on the Virginia coast, and the perfidious captain sold them to slavery or as redemptioners to pay their passage. Fortunately, they were bought by Spotswood and settled at Germanna, " where they soon throve well." Subsequently the settlement was removed ten miles farther up the river.

Twenty years after, Colonel Byrd, passing through the place, made merry at Governor Spotswood's " enchanted castle, a baker's dozen of ruinous tenements with a chapel that had been burned by some pious people with the intent to get one built nearer their own homes." Spotswood himself, turned out of his office by the intrigues of opponents, died " among his own people" at Germanna. From some of these wrecked and plundered colonists of de Graffenried, in their new and more prosperous home, was descended James Lawson Kemper, soldier of the Civil War and Governor of Virginia.

Of the various colonies sent out from the camp of the Palatines at London, the largest and ultimately the most successful " plantation," to give it the name often used at the time, was that of the Germans sent to Ireland. In all nearly four thousand colonists were sent thither, and though some returned to Germany and others finally joined the settlers in New York, it remained one of the largest settlements of these destitute people. The first section was sent off in August of 1709, just after the New Berne colony had sailed, and before the departure and return of those sent to the Scilly Islands. Other companies were sent from time to time for six months. They had their share of tribulation, discouragement, deception, and ill-treatment by the English

The Germans in Colonial Times

speculators who had them in charge, but they battled through. They were settled in the vicinity of Limerick on some waste-land, where they soon caused the wilderness to blossom as the rose. Most of them linen-weavers by trade, they had an important part in founding the Irish linen industry. They built large substantial houses with gardens and orchards. When Wesley visited their settlement of Court Mattrass in 1758 he found it built in the form of a square, around "a pretty large preaching place." They have left the impress of their character—thrifty, industrious, and conspicuously honest—upon the whole surrounding district.

From Court Mattrass in 1760 there emigrated to New York a young Palatine, Philip Embury, a local preacher who, assisted by a pious school-master of his own people, had ministered to the little flock of Wesley's followers in Ireland. He was accompanied by his wife and a few related families, among them his cousin, Barbara Heck, and her husband. Embury was undoubtedly a good man, but perhaps of a timid character, little disposed to take the initiative in anything. In the new land, amid the struggles to establish themselves which awaited the little company of poor Palatine weavers, Philip Embury demitted his humble ministry. At this juncture there "arose a mother in Israel,"—Barbara Heck. Coming one day into a neighbor's house, she found some Palatines engaged in card-playing. To the pious Wesleyan woman this was a threatening of perdition. She threw the cards in the fire, and left the terrified card-players to go immediately to Embury's house. There she knelt at the feet of the young preacher, beseeching him with tears no longer to be silent, but to preach to his backsliding countrymen. "God will require our blood at your hand," she declared. Embury responded to the appeal to his slumbering sense of duty. Barbara Heck went out, collected four other like-minded ones, and to this little company Embury preached, they sang hymns, a "class" was formed, and Embury became its leader,—the first class-leader of American Methodism. By Barbara Heck's exertions money was raised in spite of discouragements, a small, plain chapel built, help came to them from other Methodist converts, and from this poor Palatine and his handful of hearers sprang the seven million of the great Methodist Church. Of the simple German matron whose conscientious faithfulness was the seed of so much it has been testified : "She lived much in prayer and had strong faith and therefore God used her for great good."

Of all Queen Anne's *protégés* whom she sent to her colonies in America the largest number were directed towards New York. Perhaps the influence of Pastor Kocherthal is responsible for the selection of the place ; but the chief idea was to employ the Palatines in the production of tar and turpentine, naval stores of which the "Mistress of the Seas" stood in great need, for all must be brought from other nations. The trifling drawback that these husbandmen and vine-dressers from the Rhineland were entirely unacquainted with the process of making ships' stores seems not to have occurred to the authorities, who went with cheerful inexperience about the work of founding the new enterprise. The colony was to be taken out and settled upon its lands by Governor Hunter, lately appointed to the government of New York. Liberal conditions were made for the trans-

The Germans in Colonial Times

portation and settlement of these people : their fare was paid, they were to be supported for a year after arrival, tools and materials for house-building given them, and forty acres of land ultimately assigned them. But they were to be divided into gangs of workers, and all the products of their labor were to go to the Queen to recompense her for the expense she had incurred in their maintenance.

Some time in the earlier months of the year 1710— the exact date is uncertain—the expedition, consisting of ten ships, carrying altogether about three thousand souls, left England, and on June 13 arrived in the harbor of New York. A large number of the poor emigrants had died upon the passage,—nearly twenty per cent.; almost all the children had succumbed to the hardships of an ocean voyage in those times. One of the Palatine ships, wrecked accidentally or by design upon the coast of Long Island, has given rise to the legend which Whittier has immortalized in verse in his pathetic "Wreck of the Palatine." But when the miserable people were at last in "the haven where they would be," so much sickness still raged among them that the frightened inhabitants of New York insisted upon their being encamped on Governor's Island until danger of infection was over, and many died there. About eighty orphan children cast upon the charity of the community were apprenticed by Governor Hunter, and among these appears the name of John Peter Zenger, afterwards so celebrated in the history of the liberty of the press in America.

The governor endeavored to find a place on which to settle the remainder of his colony, and finally selected a tract, part of Livingston Manor, which was recommended to him by the proprietor as very suitable for his purpose. In this it is probable that Hunter—a bluff, ignorant, honest soldier, and nothing else—was deceived by Livingston, who was a canny Scot grown rich through unscrupulous practices as Indian agent, and even—it was suspected—as a partner of Captain Kidd in the latter's piratical ventures. The Earl of Clarendon called Robert Livingston "a very ill man," and such poor Governor Hunter seems to have found him to his cost.

The Palatines, divided into six companies with headmen put over them who were appointed justices, were finally sent, in the autumn of 1710, to the scene of their future labors. They were settled in two villages,—East Camp, now Germantown, and West Camp, whose name still survives. Most of the settlements in the west were embraced in the town of Saugerties. After the troubles in East Camp, the settlers there founded Rhinebeck. It may be noted that most of the trouble later experienced was localized in the eastern settlements in the Manor, while the people upon the west bank of the Hudson pursued the even tenor of their way, sharing the blessing of those who have no history.

Of course, nothing could be done until spring, so through the long winter they were supported in idleness, and "Satan found some mischief still for idle hands to do." The more industrious formed a school for the instruction of the few poor children who had survived the sufferings of the journey; they also erected houses, or, more properly, huts, for shelter. The next summer they were too busy in sowing grain for their future sustenance to give much attention to the provision of

6

the tar which was the *raison d'être* of the colony. They were also interrupted by the expedition against Montreal in this year, on which three hundred of them served their adopted country, faithfully it appears, though they did not receive the promised pay, and were disarmed as soon as they returned, for fear that they would rebel against the government if armed. It had been arranged that four hundred of the Palatines settled around New York should be recalled to the camps when their help was needed, but ultimately Hunter was glad to be freed from the obligation of subsisting these, and they were left to support themselves wherever they might have settled. At the end of the third summer which the Palatines had spent in America, Hunter, having "exhausted both substance and credit," sent despairing orders to the East Camp to have the people called together and told that they must now "shift for themselves;" he could no longer support the colony.

The colonists were in despair. Winter was at hand and starvation seemed imminent. In their extremity they remembered that when in camp, in London, at the first beginning of their weary wanderings, they had been visited by some Mohawk chiefs, who had promised them a portion of rich and fertile land called "Schorie." For this—literally the promised land—a number of the colonists now set out. Their headmen—"chiefs," as they are sometimes called in apparent imitation of their Indian friends—went first under the leadership of the elder Weiser, and asked the little band of Indians settled in the valley for land. This was given them, and the Indians always showed themselves friendly to the little company of Germans. They guided them through the forest, used for them the red men's woodcraft by pointing out edible roots and herbs, and when the first white children were born in the valley, gave the poor German mothers fur robes on which to lie.

The German "chiefs" bought from the Indian ones land for the colonists. In a short time fifty families left the unlucky scene of their servitude and came into the Schoharie Valley, making a road fifteen miles long through the trackless forest. The governor sent after them an order "not to goe upon the land and he who did so should be declared a Rebell." It does not appear why Hunter, who had just told them that they might go anywhere and "shift for themselves," should have breathed out threatenings when the Palatines went to Schoharie ; but so it was, and his resentment was implacable and undying. But the Germans "seriously weighed matters amongst themselves and finding no likelihood of subsisting elsewhere . . . found themselves under the fatall necessity of disregarding the Gov^{rs} resentment, that being to all more eligible than Starving."

In March of the next year, 1713, a large number of their kindred joined them, breaking a way through snow three feet deep, and the numbers of the settlers were increased to nearly seven hundred people.

Seven villages were laid out, named after their seven "chiefs," huts erected, and a tailor acted as lay preacher and read service ; in the total lack of any implements for tillage, sickles did duty for ploughs, and they ground corn in stone mills after the Indian fashion ; as there was not a horse or cow in the settlement, nor a wheelbarrow, they packed their few belongings into the valley on their backs, like our miners of the Klondike. In the same

way salt was brought nineteen miles from Schenectady ;
the first seed wheat for the little settlement was carried
in the same fashion, and we are glad to know that it repaid its transportation with a yield of eighty-five-fold.
For a generation, until the first mill in Schoharie was
built, the pioneers, men and women, carried their grain
upon their backs to Schenectady to have it ground into
meal, large companies of them going together and
camping overnight in the woods on the way.

During the first hard winter of the little handful just
escaped from Hunter's camp on the Hudson, Weiser,
one of the " chiefs," was asked by his Indian friends to let
his son, the afterwards well-known Conrad Weiser, spend
the winter among the red men that he might learn their
language. This was a proposition which was equally
dangerous to accept or refuse, but Weiser trusted his
son, as half hostage, half pupil, to their savage friends,
and the future interpreter of Pennsylvania was returned
to him in the spring safe and sound, having narrowly
escaped starvation and death at the hands of drunken
braves, but with a perfect knowledge of the Indian
language and, better still, the way to Indian hearts and
minds ; probably never was a severe apprenticeship
better rewarded.

To the common trials of pioneer life, in the case of
these harried Germans, was added the unsleeping hostility of the government. Their land was granted away
from them thrice, and these proprietors endeavored to
settle on their grants, or sell them to the Palatines or
dispossess the latter. To most of this worrying persecution the Palatines offered the passive resistance of
abiding upon their lands ; but finally they rebelled, drove

The Great Exodus of the Palatines

off the Albany sheriff who attempted to eject them, and tried in vain to worry out a persistent Dutchman who settled on their lands.

After five years of this warfare the Germans decided to send representatives to England to make an appeal there for their rights. They selected the elder Weiser and two others to go to London and lay their case before the Board of Trade. The delegates took ship for England, but were captured in Delaware Bay by pirates, who tortured and flogged Weiser until they extorted from him all the money with which the delegates had been supplied. Landed penniless in London, they were soon thrown into a debtors' prison, and Weiser's two companions died from the effects of ill treatment there. Weiser remained in London about five years, endeavoring to obtain for his poor people a title to the lands which they had settled with so much peril and hardship, but in vain. Governor Hunter, who arrived in England during Weiser's stay there, used his considerable personal influence against the "poor Palatine," and finally even the courageous and persistent German gave up in despair. He had become convinced that there was no justice to be had for the Palatines in New York, and advised his countrymen to go to Pennsylvania.

We do not know exactly what influenced Weiser in favor of the Quaker province; his son says that Governor Keith of Pennsylvania was in Albany upon Indian business, and "hearing of the unrest of the Germans, lost no time to inform them of the freedom and justice accorded to their countrymen in Pennsylvania."

But the settlers of Schoharie were not all of one mind; some desired to stay in their hardly won clear-

85

ings, and so submitted to necessity and bought their land again from the government. They lived a peaceful life after this in their secluded fertile valley ; almost the only man of note from among them was that William Bouck, Governor of New York in the forties, who was descended from the first of those Palatine children born a week after the entrance of the little community into the valley, whose mother was wrapped from the cold in the Indian gift of furs.

Some of the Schoharie settlers were willing to accept the offer of the new governor, Burnett, of lands elsewhere, and they, under the leadership of one of the seven chiefs, Elias Garloch, emigrated to the Mohawk Valley, and were followed by such a stream of emigration and so increased and multiplied as to make the Mohawk for thirty miles a German river ; from Herkimer and German Flats through Mannheim, Oppenheim, Minden to Palatine Bridge, Canajoharie and Stone Arabia, names of places or people testify to the Germanizing of this country. The story of the French invasions and of Herkimer's glorious death at Oriskany make this lovely valley classic and epic land to the annalist of the colonial Germans ; but it is "another story" which must be told in its place. Let us follow the tale of the exodus to Pennsylvania.

About two-thirds of the Schoharie people, unwilling to buy their land, and also to be settled on the Mohawk at the governor's pleasure, started for Pennsylvania, feeling that there at last might be found a refuge from oppression and injustice. Under the guidance of their faithful Indian friends, they cut a road through the forests from Schoharie to the head-waters of the Susquehanna ; there they built rafts and canoes, placed on them the women and children and their furniture, and floated down the river, the men driving the cattle along the land. Arrived at the point where the Swatara empties into the Susquehanna, they ascended this stream until the expedition reached the mouth of the Tulpehocken. Here the Germans selected their land and settled, finally, after fourteen years of wandering from place to place— from the Palatinate to London, from London over-seas to the camps on the Hudson, thence escaping to Scho- harie, they were finally at rest in Pennsylvania. The story of this exodus of these poor Palatines, cast down but not destroyed, baffled, oppressed, plundered, but never discouraged, is a tale with few parallels, and one of its most marvellous incidents is this journey through the forests ; yet the people themselves seem not to have thought it anything worthy of note.

Of course, they owed much to their Indian friends, with whom they seem always to have preserved a praise- worthy amity, probably owed largely to the influence of both the Weisers. Neither of these men came with the settlers to Tulpehocken in 1723. Five years after the first emigration, the Tulpehocken colony received a large accession from Schoharie, but even then Conrad Weiser did not accompany them, but came independently a year later.

His father only journeyed to Pennsylvania twenty-five years after, an old man of ninety, who came to end his days with "his Joseph," the son who had then attained a place of honor and trust in his adopted state. Muhlen- berg gives a touching picture of the old patriarch's death. "In the year 1746," writes Muhlenberg, "my wife's grandfather, the old Conrad Weiser, came to my house; he had lived in New York since 1710. The reasons of his coming were: first, it was very dangerous to live at his place as in the present war-times the French Indians rove about and kill the English subjects in a cruel manner." He then describes the practice of scalping to the fathers in Europe, and continues the story of the old Weiser's coming. "As several Germans in his neighborhood had been massacred and were treated thus, he was unwilling to give his gray head into the hands of the savages. He desired, too, to see his children and children's children once more, and to speak with me of the way of salvation. He was so wearied by his long fatiguing journey and his great age, that he was nearly dead when brought to my house. But he revived again and in half-broken words began to pray. His eyes were very dim, his hearing gone, so that I could not speak much with him, but I could not listen to him without tears of joy. I had everything quieted around, so that he did not know or notice that any one was present, that he alone and in spirit might hold converse with the omnipresent God." After recounting "the short edifying conversation" which he had with the old man, and his partaking of the sacrament, Muhlenberg says, "In the meanwhile my father-in-law (Conrad Weiser, the interpreter) sent a wagon and a bed, had him brought to him fifty miles further up the country and when he had blessed us, he reached the place with great fatigue and living yet a short time with his Joseph in Goshen, he fell asleep amid the affectionate prayers and sighs of his children and children's children standing about him, after wandering on this pilgrimage between eighty and ninety years." The old man might have said with the patriarch to whom Muhlenberg compares him, "Few and evil have the days of the years of my life been." After the toils and dangers, injustice and suffering of his emigration to America, his settlement in New York, his perilous and unavailing journey to London to get justice for his people, it is good to think of his pilgrimage ending in the house of his beloved and honored son, with peace and prayer and love.

This settlement on Tulpehocken Creek was then the remotest outpost of white colonization in Pennsylvania. But it did not long remain so. The tide of emigration was setting more and more strongly towards Pennsylvania as the only safe place to which Germans might emigrate. The region of country into which these adventurous pioneers had been so strangely yet safely conducted was one which afterwards became a very stronghold of the Pennsylvania Germans. When subsequently erected into a county it was given the name of Berks—"alt Barks" the German affectionately calls it in his dialect.

The eastern portion had furnished another nucleus for settlement, when de Turck, a Huguenot who had first sought refuge in the Palatinate, then in New York, finally decided, about five years previous to the emigration from Schoharie, to transfer himself, his family, and a small band of friends to Pennsylvania. There had been a constant, if small, influx of individuals into the future Berks County, beginning about the time of the two emigrations from Schoharie, and so the fertile country rapidly filled with its characteristic Pennsylvania German population. It would seem that there was no emigration by communities, with the single exception of the Tulpehocken settlers ; each family came alone, probably influenced by the favorable report of Pennsylvania which went back gradually across the ocean and penetrated each little community and influenced one man here, one there, to a hazard of new fortunes in the New World. Not only the praises of Pennsylvania must have influenced this small but constant stream to flow, but as well the unfavorable accounts from all the other directions in which the Great Exodus of Queen Anne's time sought to go. The massacres in North Carolina, the injustice experienced in New York, the sufferings at the first foundation of the colony in Ireland, all contrasted with the good fortunes of the Germans in the land of Penn.

One of the most unfortunate colonies was not, it is true, part of the Great Exodus. This was the experiment in Louisiana, begun under the glamour of that curious antitype of De Lesseps and Barney Barnato— John Law. This fantastic financier had just then set all France wild by his speculative miracles. With all the revenues of French taxation in his hands, princes and nobles bowing before him for an opportunity to make their fortunes by a lucky operation in the shares of his "System," with the Western Company of the Indies formed to monopolize the colonial trade of France and rival, if not crush, the British East India Company, Law yet found time for a little private enterprise in colonization. He took up a "duchy," a concession in the province of Louisiana which he was so industriously exploiting, and "purchased from one of the princes of Germany twelve thousand Germans to colonize" his new possessions. Not nearly this number ever arrived, and perhaps the fact of the "purchase" is equally erroneous, but so it is stated by Penicault in his annals of the little colony.

The Germans on their arrival in October, 1719, were first landed at New Biloxi, where, owing to the non-arrival of provision-ships, the poor colonists almost starved ; many of them ate poisonous food in their ignorance and extremity and were found lying dead. From this place of misery they were transported up the Mississippi to the farthest point of French settlement, —the Germans seemingly being considered the best pioneers,—and were settled at "Arcansas," where they built homes, being most of them married men, in which they differed from the soldiers and vagabonds who formed an undesirably large proportion of the first French colonists.

But just as their post was becoming established and flourishing, news reached them from Europe of the ruin of Law, the crash which had followed his daring speculations and driven him a fugitive over the continent. The settlers, dismayed at the fall of their master, started for New Orleans, hoping to return to their German homes, but the government would not permit the escape of such useful and industrious citizens as they had already proved themselves to be. It settled them again, independently and not in a colony, at the place which still bears in their honor the name of Côte d'Allemande. A French missionary, encamping "aux Allemands" in 1727, found "great poverty visible in their dwellings ;" but the place soon became a garden spot through their German thrift and hard work. Still, it was evident that these half-tropical countries were not for the Germans ; then, too, the Louisiana authorities exacted that all settlers in the lands of his Most Catholic Majesty should be Catholic likewise ; and the thoughts of " those intending for America" in Germany, warned by the experiences of their brethren in New York and in the South, turned more and more exclusively to Penn's province, where were found freedom, a temperate climate, the society of their fellow-countrymen, liberality in the dealings of the government, and, most valued of all, religious freedom.

CHAPTER IX

PEQUAE AND THE MENNONITES

We have seen the settlement of Berks County beginning in its eastern and western part almost simultaneously. For some reason the population of Berks was largely made up of the "church people"—Lutherans predominantly—in contradistinction to the people of another county settled by German pioneers,—that is, Lancaster. This was from the beginning a stronghold of the "sects," and first and foremost both in primacy of settlement and subsequent strength were the Mennonites.

These peaceful people had been the pioneers of Germantown, and from there, in the years which had followed Pastorius's foundation of the "German township," they had spread, slowly and quietly, as beseemed the sect, over the contiguous territory, the present county of Montgomery. But now re-enforcements arrived and did not tarry in the neighborhood of the Skippack and the Perkiomen, but pushed on to the frontier, where land was cheap and plentiful.

The impulse to this renewed Mennonite emigration came from a recrudescence of persecution in Switzerland directed against the "defenceless Christians." It is melancholy to observe that the free Swiss amid their mountains were not lovers of liberty in religious matters, and for the centuries since Anabaptist became a name of terror and reproach, an almost constant persecution had been waged against these feeble folk in the Alps.

The Germans in Colonial Times

Sometimes the zeal of the authorities slept, again it capriciously awakened. Just now occurred one of these times of renewed vigilance.

In the spring of 1709 a few families of Mennonites— Swiss exiles who had sought a later refuge in Worms and Frankenthal, but had been driven thence—arrived in Rotterdam, and made themselves known there to the "Committee on Foreign Needs," who were charged, during an existence of more than eighty years, with the relief of their persecuted co-religionists outside the tolerant country of Holland. The hearts of the committee warmed to them : "they are altogether very poor men who intend to seek a better place of abode in Pennsylvania," they said of them, and recommended them to English friends in London, who also "helped them liberally" to the extent of fifty pounds. The "poor men" went on their way to Penn's province, pushing into the wilderness "about sixty miles from Philadelphia, where they proved quiet and industrious," as James Dickinson testified of them.

They were quaint, simple people, the men wearing long, red caps, the women no head-dress but a sort of Scottish snood, "a string to keep the hair from the face." Among them was a certain Meylin, who was the descendant of a martyr, Hans Meylin, who had died for his faith in Switzerland many years before ; the son of this colonist was the first gunsmith of Lancaster County, rather a strange trade for one of this peace-loving sect ; another son fell under the spell of the Ephrata community, and became Brother Amos in that cloister. But we anticipate.

The little colony of eight families was but just settled,

huts were built, and land on Pequae Creek taken up when they felt an impulse to share with those persecuted brethren whom they had left behind the good news of their refuge in the forests of America. They decided to send some one to Europe, and, casting lots in the true Mennonite fashion, the lot fell upon their preacher and leader, Hans Herr. The brethren were dismayed at the prospect of being left alone "in Pequae," when Martin Kendig, another prominent man of the little circle, offered himself to go in Herr's stead. The offer was thankfully accepted. Kendig returned to Europe, and in the next year came back to Pequae, the leader of a new band of seekers after "freedom to worship God."

Meanwhile, in Bern the old persecuting spirit had revived. The magistrates of Bern had thrown many of the "defenceless Christians" into prison, where, in the terrible winter of 1709, whose severities were long remembered, many of the poor prisoners succumbed. The council was minded to put to death, by due process of law, those who were left, but some of the councillors "could not consent to such cruelty," so they sent them down the Rhine by boat to be deported to Pennsylvania. At Mannheim, in the Palatinate, the women and children, the old and sick, were put ashore, but a score of the men were taken on by their guards as far as Nymwegen in Holland. Here they were free, on touching the soil of that country of liberty, and went to appeal to the Mennonite brethren in that town for help. The preacher there wrote, "After they were entirely refreshed, they departed though they moved with difficulty, because stiffened from their long imprisonment. They returned to the Palatinate to seek their wives and children who are scattered everywhere in Switzerland, in Alsace, and in the Palatinate, and they know not where they are to be found. They were very patient and cheerful under oppression, though all their worldly goods were taken away. They were naturally very rugged people, who could endure hardships ; they wore long and unshaven beards, disordered clothing, great shoes which were heavily hammered with iron and large nails ; they were very zealous to serve God with prayer and reading and in other ways and very innocent in all their doings. But we could hardly talk with them, because their speech is rude and uncouth and they have difficulty in understanding any one who does not speak just their way."

These Swiss brethren returned to the Palatinate and tried to find a home there, but after an endurance of seven years, concluded that they could not hope for peace or tolerance where all depended upon the whims of the prince or his officials, and in 1717 the wanderers set out for Pennsylvania, the great asylum of the oppressed, and at length we find them at peace among their brethren on Pequae.

In 1726 another large emigration of Palatinate Mennonites took place, probably to the same district of country, and the Committee on Foreign Needs was in a strait betwixt two : their sympathies were much excited for their "brethren and fellow-believers," yet they feared to be overwhelmed by a tide of emigration from the Pfalz, far beyond their means to assist. So they passed many resolutions declining to help, yet when a company of "friends" appeared, their faces set towards the promised land of religious liberty, they compassionately "considered whether it would be possible for them to arrange for the many and great expenses of the passage."

Finally, in 1732, the committee refused any more to help intending emigrants, and requested the friends in Pennsylvania to have notice given in their churches that no one should write his acquaintances in Germany urging emigration or describing the advantages of the land. This had the desired effect, and the brethren of the Netherlands were freed from a burden beyond their means to support. The measures seem hard, but were no doubt necessary. The request to the congregations in America shows how the large persistent stream of emigration took its rise and course by a hundred, nay, a thousand, little rills of personal testimony from those persecuted people who had at last found a safe harbor in the land of Penn.

CHAPTER X

SOME years after the emigration of the Mennonites into Lancaster County, another persecuted sect, whose principles are in many ways similar to those of the "defenceless Christians," came to the same haven of refuge. But these sectaries, instead of a history reaching back for centuries, had a very recent origin.

It was in 1708 that Alexander Mack, a miller living near Schwarzenau in the little principality of Wittgenstein, became convinced that the beliefs and practices of the established churches upon the subject of baptism were wrong. Eight others, men and women, were of his own way of thinking. He baptized them all in the river Eder, having concluded from his study of the Scriptures that baptism by immersion was the only right mode. From this peculiarity they were nicknamed "the Tunkers," from the rather contemptuous German word meaning "to dip;" they themselves prefer the expression "Brethren." The tenets which the miller of Schwarzenau and his associates thought out for their little brotherhood were strikingly like those of the Mennonites, with the single exception of their insistence upon immersion. The Mennonites, while also rejecting infant baptism, have never made a point of the manner of its administration. "The Brethren" agreed with them in their opposition to war, to lawsuits and judicial oaths, and to richness of dress or furniture.

98

The Dunkers and Ephrata

The little society grew and prospered, but the authorities objecting to these public immersions in the Eder, they withdrew to Crefeld, the old home of the Germantown colonists. Here they found toleration, and, perhaps in consequence of this,—for persecution is the breath of life to sectarianism,—they also found lukewarmness and dissension.

Part of the little band came to Pennsylvania in 1719, led by their preacher, Peter Becker, and ten years later the rest followed. They settled among the other Germans, if we may judge by the places which Peter Becker and a few others visited on "a religious journey"—as Friends say—which was undertaken in 1723 to kindle again the old flame of devotion in the hearts of the scattered brethren. It was to the banks of the Schuylkill, to Falkner's Swamp, Oley, Conestoga, that these apostles of the Dunkers went, and at Pequae that they encountered a man who was to be the beginner of one of the strangest phenomena of colonial times in Pennsylvania,—Conrad Beissel, the head of the cloister at Ephrata.

He was a Palatine by birth, a baker by trade, who had come under the Pietistic influences so rife there. He would have been merely a harmless, if crack-brained, fanatic if he had not attracted the notice and the persecution of the too orthodox authorities of Heidelberg. Exiled from the city, with a halo of persecution about him, the young baker consorted with the Dunkers, who were not sufficiently separatistic for him ; even the loosely constituted sect of these Baptists was a "church," a Babylon, an abomination, and various other unpleasant things to a thorough separatist of

Beissel's kind. He sympathized rather with the "In-spired," the convulsed followers of the wild prophets of the Cévennes, who had taken refuge in Germany after the failure of their frantic revolt; even Spener listened for a time to the hysteric inspirations of prophetic maid-servants; and the inspired saddler Rock, a pet of the little Pietist court of the princes of Büdingen, was a friend of Beissel. But Germany was too worldly for our hero, and in 1720 the staid Puritans of Boston en-tertained, if not angels, then prophets unawares, when Beissel and a few friends landed there and straightway set out for Pennsylvania.

Here Beissel found his Dunker friends grown cold and worldly in the pressing occupations of building log huts, making clearings, and establishing themselves in the New World; they had, he said, "hung up their holy calling on a nail." True, Peter Becker, their preacher and leader, made a journey through parts of Pennsylvania and great revivals followed him. Beissel was baptized by Becker, though not in sympathy with him, and defended his course by the modest and rever-ent parallel that Christ allowed himself to be baptized by John.

But Beissel soon founded a new and schismatic com-munity among the Dunkers on Pequae, where he had by this time settled as a hermit, with a few like-minded brethren living near him, each in his little log hut. Within a few years after his arrival he had come to a consciousness of differing views on many points. He taught, with extraordinary mystical language, the praise-worthy virtue of celibacy, the keeping of the Sabbath on the seventh day of the week, and urged all his followers to leave the world for a hermit's life in the wilderness, "the upper country known as Conestoga."

Beissel, though his own adherents acknowledged that "his leadership was a stern and strange one," seems to have had an inexplicable influence over men and women far superior to himself. He persuaded a well-to-do farmer to build a house for his community on condition that the donor's two daughters should have a perpetual home in this convent; he ruled his followers with a rod of iron, and scarcely a whimper of dissent was audible; men of affairs like Israel Eckerlin or the far more gifted Conrad Weiser, men of extraordinary learning and piety like Beissel's successor, Peter Miller, put themselves under his yoke, while enthusiastic girls like Annchen and Maria Eicher, proud women such as she who was known first as Thekla, and after her quelled revolt as Anastasia, the reborn, yielded obedience to him; the wife of the elder Christoph Saur left home and husband and child to become Beissel's disciple, while hundreds of devout and devoted souls of simpler mould were his followers, heart and soul, and gave up their lives and property to his community.

In a decade after Beissel's arrival in America he had founded a community of celibates numbering at least eighty members; in its palmiest days the cloister had three hundred inmates. A number of buildings were erected for the use of the brethren and sisters, a *bet-saal* or prayer-house—for Beissel was too thorough a separatist to speak of a church—and many other houses, all baptized with quaint Old Testament names: Zion, Sharon, Kedar, Peniel, Bethany. The community itself took, about 1736, the name of Ephrata, in allusion to

The Germans in Colonial Times

Ruth 4 : 11 ;* before this it had been simply known as "the Camp ;" probably it was the last clause of the verse which was taken, for the passage as a whole is grotesquely inappropriate to a celibate community.

The soil was thin, the community about them one of poor and struggling frontiersmen. "Canestogues," wrote Miller, "was then a great wilderness and began to be settled by poor Germans, who desired our assistance in building houses for them ; which not only kept us employed several summers in hard carpenter's work, but also increased our poverty so much that we wanted even things necessary for life." This poverty it was, as much as any religious ideas, which dictated the employment of wood at Ephrata to so many purposes for which metal is commonly used. The buildings are put together with wooden pins, the doors hung on wooden hinges ; the community ate from wooden platters and cups, and even slept, their heads supported on blocks of wood instead of pillows. The brethren in the early times of the community drew the plough themselves, having no draught animals. They wore a habit of white, with a hood, somewhat like the dress of the Capuchins, and their feet were shod with wooden sandals.

Afterwards the community became prosperous, and this was mainly owing to the business ability and energy of Israel Eckerlin, one of four brothers, all of whom entered the convent, fascinated by Beissel's charm and urged also by old Conrad Matthäi, the Swiss survivor of

* "And all the people that were in the gate, and the elders, said, We are witnesses. The Lord make the woman that is come into thine house like Rachel and like Leah, which two did build the house of Israel : and do thou worthily in Ephratah, and be famous in Beth-lehem."

The Dunkers and Ephrata

the Hermits of the Wissahickon. But Eckerlin's gifts, though for a time they benefited the community and inured to the glory of Beissel, were too great to be tolerated by that jealous leader. At one time Brother Onesimus, as Eckerlin was called in religion,—for Beissel followed the Catholic custom of giving his disciples new names,—had supplanted Beissel as head of the community; but the brethren, and still more the sisters, refused obedience, and the Eckerlins finally left the community and set out alone for the western wilds to become hermits there. On their departure the brethren in a childish revenge burnt Eckerlin's manuscripts, cut down an orchard of his planting, and sold a bell which he had recently ordered from Europe with his name, as head of the community, cast upon it; the bell, after varied service in a church in Lancaster and in a fire department, finally came back to its original churchly use, which it still fulfils. The Eckerlins went to the remote forests of Virginia on the "New River," which we now call the Great Kanawha. There, protected by friendly Indians,—for all German pioneers seem to have had originally the kindliest relations with the red men,—Brother Onesimus and his brothers after the flesh lived a studious, peaceful life, until a band of fierce Iroquois burst upon them and dragged them captive to Montreal; thence they were sent to France, but they sank under their hardships, and died of fever shortly after reaching the Old World.

This was in 1757, ten years before Beissel's own death, and while the convent from which the Eckerlins had been thrust out to their savage doom was in its greatest prosperity. There were practised all the monastic arts :

illumination of manuscripts, the mysteriously beautiful choral singing which moved the most worldly hearers, and the publication from the press of Ephrata in the woods of Lancaster County of some of the finest as well as earliest specimens of colonial bookmaking. The community was known and spoken about in Europe ; Voltaire noted it, the Abbé Raynal and the Duke of La Roche-Jacquelin visited and wrote of it.

In his later years Beissel took to drinking, although the chronicle of Ephrata—for, like mediæval monasteries, they had their chronicle—does not admit this, noting only that the superintendent appeared " in the likeness of one who is drunk." " He became a master in this imitation," says Seidensticker, " and on one such occasion fell down the cellar stairs." Sometimes these edifying pranks inspired Beissel to the composition of hymns, which do not greatly differ in their unintelligibility from those composed when he was presumably in his right mind.

Though Conrad Beissel was a domineering, self-righteous fanatic, we have no evidence that he was immoral or other than self-deceived , the adulation and reverence which he received from the brethren and sisters would have turned a head stronger than that of the mystical baker of Heidelberg and hermit of Ephrata. Beissel lived and ruled until 1768. He lies amid the weather-beaten remains of his cloister under a stone which tells the infrequent visitor that " Here rests an offspring of the Love of God, Friedsam, a solitary but later become a leader, guardian, and teacher of the solitary and of the congregation of Christ in and about Ephrata."

CHAPTER XI

IN 1733 there came to Pennsylvania two families who were the avant-couriers of a small sect whose pathetic history of persecution and endurance makes them interesting out of all proportion to their numbers or the influence they have had upon the history or development of the province. These were the Schwenkfelder, the followers of that Silesian nobleman of Reformation time, Caspar Schwenkfeld.

Born in 1490, a courtier, a counsellor of his sovereign, a theologian, and withal a man of the sweetest and gentlest spirit, he left the Romish church under the impulse of Luther's deeds and words, but his own line of thought soon diverged from that of the Saxon reformer. His peculiar views were not so startlingly heretical as we might suppose from the violent objurgations—such as "bond-slave of the devil"—which Luther hurled at him. Schwenkfeld, a student of Hus, of Wickliffe, and of Tauler, taught a doctrine of the Word which made it almost identical with the Inner Light of the later Quakers, who, indeed, are considered by some of their highest authorities to have derived much of their teaching from Schwenkfeld through the Dutch Mennonites. The Silesian reformer also denied consubstantiation, and held some peculiar belief as to the constitution of the glorified body of Christ. As to matters of church forms and government, Schwenkfeld said that "they had not been opened to him," and left his followers to do as they were led by that "Word of God" in whose guidance and enlightenment he trusted with so sublime and child-like a confidence. After a life of unremitting labor, of persecution, journeyings, exile, and unfailing charity towards all, Caspar Schwenkfeld died in Ulm, at the house of a faithful woman friend, and was buried in a cellar.

He had always disclaimed any purpose to found a church, but his doctrine had many followers; indeed, at the time of his death almost the whole population of some districts in his native province of Silesia were in sympathy with this pure and gentle reformer. In that period of ferocious orthodoxy which followed the Reformation and preceded the Thirty Years' War, those inclined to Schwenkfeld's opinions were often severely persecuted, but during the agonies of the long conflict Protestants had no leisure from suffering in which to persecute one another. The little groups of believers who were known, in spite of their leader's protest, as Schwenkfelder diminished in numbers, partly because the mildness of the dominant Lutheran Church drew many into her fold.

In 1718, that determined zealot Carl VI. being upon the imperial throne, it was decided to convert the Silesian heretics to Catholicism, and two Jesuit fathers were sent to Liegnitz, "in which principality most of the Schwenk-felders reside," charged with this special mission. For seven years the Jesuits tried every means, fair and foul, to convert this handful of simple peasants, but in vain. They were fined, the homestead of one man confiscated for a Catholic chapel and school, they were imprisoned;

four girls were set in the stocks in the depths of winter and kept there in a kneeling posture four days and nights until the urgent appeals of their friends procured their liberation, though they lay for weeks at the point of death from the effects of the racking strain. The Jesuits refused to perform marriages, and most lamented of all their measures was the refusal to allow the heretics to bury their dead with funeral ceremonies in the churchyards. They must be taken on a wheelbarrow or cart to "the cow-paths," and there interred without hymn or prayer. There still remain more than two hundred of these graves in "the cow-paths," and the simple rhyme in which these persecuted people recorded their sufferings recited this as the greatest of their afflictions; translated, it runs: "Throw their dead out like foul carrion; the cow-path is too good; trample not on the grass; the father may not go with his child; the wife not accompany the husband to his long home." Orphan children were put in charge of the Jesuits to be brought up in the Catholic faith. The Schwenkfelder were forbidden to sell their property or to leave the country.

The poor heretics sent two of their number to Vienna to beg clemency of the Kaiser, but in vain. Four years the humble ambassadors remained at the court, pleading for some mitigation of their trials, but in 1725 the Kaiser "once for all refused" any toleration to the heretics. The jails were now "never empty of Schwenkfelder," and the fines amounted to an enormous sum. Then the patience of the misbelievers broke down, and the only deed of violence in their existence of two hundred years took place when they broke into the dwelling of one of the Jesuit Fathers, beat him, and then fled by night, leaving their little earthly all behind them, to Görlitz and to Count Zinzendorf at Berthelsdorf. Here they were afforded shelter for a time, but the danger of protecting those outlawed Christians was so great that Zinzendorf himself advised their seeking an asylum elsewhere.

But where in Europe could such an asylum be found? They knew too well that there was no continuing city for them in the Old World, so, in spite of the endeavors of friends in Holland to dissuade them from emigration by painting the gloomiest pictures of Pennsylvania, the Schwenkfelder resolved to go thither, and, helped by generous merchants of Haarlem, the three brothers von Bynschance, they set sail in 1733 for America.

They landed safely in Philadelphia, and immediately appointed a day of thanksgiving—"Gedächtniss Tag"—which is still observed by the little congregation on the 6th of September every year. For several years after the arrival of the first members of the sect each summer brought a new accession to their number, until all the Schwenkfelder of Silesia had found refuge from their centuries of persecution in the province of Pennsylvania.

A few years after their flight, Frederick the Great, having in the mean time conquered the province of Silesia, and heard of the industry, honesty, and blameless life of these Silesian Quakers, wrote requesting them to return, assuring them of full religious toleration, for "In my dominions," wrote the King once, "everybody can go to heaven after their own fashion provided they pay their taxes." But the Schwenkfelder, having escaped from Europe, did not wish to return, and wrote the great King a simple description of their peace and prosperity in Pennsylvania, declining his invitation.

Yet they long retained a grateful interest in the few friends of their days of adversity. More than half a century after the merchant brothers von Bynschance had furnished help for their destitute fellow-Christians to flee from Europe, their firm met with reverses; the Schwenkfelder in Pennsylvania, hearing of it, made up a subscription for its aid "in grateful remembrance of the kindness shown their fathers." After the Napoleonic plunderings of Germany in 1816, they sent money to the town council of Görlitz, the city which had sheltered some of the sect when harried out of their Liegnitz homes, and which was now suffering the desolation of war.

The history of the Schwenkfelder in Pennsylvania, where alone the sect is found, is uneventful. They had the usual fortunes and hardships of pioneers. Most of them settled along the Perkiomen in Montgomery County. Here they have followed their simple customs of worship, resembling those of the Quakers, with the exception that they use singing, and, although opposed to infant baptism, bring their young children to the meeting-house to dedicate them to God in prayer. For a generation after their arrival they were without any church organization, but at the end of the Revolutionary War, their minister, Christopher Schultz, a shepherd lad at the time of the flight from Silesia, who had been taught by their old weaver-preacher Weiss, organized them into several districts, collected their records, arranged a catechism and hymn-book and their "Compendium" or confession of faith. He also regulated the school and poor funds, for to both education and charity the Schwenkfelder have ever given great attention. There are but a few hundred members of the sect now, though descendants of the early exiles for religion's sake are numerous and respectable ; the soldier of the Civil War and Governor of Pennsylvania, whose monument now adorns our State Capitol, John F. Hartranft, was sixth in descent from that "Tobias Hertteranfft" who fled across the seas with the little pilgrim band more than one hundred and fifty years ago.

The zeal of those impoverished and persecuted exiles, the Schwenkfelder, for education, is only the manifestation of a characteristic common to all the German emigrants of colonial times. To secure a school-master and a minister to accompany a colony was recognized by the land speculators and colonizers of those days as almost indispensable in order to attract emigrants ; and very unsuitable men were sometimes foisted upon the poor Germans to represent these professions.

The common opinion among the Englishmen who have written our colonial history is that the Germans were "dull and ignorant boors." This perhaps arose as much from ignorance on the part of the English historian as on that of the maligned Germans,—ignorance alike of the language, the thought, and the culture of Germany. The early immigrants, also, belonging to obscure and persecuted sects, were naturally anxious to have the tenets of these sects taught their children in the language of the fathers, and so they opposed English and "godless" schools on the ground of the Catholic opposition at the present time. But their own school-masters were often men of "light and leading" among their people ; such a man as Pastorius, a scholar, a university man, and a born leader, was of course rare—such men are never common ; but a type such as Ulmer of Waldoboro, or Schley of Frederick—cheerful, courageous, resourceful, and pious—was fortunately very often found in these log school-houses of the wilderness.

Such a man blessed and taught the German children of Montgomery County in the person of Christopher Dock, the pious school-master of Skippack. Dock did not lead his people to the triumphant taking of a fortress like Captain Ulmer, nor did he settle prosperous colonies in the wilderness like Schley, but the monument of this devout Pennsylvanian precursor of Froebel is in the affection and reverence of all who knew him. The incidents of his life are few—indeed it may be said to have none. A Mennonite drafted into the army and discharged because of his scruples against warfare, he came to Pennsylvania about 1714, taught school for ten years, then gave it up and went to farming. But his conscience was uneasy ; he felt that teaching was for him a divine vocation, and in 1738 he again resumed it. For more than thirty years he taught the fortunate children of Skippack and Salford, three days alternately. Then one autumn evening "he did not return from his labors at the usual time. A search was made, and he was found in the school-house on his knees—dead. After the dismissal of the scholars he had remained to pray, and the messenger of death had overtaken him at his devotions,—a fitting end to a life like his."

Many of his friends had long been desirous to have a description of Dock's method of keeping school, but, owing to the school-master's modesty and to his Mennonite principles which forbade him to do anything tending to his own praise, it was difficult to win Dock to write it. The precious manuscript was mislaid while in the hands of the printer Saur, upon which the author joyfully remarked that "it had never been his opinion that it ought to be printed in his lifetime and so he was very well pleased that it had been lost." But it was found, printed, and so a picture of the ideal school and home life of the Pennsylvania Germans in the second and third generations after the founding of Germantown is placed before us.

A modern writer has said that it is evident that Dock's scholars were "the children of a very rough peasantry who had to be prevented from living like animals,"—which is about as well founded as most of this author's easy generalizations from insufficient knowledge. The rules of etiquette which George Washington copied from an English work for his own guidance in Virginian society, about the same time, show that our ancestors were none of them particularly refined.

Dock's book pictures for us the little Germans "rising without being called, dressing themselves quickly but neatly," and after the morning prayer and a greeting to "those who first meet you," going to school at the right time. "If any known or respectable person meets you, make way for him, bow courteously. Dear child, when you come into school incline reverently, sit down quietly in your place, and think of the presence of God. Although after school you are out of sight of your teacher, God is present in all places ; be circumspect before Him and His holy Angels." "In church sing and pray very devoutly, since out of the mouth of young children will God be praised. . . . When the name of Jesus is mentioned, uncover or incline your head. Be never idle, never listen at the door. Make your reverence deeply and lowly with raised face. Never go about nasty and dirty. If anything is presented to you take it with the right hand and give thanks courteously. Do not laugh at everything and especially at the evils and misfortunes of others. If you have promised anything try to hold to it." So the gentle school-master instructs the little boys and girls, and tells us, too, how he "treats the children with love," and endeavors to train them so that "the honor of God may be increased and the common good be furthered." Perhaps Penn's ideal of the Christian commonwealth in the wilderness was never better expressed than thus by the pious German school-master.

CHAPTER XII

THE PROGRESS OF SETTLEMENT IN THE VALLEY OF VIRGINIA AND IN MARYLAND

So much of the province of the Penns as had then been purchased from the Indians—and the proprietors were very careful to extinguish the Indian title before selling the land to white men — lay in the form of a quarter-circle around the city of Philadelphia. It stretched westward to and across the Susquehanna, and northward vaguely to "the mountains." The Germans had now spread around the outer rim of this segment of a circle. Near the city, with the exception of the Germantown settlers, the colonists were of British blood ; Chester, Delaware, and Bucks Counties were English. But outside of this, on the frontiers where land was cheap, the Germans settled, toiled, endured hardships, lived their lives after the economical and religious pattern showed in the Fatherland, and prospered.

Montgomery County was first entered in 1702 ; an interval of a few years, and the Oley Huguenots of Berks and the Pequae Mennonites of Lancaster County formed rallying points for further settlement. We have seen how Miller, the Prior of Ephrata, found " poor Germans" on " Conestogues" in need of the brethren's help. In two or three years came the fugitives from Schoharie and Tulpehocken, the pioneers of the western part of Berks. Then in Quitapahilla, the "Snakes' Hole," was begun the populating of Lebanon and Dauphin Counties. A curious episode in the history of Lebanon was the coming of a Jewish colony, which settled in the vicinity of Schaefferstown in the second or third decade of the century, had a synagogue and a rabbi, and a graveyard about which they built a stone wall so substantial that it long survived the colony, now for many years but a fading memory. Crossing the Susquehanna, probably at "Wright's Ferry," German pioneers pushed on into the territory of the present York and Adams Counties, and about 1730 formed there the earliest nucleus of white occupation, the "Conewago settlements."

The tide of German pioneers flowed yet farther south and crossed the Pennsylvania border. In 1732 Jost Heit with his family, his sons-in-law, Chrisman and Bowman, their families, and a number of others, sixteen households in all, started from Pennsylvania for the fertile regions of the South. From York they cut their road through the forests, forded the Potomac, which they called the Cohongoronton, near Harper's Ferry, and entered the rich and beautiful Valley of Virginia. Heit settled near Winchester, some of his company near the present Stephens City, the others took up their abodes at distances of a few miles from each other down "the Valley." In about thirty years the towns of Strasburg, Woodstock, and Shepherdstown (first called Mecklenburg) were established, all of them by Germans; but, of course, the settlements on these sites began much earlier. Peter Stover was the founder of Strasburg; Shepherd, a Pennsylvania German, whose real name was Shaeffer, settled his town with a number of German mechanics; of Woodstock, where we shall see Peter Muhlenberg exchanging the gown for the soldier's uniform, it is said by

The Germans in Colonial Times

Kercheval in 1833 that "it was settled exclusively by Germans, and their religion, manners, customs, habits, and language were for a long time preserved, and to this day the German language is generally in use by the inhabitants." And this, we know, was a full century after Jost Heit's caravan crossed the "Cohongoronton" on its way to settle the valley. Doddridge, who, of course, was not of this people, says, in his valuable "Notes" on the frontier life of Virginia and Pennsylvania, of these pioneers and their descendants, "It is remarkable that throughout the whole extent of the United States the Germans in proportion to their wealth have the best churches, organs, and graveyards."

A few years passed, and Jost Heit's trail was followed as far as Maryland and the Monocacy by other Pennsylvania Germans, who settled in the neighborhood of what is now the town of Frederick. The passage of Heit's colony, like one of the treks which founded the Dutch republics in South Africa, had called the attention of the Maryland governor to the valuable material for settlement which was passing over his country; he offered land to other Germans upon favorable conditions, and presently there arose a little settlement, commonly known, as was the custom of the time, after the stream which drained the country, as Monocacy. In 1735 an organized colony came to re-enforce the few scattered pioneers. It was led by a Palatine school-master, John Thomas Schley, who was the mainstay of school and community and church for half a century. Schlatter, the pioneer apostle of the Reformed Church in this country, wrote, twelve years after, "It is a great advantage to this congregation that they have the best school-master that I have met with in America. He spares neither labor nor pains in instructing the young and edifying the congregation according to his ability by means of singing and reading the Word of God and printed sermons on every Lord's Day." This excellent schoolmaster, the next year, built the first house in the town of Frederick, which was laid out in 1745. The surveyor, we are told, intended to lay out its streets towards the cardinal points, but owing to his defective instruments he was not very successful. From John Thomas Schley are descended a long line of men useful in their day and generation as he was in his ; the most famous being Admiral Winfield Scott Schley, the destroyer of Spain's last fleet in that New World which she discovered.

The Palatine school-master also lived in stirring times, though the incidents of his day were but the border warfare between the two provinces of Maryland and Pennsylvania. In the same year that Schley and his fellow-Palatines came to " Monocacy," the Governor of Maryland appealed to the King to relate how he had "thought the people so deserving Encouragement that several Considerable Quantities of Land were allotted them for their Residence and accordingly not less than fifty or sixty families of that nation immediately took possession of these Lands." Presently " through unwariness and too much Credulity they suffered themselves to be prevailed on by the Emissaries of Pennsylvania to renounce openly their Submission to this Government." These Palatines then proceeded, " being people of more than ordinary Spirit, to the Commission of horrid and Cruel Violence,"—that is, they retaliated some attacks

117

by the borderer, Thomas Cresap, by burning Cresap's house. Much wordy and stately correspondence between the two governors followed, the Pennsylvania government "made some observations on the style and manners of the Lord Baltimore's letters which they conceived too peremptory;" the King was appealed to, and finally a line was run between the two provinces, as far as the Susquehanna, where it was stopped for a matter of thirty years, until the famous "Mason and Dixon's Line" was at last completed. The hostilities between Cresap, who was a typical frontiersman, and "these deluded people," the Palatines, seem to have ceased spontaneously without need of any further rhetoric, and the Germans continued the quiet settling up of the province.

In 1739 Jonathan Hagar came to reside on his tract, called "Hagar's Choice," about thirty miles west of the Monocacy settlement. In 1769 he had his town laid out, and attempted to give it the name of his beloved wife, Elizabeth, but to the public Jonathan Hagar was better known than his wife, and so the place was called Hagar's Town "in honour of its intelligent founder." By this time the Germans had spread over the whole region west of the South Mountain and as far as Conococheague Creek. Elizabeth (Hager's) Town was taking its present name ; the Moravians had begun a church settlement at Graceham ; and the subsequent Taneytown, Mechanicstown, Emmitsburg, and many other villages were being settled.

Frederick County—liberally including the western part of the province "as far as the settlements extend"— was formed in the middle of the century. All through the country Germans had settled on their "tracts," which often rejoiced in the oddest and quaintest of names : "The Bachelor's delight," "Father's Good Will," "Found it out," "Hager's Defence," "Kyser's Inheritance," "Magdalen's Fancy," "Manhim," "New Bremen," "Small Bit," "Struggle," "New Work," "Jacob's Loss," "Adam's Fall," "Small Venture," or "Thereabouts," "Bower's Struggle," "I have waited long enough."

It was a frontier community, who for the most part lived like the peasants they had been and the backwoodsmen that they were. The women in petticoat and short gown cooked plentifully, kept the rude log cabins cleaner than those of their few Irish neighbors, worked in the fields in summer and spun diligently in winter ; the men, clad in the half-Indian costume of fringed hunting-shirt and leggings, cleared and farmed their little tracts, and had rich gain in skins, furs, and game that fell to their unerring rifles.

The thrifty Palatines early established a trade with the German settlements south of them, and caravans of pack-horses carried through the Valley of Virginia as far as Georgia their manufactures of wool, flax, and leather. It was along this southern trail, first blazed by the German pioneers of the Shenandoah Valley, that most of the emigration to Maryland, Virginia, and the farther South passed. About the middle of the century we have the record of a small number of Germans who landed at Annapolis, and came to Frederick County from there. The first Lutheran minister of the town came with this colony, and there is a letter from Cæcilius Calvert, Lord Baltimore, which vaguely recommends the authorities "to forward them to Manockesy (which I understand is in Frederick County)." The arrivals of ministers, the foundation of churches and building of houses of worship, represent the intellectual as well as the spiritual side of pioneer life, and, judged by this standard, the Palatines of the Maryland wilderness were neither backward nor neglectful of these higher things.

But while they were clearing the forests, building log churches, laying out towns, and sending tinkling trains of pack-horses through the southern wilderness, German settlement in the South, in Georgia and "the Carolinas," had begun there almost contemporaneously with that of Western Maryland and the Shenandoah Valley, and was increasing and multiplying from centres of its own foundation.

CHAPTER XIII

THE GERMANS IN SOUTH CAROLINA

THE first German settlement of the Southern States was the unlucky colony of Purysburg, in what was subsequently South Carolina. A certain Jean Pierre Purry, of Neufchâtel in Switzerland, conceived the design of planting a colony in the Carolinas. It was with him a matter of business and hoped-for profit; no religious or humanitarian ideas entered into it. Purry had been a director in Law's "Compagnie des Indes," and seems to have inherited to the full the visionary and magnificent spirit of that blower of bubbles. After his superior's fall Purry visited South Carolina, was enamoured of the climate and land, and published a curious pamphlet setting forth the advantages of countries under the influences of the sun at the precise angle of the thirty-third degree of latitude. This favored situation Carolina occupied, and he, therefore, desired to lead a colony thither.

The proposition apparently fell flat; but in 1731 the indefatigable "Mr. Peter Purry" sent out another pamphlet informing the public that he had secured a grant of land "on the borders of the river Savanna proper to build the town of Purrysburg upon." He paints the prospects of the colony in most alluring colors: "A man who shall have a little land in Carolina and who is not willing to work above two or three hours a day, may very easily live there. If you travel into the country, you will see stately Buildings, noble Castles, and an infinite number of all sorts of Cattle. . . . The people of the Palatinate, those of New York, New England, and other parts sell all that they have to come to Carolina." The reader wonders that any one resisted the attractions of this earthly paradise, but the cold fact is that Purry was only able to collect one hundred and seventy Switzers who sailed with him the next year for this "excellent country."

Arriving there, the governor gave them forty thousand acres of land about thirty miles from the mouth of the Savannah River, and also provisions for their maintenance until they should be able to support themselves.

But the colony, in spite of a re-enforcement of two hundred souls, would not prosper. Sickness, the hardships of life in a new land, and discontent were among them. They had brought their own minister, one M. Bignion, who had received Episcopal ordination at the hands of the Bishop of London when the colonists tarried there on their way ; but in a few years he departed for the settlements on the Santee. When, about the same date, the period arrived to discontinue the allowance for the support of the colonists, the poor Swiss were not able to take care of themselves as they had expected. True, we hear how in 1736 a deputation from Purysburg, a patrician of Berne and other gentlemen, waited upon Governor Oglethorpe of Georgia with polite speeches, and how when Oglethorpe repaid the visit "he was lodged and handsomely entertained at the house of Colonel Purry ;" but the majority of the colonists were in no such circumstances as their leader.

The Germans in South Carolina

Two years after this the founder died, and the prosperity of the colony seems to have died with him. It maintained a struggling and dwindling existence until the Revolution.

The coast country of South Carolina was by this time ascertained to be—save in exceptional places—malarious, and impossible for the continued residence of white men. The plantations were deserted for the "upper country" in the dangerous summer, and the gay little city of "Charles-Towne" in winter. The tide of German emigration set towards the high lands in the centre of the province ; in a few years a score of colonies had been settled there, and "by 1775 they had spread themselves over the entire western portion of the colony."

Undeterred by the misfortunes of the Purysburg colony, perhaps encouraged by the hard-won success of the pious Salzburgers at Ebenezer, many persons were anxious to "undertake the transport of Palatines" to Carolina. Among the state papers are letters setting forth that the writers "hear upon good authority that the agents for the Penn family have quarrelled with the Palatines and have refused to let them have any more land in Pennsylvania. This will put a stop to any more going to that colony. Next year a number of the better sort of the inhabitants must be forced to quit the Palatinate on account of their religion. If proper encouragement were given to a few families to go and settle in South Carolina so that they might acquaint their countrymen with the goodness of that province, South Carolina might very soon be peopled with honest planters." Then we have an enthusiastic account of "some Palatines who were sent by their countrymen to

South Carolina. They very much approve of the country and have made an advantageous report."

These personal reports seem to have been the chief
cause of the emigration of Germans to the South. Few
large bodies of emigrants seem to have come ; but in
1735 an emigration *en masse* took place to the settlement afterwards named Orangeburg, "because the first
colonists were subjects of the Prince of Orange."
Subsequently this name was given to the whole
"District," which is the first of the counties on the
range back from the ocean to be colonized. Two years
after the first comers, a third re-enforcement arrived,
bringing with them, in the German fashion, their pastor,
the Rev. John Ulrich Giessendanner. Shortly after his
arrival he was married to the person who had been his
housekeeper for more than a quarter of a century ; both
were well stricken in years, and shortly afterwards this
first German pastor of South Carolina died.

He was succeeded by his nephew, who bore the same
name, but probably to avoid confusion soon dropped his
middle name and was known as the Rev. John Giessendanner ; he, like his uncle, was a Swiss, and labored for
many years among the pioneer Germans with general
acceptation, as was shown in the disturbance which was
shortly after brought into the little settlement by a certain itinerant minister who rejoiced in the name of the
Rev. Bartholomew Zauberbühler. This worthy was not
only a minister but a colonizer, a land speculator, and
not impossibly one of those hated agents in collecting
"Palatines" for the New World whom the Germans
branded with the name of Neuländer. It seems that
the settlers of Orangeburg had degenerated somewhat

in the roughness of pioneer life, and when their young and energetic pastor attempted to bring about a reformation, there was some disaffection among them. Zauberbühler heard of this : he was at the time occupied—and one would think sufficiently so—in settling the colony of New Windsor on the Savannah River opposite Augusta. But he found time to intrude into the Orangeburg parish, and in 1742 appeared before the provincial council with a petition reciting that "there were a great many Germans at Orangeburg, Santee, and thereabouts who are very desirous of hearing the Word of God preached to them and their children," and also very desirous that Zauberbühler should be the preacher. He asked the council to grant him five hundred pounds money to go to London to be ordained to the position of minister in the established church at Orangeburg on his return ; in recompense he proposed " to bring over a number of foreign Protestants to settle in this province." But before the Rev. Bartholomew could take his departure for England on this very mixed ecclesiastical and colonizing mission, the Orangeburg settlers sent a most indignant petition to the council " to permit the said Mr. John Giessendanner still to officiate for them in divine service free from any further disturbance or molestation." Upon this, Zauberbühler subsided and we hear nothing more of him.

But a few years after Giessendanner took the step threatened by his rival, and went to London for Episcopal ordination. The Anglican was the established church in the colony ; the Society for the Propagation of the Gospel, though originally a non-denominational missionary society, now threw its influence on the same side in appointing its clergyman for work in the province, and many of the early Lutheran congregations were thus transferred to the Episcopal fold.

Meantime, settlement advanced. Governor Glen wrote to the home government in 1745 of "Orangeburg, Amelia, Sax Gotha, and Fredericksburg, towns chiefly settled with German Protestants." Amelia Township is northeast of Orangeburg; "Sax Gotha" is the governor's mistake for Saxe-Gotha,* the original name of the district or county subsequently called Lexington; it formed the northwest corner of Orangeburg district. It was settled in 1737, two years after the elder colony; in 1741 Bolzius of Ebenezer wrote, "We had heard nothing before of Saxe-Gotha in America, but we have just heard the intelligence that such a town (township) is laid out in South Carolina, one hundred English miles from Charlestown on the road that passes through Orangeburg, and settled with German people. They have a Reformed minister among them with whose character we are not yet acquainted." This clergyman was the Rev. Christian Theus, a painstaking and godly man, who labored for fifty years in this pioneer community, and now rests under a tombstone whose half-effaced inscription says, "This faithful divine labored through a long life as a faithful servant in his Master's vineyard, and the reward which he received from many for his labor was ingratitude."

Very probably this melancholy tribute alludes to the opposition and personal danger in which Pastor Theus

---

* Mills, speaking of Saxe-Gotha, says quaintly, "The inhabitants are mostly of German extraction and a good deal of equality is kept up among them."

then stood from what is known as the Weber heresy. This wild sect, reminding us of some of the fanatical developments of Russian sectarianism at the present time, was founded by a certain Peter Weber, who announced to his believing followers that he was God ; another of the sect claimed to be the second person of the Trinity, and the principal doctrine of the sect seems to have been the scourging of members at the hands of these frantic fanatics, that they might "be healed by stripes." Finally the leader selected one of his people as the incarnation of Satan, who was commanded to be destroyed, which was carried out so literally that the man was killed ; for this murder Weber was hanged, and the sect perished with its poor deluded founder.

This half-insane tragedy would give a very false impression of the early German settlers of South Carolina in general, if we took it as representative of the pioneers, who, patient, industrious, brave, and God-fearing, were all these years filling up the central and western part of the State.

The fertile fields of the well-named counties of Richland and Fairfield were first tilled by them, overflows probably from the Saxe-Gotha settlements, as was the case in the Newberry district. We have seen that speculative minister of the Word, Zauberbühler, founding the settlement of New Windsor ; this later received large accessions through the efforts of an assister of emigration, Hans Riemensperger, who also was instrumental in bringing many persons, chiefly orphans, as redemptioners into the Saxe-Gotha settlements. The story of the Carolinian redemptioners has never been told, though we know from the scattered notices in the

The Germans in Colonial Times

Urlsperger reports that this useful but misinterpreted kind of emigration made up a large part of the whole in the Southern as in the Northern States.

About the middle of the eighteenth century there came to South Carolina one of the latest colonies from the Fatherland, a number of Germans, who "after some delay settled so near the Northern border of the province that part of their settlements are in North Carolina and part in the counties of Chesterfield and Lancaster in South Carolina." They brought with them, as was common, a minister, or rather a school-master, who served them in divine things, subsequently studied theology and was ordained, and finally led the greater portion of his people to "the Forks of Saluda and Broad" (Newberry County), where they seem to have re-enforced the previously mentioned settlement, and from this apparently it was sometimes called "Dutch Forks."

The last Germans to settle in a body in the province of South Carolina was the much-tried colony of "Hard Labor Creek," a name probably bestowed by the pioneers out of the fulness of their hearts. An officer of the victorious army of Frederick the Great, one Stümpel, found himself after the conclusion of peace discharged and poor, like the hero of Lessing's immortal play "Minna von Barnhelm." But Stümpel was very unlike the heroic and scrupulous Major von Tellheim. *He* set about retrieving his fallen fortunes by speculating in German colonists. He procured five or six hundred of them, a tract of land from the British government, and transported his "poor Palatines" to London with the intention—it is to be hoped—of taking them to America. For some reason he was unable to do this, whereupon the valiant officer decamped, leaving his helpless colonists penniless and starving in a strange land. Their pitiful case was brought to the notice of benevolent Englishmen. Food, money, medical attendance, and transportation were given them, and in the spring of 1764 two ship-loads of them arrived at Charleston and were presently sent up the country, "conducted by a detachment of the Rangers," through the forests and swamps to the very verge of white settlement on a tract very inappropriately named "Londonderry." The other name we have cited, as well as that of Cuffeytown, was also given to the place which was in the present county of Abbeville. Here the deserted and beggared Germans, who had so wonderfully found friends in their distress, settled, increased, and multiplied, and at one time had a church of their own— "St. George on Hard Labor Creek"—where they heard the gospel in their own language ; but in the storms of the Revolution this passed from existence.

CHAPTER XIV

THERE were in New England two attempts at German colonization, one at Waldoboro in Maine and the other at Braintree in Massachusetts. Neither was very fortunate in its outcome, and, as they were somewhat connected, their stories may be told together. The settlement of Germans in the present State of Maine, then the eastward frontier of the province of Massachusetts, began about 1739; in the next year two or three families added themselves to the colony, but the main body came in the autumn of 1742; and, indeed, so slight is the evidence for any earlier settlement that this may be taken as the true date for this beginning of German settlement in Maine. These emigrants had been procured for General Waldo, the owner of a large tract of wilderness "on the confines of New England," by Sebastian Zauberbühler, the son ot that minister, colonizer, land speculator, and sharp business man whom we have seen in South Carolina, colonizing Germans at New Windsor, and concurrently vexing the righteous soul of the pastor of Saxe-Gotha.

Waldo himself was of German descent. His grandfather was an officer in the army of Gustavus Adolphus, and a branch of the von Waldow family still exists among the Prussian nobility. The father of the provincial proprietor, however, dropped the von and the nobility to become a prosperous merchant in Boston; his son was

born in London during a business residence of the
father's in that city. He became a typical American,
an energetic, resourceful, not too scrupulous merchant,
a colonizer of vast plans and promises, a soldier when
occasion arose, who could take from the King of France
his great fortress of Louisburg with an army of provincial husbandmen and mechanics. This, however, was
not the result of native and untutored military genius.
He had served the Elector of Hanover for ten years in
his army, rising to the rank of major, and when the
elector became George I. of England, Waldo resigned,
receiving the rank of captain in the colonial militia of
Massachusetts.

He made many journeys to Europe, and it was probably on one of these that he began the project of colonizing the tract of land which he had acquired in Maine,
with Germans. He appointed Zauberbühler his agent
for the collection of the emigrants. The specious Sebastian established himself at the inn of the "Golden
Lion" in Speyer, the old Palatinate city, and thence
issued a circular glowingly describing the charms and
fertility of the coast of Maine. Land was promised the
colonists, the support of a minister, "chirurgeon," surveyor, and school-master for ten years, good food on the
voyage, two large houses for their shelter during the first
winter, and a church, while Waldo promised to support
the colonists for a year after their arrival.

With these enticements Zauberbühler induced three
hundred Pfälzer and Würtemberger to accompany him
to the promised land. They were chiefly Lutherans in religion, and at that time a coalition between the Reformed
and Catholic churches of the Palatinate made life bitter

for these poor Christians : they were assured of "the free exercise of all Protestant religions," and so they went, the Palatines gathering at Mannheim, the Würtemberger at Heilbronn, for the tedious journey down the Rhine. At Cologne they were detained two months, no ship being ready for them. If they had been allowed to enter Holland, by the terms of the contract, Waldo's Rotterdam agents would have been obliged to subsist them. They were kept at the frontier until their money and patience were almost exhausted ; a number diverted their emigration to Pennsylvania, some returned home, many of the young men enlisted, and the remnant finally sailed for New England.

At Boston they were welcomed by Governor Shirley and by Waldo, who accompanied his colonists to Broad Bay, but soon quitted them, leaving them without the promised shelter or church, without clothing, chimneys to their houses, mills to make flour, or ovens to bake bread ; the chief subsistence of these German pilgrims during the first winter on the stern and rock-bound coast of Maine was rye bruised between stones and made into broth. If there were any colonists of their own race who had preceded them, they were too poor to be of much assistance.

Their minister left them during their first hardships, but his place was filled by John Ulmer, a school-master, who for years read service and sermons to them in barns, or whatever rude shelter could be found when the inclemency of the weather made their customary service in the open air impossible. He "conferred" with the Indians when the mutterings of alarm came before the Spanish War ; he led the German soldiers in the siege of Louisburg; he was their magistrate, prince, priest, and military commander, and withal put a cheerful courage on and solaced himself with jokes now and then. Once at Pemaquid, "hailing the people in the dusk of the evening to set him across the river," he gave his name "with such a string of Dutch titles that they expected to find a large number of persons" and were surprised to discover only the German school-master of Broad Bay waiting at the ferry.

The colonists presently sent a petition to the Massachusetts General Court begging the redress of their wrongs, but this worshipful body was evidently afraid to molest the wealthy merchant for his broken promises to "the Palatines." A committee finally reported that the Germans and Zauberbühler were both at fault, and that "Mr. Waldo did conceed to fullfill his part of the contract which, notwithstanding he has not in all respects done, he has shown forth heretofore, and now declares is ready to do it whenever it will suit with their convenience." It is also suggested that as "said Palatines will be left in starving condition 'tis humbly proposed this Court grant a sum of money to be laid out in Provisions and Clothing to help 'em thro' the winter;" but neither this nor any other help for which they asked was ever given them.

When the siege of Louisburg was resolved upon, the Germans, as we have seen, went to war under the leadership of Ulmer. Many of the settlers took their families with them to Nova Scotia, and the little cluster of log-huts was almost deserted; some of the Germans remained in the neighborhood of their conquest. The remnant, left behind, defenceless, were attacked by the

Canadian Indians, their cabins burnt, some men killed and others dragged away to a savage captivity, and the place lay desolate for the next three years. Then some settlers, led by Ulmer, returned; a saw-mill was built; other colonists came in 1752, and Samuel Waldo, son of the provincial general, was sent to Germany to enlist still more. He revamped the circular used by Zauberbühler ten years before, and by means of it collected about fifteen hundred colonists.

These were brought over under the leadership of Crell, a merchant and printer, and emigration agent of Philadelphia and Boston and Germany. He seems to have been as unstable as this description would imply, but by a curious combination of circumstances he had been brought into relations with Waldo on the one hand and the Palatinate on the other; he was in the main an honest man, sincerely desirous that the then growing abuses of German emigration to the New World should be reformed. Through a short-lived German newspaper which Crell, among his other enterprises, once printed in Philadelphia, he had become acquainted with Heinrich Ehrenfried Luther, a type-founder and merchant of Frankfurt, an "Aulic Counselor," and an upright, honorable man. He was much distressed by the abuses which the agents and ship-masters of Rotterdam inflicted upon the plundered and deluded emigrants, and desired to start an emigration to New England and Nova Scotia which should be free from these faults. At first Crell appeared to Hofrath Luther to be the man for the place, and he encouraged him to go up and down the Rhine Valley collecting emigrants for New England. But Luther had overrated Crell and underrated the strength of the ship-owners' combination. He was forced to give up his attempt to reform the abuses from the German side of the ocean ; this reformation was reserved for the humble but practical " German Societies" formed in the cities of America where Germans resided. But this is another and a most interesting and honorable story, to be told in its own place.

Before Luther ceased to patronize him, Crell had procured a small number of Germans, whom he accompanied across the ocean and settled, some in Waldoboro, where they were for a time dependent upon the charity of the province and of the struggling pioneers who had preceded them and were just beginning to repair the desolations of war and Indian forays ; some Crell sent to begin the colony of Frankfort in Maine, and some to settle about " Fort Massachusetts." Some were also assigned to the settlement in the town of Braintree, Massachusetts, which was to be named " New Germantown," and to rival the old one near Philadelphia, which had now been for nearly seventy years the first home of German immigrants in Pennsylvania, and a centre of Teutonic life, language, and culture.

The stories of the two Massachusetts settlements are soon told. The settlers in " the German townships so-called at Fort Massachusetts" petitioned the General Court in 1753 to lay them out land, grant them lots " for the first settled Protestant minister, for the Ministry and for the School." They tell how they " were induced at a very great expense to come over to America, that a number of us not being able to pay so great an expence as our passage from Germany necessarily involved us in, we have been obliged to go to labour with our hands in order to Discharge said expence, which some of us have now cleared." The records add that "Mr. Crellius has failed of bringing forward said settlements and that the poor petitioners are to be left without any aid." Among the names signed to this petition is that of Daniel Sachs, the great-grandfather of John G. Saxe the poet. The settlers called their little colony "Leydensdorp," in memory of the sufferings (leiden) which they had endured in their pioneer days. But later information fails to give us any account of this frontier post of Germany in the wilderness of Massachusetts.

Of New Germantown we have more knowledge. For a time it appeared destined to prosper: Benjamin Franklin invested in a few town lots, thus evidencing the faith of that usually sagacious philosopher in the Yankee project. On Crell's failure to carry out his plans for the settlement, two Englishmen, Palmer and Cranch, undertook to employ the "Palatines" in some glass-works to be established. The pressing needs of the people were relieved by public charity, dispensed through "Mr. Elter," the provincial interpreter, who supplied them with beds and blankets. A few additions came to their number. But the glass-works persistently refused to be profitable, perhaps because only the coarsest and most inferior grades of goods were manufactured. The General Court, who must have been heartily tired of their Teutonic speculation, were again appealed to, this time to permit a lottery for the benefit of the "infant industry" of glass-blowing. Even this mode of encouragement (often applied to church-building by our pious ancestors) failed to galvanize into life the glass-works of "Germantown." The colony in Braintree broke up after a brief and unfortunate existence of about seven years, the colonists—many of them—joined their fellow-countrymen in Maine, and "New Germantown" as a Teutonic community ceased to exist.

The colonies on the coast of Maine—at that time, of course, part of Massachusetts—seem to have been more attractive to emigrants, in spite of the hardships of the pioneers and the attacks of the Indians, who, after Braddock's defeat, constantly harried the settlers. The details of their sufferings are the same that we meet with all along the frontier upon which the Germans were settled, from the coves of "hundred-harbored Maine" to the log-cabins of the Carolinas, and they need not be recapitulated. Everywhere are the same stories of pioneers shot down or tomahawked in their little clearings, of women defending their cabins or fleeing with babies in their arms to the nearest fort, of boys taken into an Indian captivity from which they were often reluctantly ransomed years after, of a blue-eyed Gretchen who weeps over the death of "Indian Margaret's" baby, its brains dashed out by a furious white ranger. Of these alarums and excursions the Germans of Maine had their full share, but in the later years of the French and Indian War they seem to have been exempt from attack.

As soon as the settlements were freed from fear of savage foray, German colonization proceeded rapidly. We have seen the arrival in the Christmas-tide of 1753 of the pioneers of "Frankfort on the Kennebec." A German newspaper presently gave its readers a glowing account of this rival of Frankfurt-am-Main, in which forty families already resided ; the population was to be increased to one hundred families,—a thing more easily said than done. The poor children of the Fatherland were meanwhile employed in building a fort for defence against the savages, in patrolling the woods as a company of rangers for the same purpose, and enduring all the hardships of pioneer life. By 1756, however, most of the emigrants had served out their passage money and were able to buy themselves farms. In a few years the neighboring town of Dresden was laid out, and into this Frankfort was incorporated, its name lost, and so disappears from the page of history the rival of the two German cities on the Oder and the Main.

About the same time, a little later than the foundation of this metropolis of many hopes, was that of Fryeburg, in the eastern foot-hills of the White Mountains on the New Hampshire border. To this romantic spot, reminiscent of their Swiss mountains, Joseph Frey led a colony from the Bernese Oberland. They tarried for some years after their landing, in Boston, on account of the disturbed condition of this frontier, and here was born the subsequent pastor of their village church, Wilhelm Fessenden. His grandson, William Pitt Fessenden, and the descendant of the town's founder, Senator Frye, have represented their State in the United States Senate, and the last named was one of the commissioners to negotiate the treaty of peace which closed the Spanish-American War of 1898.

But new troubles were gathering round the Waldoboro settlers. In 1759 an expedition was sent up the Penobscot River to build a fort which should take possession of that country ; Waldo accompanied the soldiers, for he believed his patent to extend thither and wished to see his land. Arriving at a point opposite Bangor,

he withdrew a few paces, looked around, and exclaiming,
" Here are my bounds," instantly fell dead of apoplexy.
His sudden death was regarded by the colonists as a
punishment for his dishonest treatment of them and the
sufferings which they had endured from his criminal
carelessness of his promises. After his death uncer-
tainty arose as to the limits of his patent, and the outcome of tedious and involved negotiations was that the
Broad Bay settlers were obliged to buy their lands a
second time from the representative of the Pemaquid
Company. Many did so, but a number, indignant at
the dishonesty, as they considered it, of requiring them
to buy their lands twice over, resolved to leave their
hard-won plantations in the wilderness and emigrate to
the South.

The reasons for this are bound up in the ecclesiastical
history of the little settlement. We have seen how persistently the Germans endeavored to keep up some sort
of church service under the leadership of their school-
master Ulmer. In 1760 the congregation erected a
church ; a very humble specimen of architecture it was,
but no elaborate cathedral of their Rhenish home could
have represented more devotion or sacrifice. The floor
was of logs " hewn as smooth as their tools could make
them," the windows of sheepskin in default of glass, and
the pulpit was for ten years unpainted until the first
craftsman of that sort in the settlement decorated it with
a coat of paint. But it was dedicated with great joy,
amid the tears of some old people who had worshipped
in the churches of the Fatherland, and " wept when they
remembered Zion."

Their clergyman—" Dr." Schaeffer as he was called,

for he united the medical and clerical functions—was of a kind grievously abundant in pioneer times. It proved that the beautiful woman whom he brought with him to Broad Bay was the seduced wife of another ; his learning, both medical and religious, was as problematical as his moral character, and avarice, dishonesty, and impudence seem to have been his most distinctive qualities. His disgusted flock made futile efforts to rid themselves of him, but he retained his place until his Toryism in the Revolution made his downfall inevitable.

It was not strange that when a pious Moravian brother, George Soelle, came to the little flock in the Maine woods that they heard him gladly, and also listened to his project of a removal to a settlement of his church in Carolina. In 1767 they were favored with a visit from Bishop Ettwein of the Brethren's Unity, who described the advantages of Salem in North Carolina, a Moravian settlement, so enticingly that a half dozen families went thither from Maine ; in the next year others went and their pastor with them.

Two years later a large number of the settlers of Broad Bay (which was to be named Waldoboro when shortly after incorporated) left their homes which they had won by such sacrifices from the wilderness, and followed their townsmen to the South. In the despair and exasperation which possessed them, as they were again and again annoyed by claims of ever-new "proprietors" to own their land, some of the emigrants destroyed with their own hands their houses and barns, pulled down their fences, and filled their fields with stones. It is said that three hundred people left Waldoboro in this despairing flight. This later emigration went not to Salem, but to Buffalo Creek, in the present Cabarrus County, North Carolina. It is probable that this last emigration did not consist of Moravians, for we subsequently find them served by a Lutheran pastor, the Rev. Adolph Nussman.

Many of the Waldoboro colonists remained behind, accommodating themselves to circumstances, purchased their land from the self-styled proprietors, and formed the only Teutonic community in New England which retained for generations the impress of its German origin. It is not strange that the endeavors which were made to draw to the waste places of New England the stream of German colonists which was so enriching Pennsylvania, were not successful. Forsaken to starve and freeze, cheated and plundered on every hand, the determination of the Germans towards the honest land of Penn was but the natural conclusion of the whole matter.

CHAPTER XV

THE SALZBURGERS IN GEORGIA AND THE PENNSYLVANIA GERMANS IN NORTH CAROLINA

About two years after the unfortunate experiment of Purysburg had been begun, another colony was started in the neighboring province of Georgia. The foundation of this colony, and the character of its founder, General Oglethorpe, recalls to us in many ways the pious and idyllic beginnings of Pennsylvania and the lofty purposes of William Penn. To be sure, Oglethorpe was not the only powerful representative of a persecuted sect; he was a soldier as well as a philanthropist, and we shall see him later founding an outpost against the power of Spain, daring "to singe the Spaniard's beard" in a spirit worthy of Drake himself, and gallantly defending his little fort of Frederica with a handful of soldiers against a Spanish attack apparently overwhelming in numbers. He was anxious to secure industrious colonists for his new plantations in America, but doubtless sympathy with persecuted Protestants had much to do with attracting him towards the Salzburgers.

These devout Lutherans were the remnants of men who had kept their faith pure in the Tyrolean Alps for two centuries, often in the face of bloody persecutions. In intervals of quiet they had greatly increased in numbers, until in the great persecution of 1729–32 thirty thousand of them were exiled from their Tyrolese homes. The Archbishop of Salzburg, Leopold, Count

The Salzburgers in Georgia

Firmian, was zealous for his faith, and fancied that by severe measures of persecution and repression he could rid his orthodox land of the Lutheran heresy. But he little understood the faithful, simple, resolute peasants with whom he had to deal. Their Bibles and Lutheran books were confiscated and burnt, the owners whipped and imprisoned; the property of the Protestants was taken from them, they were exiled from the mountain homes which they loved with all the passionate tenacity of the dwellers in the Alps; worst blow of all, their children were taken from them to be brought up in monasteries in the Catholic faith; yet the Lutherans of Salzburg never faltered. They took joyfully the spoiling of their goods and left homes and hearths singing Luther's high-hearted hymn :

> " Nehmen sie den Leib
> Gut, Ehr, Kind und Weib,
> Lass fahren dahin.
> Sie habens kein Gewinn.
> Das Reich muss uns doch bleiben."

Long trains of these exiles for conscience' sake passed through Germany, exciting generosity and admiration wherever they came. One of the favorite hymns sung on their marches was the exiles' song composed by one of their number, Schaitberger, who had himself tasted the bitterness not only of exile, but that of having his two daughters rent from him to be trained in the abhorred faith which persecuted him. Yet he could say, bravely,—

> "Thy will, O God, be done! May I
> Still cheerfully obey thee.
> And may thine arm of power and love
> Encompass still and stay me ;

The Germans in Colonial Times

Forth from my home I now must go.
My children ! must I leave them ?
O God, my tears in anguish flow.
Shall I no more receive them ?
My God, conduct me to a place,
Though in some distant nation,
Where I may have thy glorious word
And learn thy great salvation."

By far the largest number of these exiles, twenty thousand of them, settled in Prussia. But a small band arriving at Augsburg in 1733 so excited the compassion and admiration of Pastor Urlsperger, of that city, that he busied himself to collect money, clothing, etc., to relieve their immediate needs, and then, through the London "Society for Promoting Christian Knowledge," planned the emigration of these persecuted Salzburgers to Oglethorpe's new colony. The Tyrolese naturally felt fear at going so far from home, to distant wilds beyond the seas, and the stories of the ill-treatment and the broken promises suffered by the "poor Palatines" of the Great Exodus were known even to these peasants from the Alps. But Urlsperger succeeded in allaying their well-grounded distrust. Large promises (which, it is good to be able to say, were afterwards performed) were made of free passage and support and land to be given the colonists in Georgia. Pastors and school-masters were provided ; the emigrants were taken to England and sailed from Dover in January, 1734, under the care of a devout and upright young nobleman, Baron von Reck, and with two pastors, Bolzius and Gronau, trained at Halle and representing the spirit of that noble foundation in its best days.

The voyage was uneventful and fortunate ; on the 11th

of March their ship, the "Purysburg," reached their desired haven, and the devout Salzburgers recognized with delight that this was "Reminiscere Sunday" and that the gospel for the day related how their Master had that day come to the sea-coast fleeing from the persecutions of his own people. Recognizing the good hand of their God upon them, they resolved to keep the day annually as one of thanksgiving, and this was observed "for a very long time." Their settlement from the same pious motive was to be named Ebenezer,—"Hitherto hath the Lord helped us."

Oglethorpe was at Charleston ready to embark for England on a mission in the interest of his infant colony, but he delayed his departure to go with von Reck and a few of the leaders of the Salzburgers to choose a site for the new settlement. One was selected, about twenty-five miles up the Savannah River. It was thought to be at once healthful, beautiful, and convenient of access from Savannah, the capital of the new colony, though it ultimately proved to be none of the three.

Here the infant settlement passed through those trials incident to new "plantations." The first colony, which consisted of seventy or eighty persons, contained no mechanics, and the Alpine peasants proved, as might have been expected, awkward pioneers. Sickness broke out, and there were a number of deaths; but the Germans endured all in triumphant courage. With the next year brighter days dawned. A number of their fellow-countrymen joined them in 1735, and among them were artisans who built houses and a boat, mills and causeways and bridges for Ebenezer. The days they were obliged to stagger along the swampy roads from Savannah with packs of provisions on their backs were over.

In 1736 occurred what was known as the "Great Embarkation." Two ships arrived in Savannah, containing a number of people, and rarely have the small emigrations of that early time brought in one "transport"—to use the phrase then common—the seeds of so many various projects and tendencies. Besides the Salzburgers, who were conveyed by their noble friend Baron von Reck, came a company of German soldiers under Captain Hermsdorf, destined as the garrison of Oglethorpe's new defence against the threatening power of Spain,—Frederica, the fort of St. Simon's Island. There were a score or so of Moravians under the conduct of their bishop, Nitschmann, the first representative of the sect which was in a few years to become so prominent, and in the main so happily active, in German-American life. And there were also an intolerant, ascetic young English clergyman and his gentler, humbler brother, going "to teach the Georgia Indians the nature of Christianity." On the voyage over a fearful storm had torn the rigging and threatened to engulf the ship; yet amidst the wild or speechless terror of the English passengers, the Germans sang hymns unfalteringly. The young ascetic, himself trembling at the prospect of an eternity for which he felt entirely unprepared, asked one of the Germans, after the storm was over, "Were you not afraid?" "I thank God, no," answered the man. "But were not your women and children afraid?" "No," replied the Salzburger, "our women and children are not afraid to die." John Wesley, for it was he, pondered these sayings in his heart, and they were destined, with the influence of the subsequent teaching of the Moravians, to lead his feet into the way of peace.

Meanwhile, the Salzburgers, unconscious of their influence on the development of one of the moral and religious forces of the century, passed on to the little village in the swamps of the Savannah or to the new fort of Frederica. To the latter place most were unwilling to go, "as fighting was against their religion;" but we find in the next year a Lutheran church was organized there, its members consisting apparently of the German soldiers under Captain Hermsdorf and a few "Saltzburghers who fish and hunt for their subsistence." The minister sent them—the Rev. Mr. Driesler, who served also as school-master—lived only a year, and his widow soon sadly reported that there was no service of any kind held in Frederica. The Swiss minister, Zübli, a prominent figure of later times in Georgia, shepherded this flock until driven away by the desperate attack of the Spaniards upon the place in 1742. What part, if any, the few German inhabitants took in the gallant defence of the place, we cannot tell; but in a few years the whole settlement—Germans, Highlanders, and English, fort and village, and "Mr. Oglethorpe's Farm"—had disappeared; and now only the ruins, overgrown with luxuriant creepers, remain to show that here was an outpost against the power of Spain, where obscure Germans bore their frequent part as colonists and pioneers.

The Salzburgers who had been taken to Ebenezer to re-enforce that place were dissatisfied at the condition of things which they found there. The site was proved to be unfortunate and unhealthy. The creek which was to furnish communication with the town of Savannah was either a shallow "branch," or, in rain, swamped the village. The soil was thin and unfit for farming. So the two ministers of Ebenezer, who led their people in all things, temporal and spiritual, went to plead with Oglethorpe for a new location, and the general, though convinced that the same trouble would follow on a new site, acceded to the wish of the Salzburgers in order to content them.

The new Ebenezer, contrary to Oglethorpe's opinion, proved a better site than the old, and the Salzburgers felt satisfied with the change. For the next few years there were constant accessions, but no large "transport" arrived until 1741, when a number of Germans, not only Salzburgers, but Swiss and Pfälzer as well, came to swell the population of Ebenezer. There were now about twelve hundred Germans in the colony of Georgia. Among the later arrivals came many who "served" for their passage,—what were known in Pennsylvania as "redemptioners,"—and they commonly became both prosperous and respectable after serving this apprenticeship in the new country. The people in Ebenezer now laid out their town, following the plan of Oglethorpe, which has made the present city of Savannah the lovely tree-shaded town that it is. The Salzburgers, however, only built a school and an orphan-house on the model of the Halle Orphanage where their beloved pastors were trained, and in this building they worshipped for years, until they were able to erect the church, now the only relic of Ebenezer—then a fine structure, according to the standard of the time, and surmounted by the rather unusual emblem of a swan, the Luther coat-of-arms, in allusion to Hus's triumphant dying prophecy : "To-day

you burn a goose, but from my ashes a swan shall arise ;
him you cannot destroy."

Other churches through the country ministered to the
religious wants of the large German population, and these
churches bore scriptural names,—Jerusalem, Bethany,
Zion, Goshen ; as far as Savannah their ministers labored.
The Ebenezer people were much favored in their ministers ; Bolzius in particular was a man not only of godliness, learning, and a lovely spirit, but of great practical
and executive ability. He labored with especial earnest-
ness to introduce the manufacture of silk, but this finally
proved unprofitable, and only the mulberry-trees around
the Ebenezer church remain of it. In 1752 a large
number of Germans came to this part of the country,
St. Matthaeus's parish, as it was then designated : they
were Würtembergers, and were led by the Rev. Mr.
Rabenhorst, who became an assistant pastor at Ebenezer. The period from that time until the Revolution
desolated the settlement of these pious people was the
high-water-mark of Ebenezer's prosperity.

It was probably the most fortunate of all the German
settlements in the Southern States, which were now numerous. Beside the large number of Germans residing
in the two cities of Charleston and Savannah, and ex-
cluding the abortive attempts at colonization at Frederica
and Purysburg, there were large tracts in South Carolina,
such as Orangeburg and Saxe-Gotha, which were purely
German in origin, life, and language ; there were other
isolated settlements in the Carolinas, and from the
northern settlements of Pennsylvania along the Monocacy
and the frontier of Maryland, through the great Valley
of Virginia, by Winchester and Shepherdstown, Stras-

burg, and Woodstock, a new movement was beginning: the emigration of the Pennsylvania Germans into North Carolina, which filled the mountain counties on the western frontier of the old North State with German pioneers.

They came overland through the Valley of Virginia, having their furniture, bedding, etc., packed in the big wagons which were as characteristic of Pennsylvania Germans as the schooners of the Massachusetts coast of the trading Yankees in that part of the country. The cattle, sheep, and hogs were driven with the train ; so, slowly they went southward until the highlands of North Carolina were reached. Here the Germans settled, made a clearing, built a log cabin, and soon a little transplanted bit of " Pennsylvania Germany" was seen there, and only the patois of " Pennsylvania Dutch" was heard. Hard-working, thrifty, and simple, they were anxious to have the Gospel preached among them after their own fashion, and many " union" churches, in which Lutheran and Reformed worshipped side by side, arose among them. In the dearth of settled ministers, the school master filled the same place which he had done in earlier German settlements : read service and sometimes a sermon, baptized children in apparent danger of death, —the so-called " Noth-taufe," which the Lutheran, like the Catholic, Church permits,—and read over the dead of the pioneers some liturgy of the Fatherland.

The first fringe of German settlement was overleaped by the Scotch-Irish, who pressed to the frontier, but they again were passed by the Germans, who settled in the extreme western counties of North Carolina ; thus "the different European nationalities from which these settlers

originated, occupying strips of land across the State
mostly in a southwesterly direction, like so many strata
of a geological formation." But the German colonizing
of North Carolina was very slow in comparison with
that of the provinces of Georgia and South Carolina.
No ship-loads of emigrants came, as to Ebenezer and
Saxe-Gotha ; the emigration was not from Germany,
but from Pennsylvania, and came slowly, drop by drop,
not in communities, but as isolated families, until by
the outbreak of the Revolution the whole west of the
State was permeated with German influence.

CHAPTER XVI

THE colonization of North Carolina was, as we have seen, a Pennsylvania German movement in distinction from the emigration of European Germans. It was one of the manifestations of the life evolved from new conditions by the descendants of the Palatines amid the forests of Pennsylvania. This life, social, intellectual, and religious, was showing itself in many forms. One of the most interesting, and one perhaps least known to the outside English-speaking world, is the development of the German press.

It is the common belief among Americans of what they call the Anglo-Saxon race that the colonial Germans were utterly ignorant, illiterate, and destitute of any form of intellectual life. Many of them, doubtless, were so ; the numerical majority of pioneers must always be such,—hewers of wood and drawers of water, fitted for the rough tasks and hardships of their life. But we have seen among the early German immigrants men like Pastorius, the founder of Germantown, learned in all the wisdom of the Fatherland ; deeply read mystics like Kelpius ; leaders and organizers. such as the Weisers, or Bolzius of Ebenezer ; men, at least of ability, such as Beissel must have possessed to obtain over many men of many minds the ascendency which he had. Such men were certainly neither ignorant nor stupid.

The German Press

Seidensticker, the authority on this as on other parts of the history of the Pennsylvania Germans, remarks that in printing, as in immigration, the sects take the lead. Conrad Beissel and some of his Ephrata brethren, perhaps the most classical examples of the Pennsylvania German sectarians, were the first to commit their teachings to print in the German language in America. They published several tracts and poems setting forth the views of Beissel—for the others were simply followers and echoes—upon religious matters, Sabbath observance, celibacy, and mysticism.

Some of these works issued from the press of Andrew Bradford ; but the later ones were given to the world through the medium of that most practical and irreligious philosopher, " Poor Richard." The imprint of Benjamin Franklin upon the title-page of the Ephrata brethren's theosophic lucubrations is absurdly comic. These first pamphlets were printed in Roman type, but in 1739 there issued from the newly founded press of Christoph Saur, of Germantown, the first book printed in America with German type,—the " Zionitische Weyrauchs-Hügel," or Zionite Hill of Incense, a collection of the mystical hymns of Ephrata, as queer as was their title.

The press of Saur, and the life and character of the man himself and his son and successor, merit a more than passing notice. Born in Laasphe, Westphalia, in 1693, Christoph Saur the elder (as we must call him to distinguish him from his son and successor) grew up in an atmosphere of the queerest religious ideas as well as the widest possible toleration of them. The tiny county of Wittgenstein was a nest of sectaries,—the sects of the "Awakened," the "Inspired," and all manner of solitary mystics and hermits ; at Schwarzenau, in this country, as we have seen, the Dunkers took their rise. Christoph Saur was a married man, nearly thirty years of age, when he came with his wife and child to Pennsylvania. There he settled in Lancaster County, not far from the cloister of the mystical and celibate Dunker Beissel, whom Saur had known in Germany. He found little in common with this domineering fanatic, but his wife, Maria Christina, fell so completely under the influence of "Father Friedsam" that she left her husband and her little son and entered the cloister, living there for nearly a score of years as "Sister Marcella."

This destruction of his domestic happiness may well have embittered Saur against the home near Ephrata. He soon quitted that neighborhood and settled in Germantown, where, in 1738, he announced the foundation of the first German press of America. "I could find no more convenient device," he says, "to make it known throughout the land than to print an almanac." This, as well as the long line of its followers up to the Revolution, contained what the publisher regarded as improving reading, articles upon medical, historical, or scientific subjects, intermixed with Saur's own quaint and characteristic observations. In order to spare his patrons useless inquiries he informs them that his expected invoices of Bibles, devotional works, and the like have not arrived ; he has, however, a chemical or rather alchemistic book for sale, but it is only for intelligent and curious people. Many persons having inquired whether he would not soon publish a German paper, he tells the would-be subscribers that he is not minded to misuse valuable time in collecting and printing "useless things, much less those which are only lies," but he holds out hopes that he may in time print "trustworthy news and such as would be of profit to the reader."

In the next year Saur carried out this project, and for many years continued to edify, admonish, and instruct the German public through the columns of a paper which bore various names. At first it was called "Geschichts-Schreiber;" presently noting with sorrow that his news was not always accurate, Saur changed the name to "Berichte," by this meaning to imply that these were only "reports;" finally, under his son's editorship, it became simply the "Germantown Zeitung." It had a large subscription list for the time and language, having four thousand subscribers, not only throughout Pennsylvania, but in Virginia and Georgia and the Carolinas. It was a power in the land, as the managers of the German school project found to their cost. The size of the paper gradually increased; at first a little four-page quarto like the almanac, and appearing only monthly, it grew to a folio of weekly appearance.

The contents are indescribably quaint and original; a picture of German life in Pennsylvania for the greater part of the colonial period could be painted from the simple sketches furnished by its pages. First comes the news of foreign parts, and from home ports like Boston; to these items Saur often appends comments. Any war news rouses the peace-loving Dunker to a very rage of non-resistance. His bookselling business is advertised, as also the concerns of others who have farms or merchandise to sell, or have found a gold piece upon the road, and wish with scrupulous honesty to restore it to the owner, or whose runaway negroes or servants are described with unflattering accuracy. In its columns, also, Saur conducted his numerous and vigorous controversies with others of differing religious views, or with the powers that were.

Besides all this editorial work, which would of itself have filled less capable hands, Saur carried on for twenty years a large printing, publishing, and importing business. His first book, the Weyrauchs-Hügel, was, with one exception, the largest book printed up to that time in Pennsylvania, containing nearly eight hundred pages. Four years after, Christoph Saur published the first edition of the Bible printed in a European lauguage in America, the splendid quarto "Germantown Bible." Two other editions were called for, and when, in 1776, the third edition was published, the younger Saur could still say, with pride, that no other European nation had yet printed the Bible in their language in the Western hemisphere. When at the close of the Revolution the first English Bible was printed in America, it was undertaken only when well guaranteed.

Evidently our German forefathers were neither so poor, so rude, nor so irreligious as they have been pictured by some English writers, when they could support the issue of so many editions of a large and expensive Bible in their mother tongue.

The other works issued from Saur's press were— as might have been inferred from the character of the publisher, as well as his public—largely devotional or religious works. Most of the German settlers of the New World had come here as much from religious motives as from a praiseworthy desire to better their condition. It was for them that the German presses teemed with hymn-books, catechisms, sermons, and, alas! very many and very virulent controversies attending Count Zinzendorf's visit to Pennsylvania in 1742, when he attempted a premature experiment in Christian Union among the "many-creeded men" of Penn's province. Zinzendorf's party had their printing done mainly by Franklin. Saur published the pamphlets of the church people in opposition to the scheme of the "Congregation of God in the Spirit." This unedifying subject busied Saur's press for several years. Soon after, Franklin's "Plain Truth" in regard to frontier defence roused all the non-resistance in the Germantown printer, and in 1764 another like controversy employed his press.

But of all Saur's controversies, the most important and most misunderstood is that relative to the German schools, and the dust of the quarrel still obscures the issue in our own day. The project for the establishment of these "charity schools," as they were also and offensively called, was partially religious,—or better, sectarian, —partially political. It was a section of that perennial question which led to the squabbles between the Quaker non-resistant Assembly and the militant proprietors. The German sects were nearly all opposed to war, even to the defence of the frontiers against French wiles and Indian massacre. But the German church people, Lutheran and Reformed, and the German pioneers pushing into the wilderness had no such conscientious scruples. So Saur represented and led but a section of his countrymen, though the Germans at that time, as well as later, were portrayed as sluggish and cowardly in the defence of their adopted country.

The Germans in Colonial Times

The project for the foundation of schools among the German population of Pennsylvania was begun with collections made by the Rev. Michael Schlatter, the organizer of the Reformed Church in this country. He was a Swiss German from St. Gall,—an energetic, active, hard-working man. The Reformed Church of the Palatinate had been requested by the emigrants of their faith in Pennsylvania to send ministers to their destitute churches, but the Palatinate Church, itself persecuted and poor, handed on the appeal to the brethren of Holland, who lived in wealth and religious freedom. The Dutch Reformed Church sent out Schlatter, who came to Boston in 1746, where he writes, "I was received with much love and kindness by the Hon. I. Wendel, a distinguished Holland merchant, and an officer of the Government there," and, we may add, an ancestor of Dr. Oliver Wendell Holmes. So welcomed, Schlatter's impressions of the country across which he journeyed to his place of work in Pennsylvania, were naturally favorable. "I can truly testify," he says, "that often when contemplating the houses, the level country, the climate, and the sensible inhabitants, living in the same manner, enjoying the same culture, pursuing the same business, and differing but little from Europeans, I could scarcely realize that I was in a distant quarter of the world."

Naturally, such an observer did not take the same gloomy view of the barbarity in which the Germans were sunk, as was evidenced by the later appeals for the charity school project. But Schlatter willingly assumed the superintendence of the schools, which he could easily combine with his extensive and often difficult journeyings to all the little settlements where the people of his church were to be found. We see him going as far as Lehigh, Northampton, and Bucks Counties in Pennsylvania, to Lancaster, the largest town outside of Philadelphia, to "Yorktown, newly laid out," to New York, "in the Rarentans,"—probably the German Valley churches, now long since passed over to the Presbyterian body ; or Schlatter takes his "great journey" to Monocacy, where he meets and commends that best of school-masters, Schley ; to Conococheague, where "the people built them a fort," to be improved by Braddock into Fort Frederick ; thence down the Valley of Virginia to Winchester, Woodstock, Strasburg, then nameless, or with other names.

He knew the country well, and should have known the people better than to fall in blindly with the charity school scheme, now being engineered by that perfervid Scot, the Rev. William Smith, who knew little of the conditions or characteristics of the German population, and was not so judicious in his advocacy of the scheme as he was ardent and energetic. Christoph Saur held the opinions of most Dunkers on the subject, of the uselessness of any but the simplest education, and regarded the fear of the Lord as not only the beginning, but the end of all wisdom. Smith, when he met with discouragement in his project, through the influence of Saur in his paper, published a plan for making good citizens of the Germans by taking away their votes (which strengthened the Quaker party) and by prohibiting the use of their language in legal documents, or the publication of books or papers in that language ; this last suggestion, of course, was especially aimed at Saur, who was also vilified as "a papist emissary."

The Germans in Colonial Times

The society for German schools next established a press of their own to counteract the baleful influence of the Germantown printer, and published therefrom a German paper (the "Philadelphische Zeitung"), a few books, and the "Rules and Articles of War," an extraordinary issue for an educational and benevolent society, surely. It shows the political complexion of the whole project, which soon proved a failure. The Lutherans, who had at first favored it, were not likely to be won by Dr. Smith's suggestion that through the instrumentality of his schools he could easily convert all the Lutherans to the Episcopal Church. The Reformed Church also opposed it, and Schlatter's personal popularity suffered to such an extent from his connection with it that he was obliged to give up his work as superintendent alike of churches and schools in Pennsylvania, and accept a chaplaincy in the army. The "Philadelphische Zeitung" came to an untimely end, through the ill-advised publication in it of an article abusing the Quaker party in the Assembly. For this the versatile Dr. Smith was imprisoned, the paper stopped, and Saur and the "Germantowner Zeitung" left in victorious possession of the field.

The elder Christoph Saur died in 1758, and his son of the same name succeeded him. The younger Saur was not only of the same name but of the same nature. In the simple, yet dignified obituary of his father, which he published in their paper, the son expressed his unwillingness to take upon himself "the burden of the press;" but he felt himself obliged "for the sake of God and his neighbor" to take it up and carry it on in the spirit of the founder; for, he said, "to the honor of God and the benefit of the country this press is dedicated, and I shall seek always to keep this aim in view." The younger Saur was a member and minister in the Dunker Church, and therefore as determined and conscientious a non-resistant as had been his father; but as he fell on evil times, his principles cost him more dearly. He had had charge of the printing of English books before his father's death; after the whole "burden of the press" fell upon him, he issued many important works, the most imposing being the second and third editions of the Bible. The last edition brought him in more money than he had expected, so he printed and distributed gratis "Ein geistliches Magazien," (1764) containing hymns, translations of Law's "Serious Call," the pious school-master Dock's admonition to his scholars, and the like matter. This "Magazien" was the first religious periodical published in America, and thus the Germans whom Dr. Smith portrayed as sunk in irreligion and barbarism were the founders of the religious press of to-day.

The younger Saur was a man of as various talents and as much energy as his father; he was the originator of the stoves which, improved by Franklin, attained a wide popularity under the latter's name; he was also the first type-founder of America, and the convention of 1775 urged patriots to make use of these types in encouragement of home manufactures. The opposition to the political school project, which we have seen the elder Saur fight through, was not inherited by his son; the younger man was one of the founders of the German-town Academy.

He was a wealthy, prosperous, and respected man when the storms of the Revolution broke upon him.

The Germans in Colonial Times

As a conscientious non-resistant, Saur had no sympathy with the war, but there is no evidence that he was disloyal. Taking advantage of a technical disobedience to an order of the Assembly, Saur was arrested, treated with much personal harshness and indignity, banished from Germantown, and his entire property confiscated,—house, lands, and press. Saur felt himself "not free," in the Quaker phrase, to appeal to the law to right this outrageous injustice, and "he took joyfully the spoiling of his goods," after the apostle's advice : but he smarted under the imputation of disloyalty, and inquired pathetically of the meeting of his brothers in faith, "If a man is declared a traitor without a cause, is it just to let him lie forever under that reproach?"

He survived his temporal ruin six years, living in the house of a friend, and supporting himself partially by working at his trade of book-binder. He also ministered among his brethren, and shortly before his death walked a dozen miles to preach to a little flock in the neighborhood, "returning to his home in the same apostolic fashion." There he died, at the age of sixty-three, and surely he must have had the blessing of those who suffer for righteousness' sake.

The other important German press of colonial times, that of the Brotherhood of Ephrata, is historically connected with the beginnings of the press founded by the elder Saur. We have seen that the "Hill of Incense," the strangely named hymn-book of the cloister, was the first bound book printed upon the new Germantown press. During the time it was passing through the printer's hands, Saur discovered amid its mystical doggerel the following verse,—

The German Press

"Sehet, sehet, sehet an
Sehet, sehet an den Mann
Der von Gott erhöhet ist,
Der ist unser Herr und Christ."

["Look, look, look, look at the man who is exalted by God, who is our Lord and Christ."]

He thought Beissel, the head of the community, intended himself by this, and on asking his copy-holder, a warm adherent of Beissel, had his suspicions confirmed. Saur wrote to the prior, reproaching him for such a display of spiritual pride; Beissel replied by adducing the text, "Answer not a fool according to his folly," and Saur, not unnaturally exasperated by this sort of religious polemics, retorted by an argument which was the most crushing one, to Beissel's mystical mind, which he could have devised : he proved that Beissel's name in its Latinized form could be made to yield the apocalyptic "Number of the Beast!" Needless to say, Saur printed no more hymn-books for the monks of Ephrata.

A few years after began the issue from the cloister's press of Beissel's theosophic works and a string of hymn-books, whose extraordinary names are only equalled by their wonderful contents : we listen to the "Song of the Lonely and Deserted Turtle Dove," to an "Echo" of this, and to the "Newly enlarged Song" of the same melancholy bird. We have, too, "An Agreeable Odor of Roses and Lilies," and a "Paradisaic Wonderplay." To encounter the sober verity of a title like the "Chronicon Ephratense" is a relief from this fauna and flora, until the modern student attempts to read the chronicle of our Pennsylvania monastery, with its mystical dialect, its pictures of the sentimentality of the sisters, and the unconditional surrender of the brethren to Beissel's overweening tyranny, when he feels as near insanity as was the community itself.

The Ephrata press also did some custom-work, and its most notable effort in this line was the production of that greatly reverenced Mennonite work, an account of Anabaptist martyrdoms, Van Braght's "Blutige Schau-platz," vernacularly known as the "Martyr-Book." It was printed in 1748, a splendid folio of twelve hundred pages, "the largest and in some respects the most re-markable book of the colonial period." The translation from the Dutch original into German, which was now the language of most of the Mennonites in Pennsylvania, was made by Peter Miller, the learned and devout suc-cessor of Beissel as prior of Ephrata. The type, paper, and binding, are the best of their kind and time, and the book is a monument worthy to stand by the side of the Germantown Bible, as a testimony to the excellent craftsmanship of the German colonial press.

The story of the Saurs and their rivals has carried us chronologically far beyond the time of foundation of some other German presses. There were many men who attempted, with more or less success, to publish German books and newspapers. Among these short-lived presses were those of Crell, whom we have seen endeavoring to colonize Braintree, Massachusetts, with his countrymen ; and the Armbruster brothers, who had a long and checkered career in the unsuccessful service of the "art preservative of all arts." Gotthard Arm-bruster published in 1747, a polemical pamphlet against Saur, who reprints in his paper an extract from its abuse "whereby the author wishes to prove, that *he* is a good Christian." Nevertheless, when next year Armbruster put out the prospectus of a German newspaper, Saur quoted it in his " Berichte," closing with the request that "dishonest subscribers who had never paid him should not treat his rival in the same fashion." After some time Anton Armbruster emerges, carrying on German printing for Benjamin Franklin, and publishing the paper which was designed to counteract Saur's opposition to the charity schools. But in 1763 he writes Franklin, "I do assure you the distress is very great," and he, his publications, and his paper, the "Fama," soon disappear from view. Indeed, we should not have heard any blast from this trumpet of Fame, were it not for controversies carried on with Heinrich Miller, and his paper the "Staatsbote," which was in some sort a successor to the reputation and favor of Saur's "Germantowner Zeitung."

Heinrich Miller was apparently, in his earlier years, the most restless of tramp printers. A Waldecker by birth, a Moravian in religious sympathies, a "passionate traveller" in taste, he had worked as printer in Zurich, Leipzic, Altona, London, Hamburg, Amsterdam, Rotterdam, Antwerp, Brussels, Paris, Philadelphia, Marienburg (where he established a business), again in England, Scotland, and Philadelphia, where he was employed by Franklin. He returned to Germany, set up a press of his own in London, but finally came back to Philadelphia in 1760 to found one of the most successful German presses of the period immediately preceding the Revolution. He was the printer to Congress, but during the war he retired from business to end his days in the quiet of Moravian Bethlehem, and was succeeded by Steiner and Cist.

Miller's press, in its difference from its predecessors, is very instructive as to the change which was coming over the face of things, and the attitude of the German population towards them. Miller, like all others, printed a calendar, and we have spoken of his "Staatsbote," which is said to have even outstripped Saur's paper in its circulation. He also, true to his Moravian sympathies, printed religious works, sermons, prayer-books, and the "Watchword," or daily texts of the Brethren's Unity. But a large and continually increasing proportion of his publications was of a political nature,— pamphlets for and against Franklin, addresses to various classes and conditions of men, dated, in the case of one of them, with the doggerel lines,—

> "Gedruckt zur Zeit und in dem Jahr,
> Da einem wider 'n Andern war."

On the passage of the Stamp Act, Miller suspended his "Staatsbote," "until it would appear whether means can be found to escape from the chains forged for the people and from unbearable slavery." On March 19, 1766, the "Staatsbote" issued an extra, announcing the repeal of the hated act, and headed with the verse,—

> "Den Herren lobt und beneydeit,
> Der von dem Stämpel Act uns hat befreyt."

But the patriotic services of Miller and the other Pennsylvania Germans belong to another portion of the subject.

To the presses of Germantown, Ephrata, and Philadelphia there were added, about the year 1774, those of Matthias Bartgis in Frederick, Maryland, and of Frantz (or Francis) Baily in Lancaster, Pennsylvania, besides the many attempts, extending over but a few years, to begin German printing in other localities ; but these mentioned make up the sum of living and active presses among the colonial Germans. It is a record of which their descendants need not to be ashamed.

Perhaps it is owing as much to dense ignorance as to prejudiced unwillingness to accord honor where honor is due that the Pennsylvania Germans have been portrayed as totally destitute of literary culture or aspirations, and that their presses have been described as only fountains of sermons and hymn-books. Their patronage of newspapers like Miller's and Saur's, their publication of two such monuments of typography as the Germantown Bible and the Ephrata Martyr-Book, and the character and diversity of the books printed or imported for the German market, show that they were not all so ignorant, stolid, and degraded as they have been represented.

CHAPTER XVII

THE MORAVIANS

CONNECTED with the emigration of the little sect of Schwenkfelder, and also with that of the Protestant exiles of Salzburg, to Georgia, is the appearance in America of a sect much more widely known,—that ancient church of the "Brethren's Unity, commonly called Moravians." Into the long and honorable history of this remnant of John Hus's followers in Europe we cannot enter. It is only their life and labors in America which concern us.

There is scarcely anywhere outside of Holy Writ so strong an instance of what seems the direct guidance of Providence in the affairs of men as that which brought together the persecuted remnant of the "Bohemian Brethren" and their devout protector, Nicholas Louis, Count Zinzendorf. The young nobleman had been educated in the straitest sect of Lutheran pietism on his Saxon estates by his aunt and grandmother, two "schöne Seelen" of the type which Goethe has immortalized. With a few like-minded friends, the young count, on coming of age, had designed a work for the revival of vital godliness in the Lutheran Church, such as Spener had wrought and preached in the previous century. When returning from his wedding to the lovely and pious Countess Dorothea of Reuss, the noble bridal party came upon a company of people who were erecting a house in the woods at Berthelsdorf, a newly purchased estate of the count's. On inquiry, it appeared that they were the Protestant exiles from Moravia, some remnants of the old Brethren's Church, to whom the young count, knowing nothing of them save that they were persecuted for righteousness' sake, had granted an asylum on the Hutberg. Zinzendorf dismounted, talked and prayed with the exiles, and gave to their new settlement the name of Herrnhut (the watch or protection of the Lord). Then he and his bride went on their way, little knowing that these simple peasants and carpenters were those with whom their lot was henceforth cast.

The count pursued his purpose, aided by some of his learned and noble friends, of awakening the Lutheran Church. But "his way had the Lord hedged in," as he would doubtless have expressed it, for he had a child-like, almost superstitious, confidence in the direct interposition of God in all his concerns. His favor at court gradually waned, the protection upon his estates which he was fain to afford not only to the Moravians, but to the remnant of the Schwenkfelder and all other persecuted people, became ineffectual. Finally, in 1736, he was himself banished. On receiving the decree of banishment Zinzendorf said, cheerfully, "We must collect the pilgrim congregation and proclaim the Saviour to the world. Our home will be wherever the most real service is to be done for the Saviour."

Foreseeing this likelihood of exile, Zinzendorf had endeavored to provide a place of refuge, but one plan after another fell through. He had thought of sending the Schwenkfelder to Georgia, with a little idea of establishing the refuge which he sought from European persecution in Oglethorpe's colony of toleration. The Schwenkfelder had been persuaded, while on their way to embark, to change their destination for Penn's colony. But Zinzendorf still planned to settle the Brethren in Georgia, and so, on one of the transports which took over a Salzburger colony, were a few Moravians led by their bishop, Spangenberg.

As leader of the church in its early settlements in America, he should be more than mentioned. A German university graduate, he, like Zinzendorf, had tried to work among the Lutheran Pietists, but in vain, and finally theological hatred ran so high that Spangenberg was expelled from the University of Halle, the stronghold of Pietism. He then came to Zinzendorf and the humble Moravians. Although a learned and cultured man, he did not disdain the lowliest tasks. In the early hardships of the Georgian settlement he served as cook. From Pennsylvania, two years after, he writes: "As regards my outward occupation, it is at present farm work; but this is as much blessed to my soul as formerly my studying and writing. For nothing, even in outward affairs, is in itself good or bad; but whatever is done with the blessing of God thereby becomes good, whilst anything performed without God's blessing becomes bad." Doubtless these practical occupations of the learned theologian helped him during the forty years of his service in the New World to guide the "economies" of the settlements. Meanwhile, he did not neglect preaching, and it was while laboring for the unity of Christians in America that Spangenberg wrote one of the first and finest hymns which had their birth on our soil,—" Die Kirche Christi die Er geweiht," translated in the " Lyra Germanica :"

> " The church of Christ, that he hath hallowed here
>   To be his house, is scattered far and near,
>   In North and South and East and West abroad,
>   And yet in earth and heaven through Christ her Lord
>   The Church is one.

> " One member knoweth not another here,
>   And yet their fellowship is true and near ;
>   One is their Saviour and their Father one,
>   One Spirit rules them, and among them none
>   Lives to himself."

This was eminently true of Spangenberg's apostolic life.

Yet the first visible outcome of the exertions and sacrifices of the Brethren in Georgia was complete failure. Several companies of Brethren were sent out, but their settlement was visited by sickness, their hoped-for access to the Indians did not come to pass, and finally, when the Spaniard threatened Georgia and Oglethorpe prepared for his gallant defence of Frederica, the Moravians were called upon to bear arms, which was opposed to their principles, and the remnant of the Brethren deserted their settlement in a disobedient, very un-Moravian fashion, and took refuge in Pennsylvania, near Germantown.

But meanwhile, other things were preparing for them. Re-enforcements were sent over for the Georgia settlement, under the leadership of Peter Böhler. This devout man had been a friend and teacher of the Wesleys in Oxford ; through them Whitefield had heard of him, and when he arrived in Georgia, he eagerly sought him out.

The Germans in Colonial Times

When Böhler led the discouraged remnants of the Moravian colony of Georgia to Pennsylvania, Whitefield came to him and offered a tract which he had just bought at "the Forks of the Delaware" to the Moravians if they would build upon it a stone house to be used in Whitefield's project of an orphan house. This was the "Nazareth Tract," upon which the church settlement of that name subsequently arose.

Böhler joyfully accepted the offer. The Brethren had no abiding place; Spangenberg had been recalled to Europe, the little remnant was deprived of his expected advice, and it was only Böhler's courage and cheerfulness which had kept the small company together. So they went joyfully through the woods on foot a three days' journey from Germantown, the little band of "seven brethren and two sisters, and two boys," and, arriving on a May evening, sat down under a black-oak-tree and sang hymns of praise and thanksgiving to God.

They went courageously to work, built a log house for a shelter, and began the school-house, according to their contract with Whitefield. In December of the same year (1740), a small company of brethren and sisters arrived to encourage the hearts of the beginners at Nazareth. They stood in much need of cheer, for they had just received from Whitefield a peremptory notice to quit his land "forthwith."

The reason for thus ejecting these pious and cheerful exiles, in the depth of winter, from their promised refuge was that Whitefield had had a theological dispute and difference with Böhler on the question of a "limited atonement"! Finding Böhler entertained the charitable faith that "Christ died for the ungodly," White-field evidenced his superior belief in the excellent articles of election and reprobation by turning out these miscreants from the "Nazareth Tract." But a certain Justice Irish gave them a tract upon the Lehigh. "Though not himself a professor of religion, yet he esteemed the Brethren as moral and industrious men, and highly disapproved of Mr. Whitefield's arbitrary conduct." Thus was founded Bethlehem, and here on Christmas-eve, 1741, came Count Zinzendorf and his party, and, being lodged in a house, part of which was used as a stable, "on Christmas-eve we called to mind the birth of our Saviour, and thus this new settlement received the name of Bethlehem."

From the humble settlement which began in the stable reached out influences which covered the whole country. The visit of Count Zinzendorf to America was the cause of much stir in religious circles here. The plans which he had come to carry out were many and various, and they were pursued with all his charac-teristic ardor and enthusiasm, and, we may add, without censoriousness, with all his usual lack of judgment. His first, and nearest and dearest, plan was that for the foundation of the "Congregation of God in the Spirit," a sort of informal religious league, which never aimed at a corporate reunion of Christian sects, but was "to afford to all the children of God, though of different denominations, an opportunity not only of strengthening the bond of Christian fellowship, but of assisting each other in the mutual prosecution of the work of God in this country." It was, as will be seen, a sort of prema-ture "Evangelical Alliance," appearing ere the times

were ripe, and so doomed to failure. In the reception
with which it met, the Christianity of America did little
credit to itself, as indeed Christianity in controversy
rarely does. Zinzendorf was a fallible mortal with many
errors and weaknesses, but he at least abounded in
that grace of love without which all other graces are
as sounding brass and tinkling cymbals. His opponents
could not be praised in this respect. The synods, which
were to be meetings for consultation as to the advance-
ment of Christ's cause in Pennsylvania, after many
changes of character and constituents, became the
ecclesiastical synods of one, the Moravian Church.

The controversies had at least one good effect, that
of much increasing the activity of the German press of
Pennsylvania ; pamphlets in support of Zinzendorf and
his party occupied the press of Benjamin Franklin, while
Saur's and occasionally some English presses poured
forth " Protestations," " Reports," and " Testimonies"
innumerable. "A Troubled One," Gruber the mystic,
gave voice to his distressed spirit in five pages of prose
and three in verse against the count ; Boehm, the old
Reformed minister, issued from Falkner's Swamp a
" Faithful Warning," and in the next year a "Renewed" one. The school-master of Bethlehem sent
out "Truthful Intelligence," and Zinzendorf, who held
the pen of a too-ready writer, was fertile in "private
declarations," and the like. Gilbert Tennent and other
Presbyterian ministers clamored in the pulpit against
"the damnable doctrine of the Moravians," and also
called their Moravian fellow-Christians "locusts out of
the bottomless pit," "foxes who spoil the vineyard of
the Lord," and other worse names. Muhlenberg, who

The Moravians

was just beginning his noble work of organization among the scattered Lutherans of the province, was not much more favorably inclined towards a party who were to occasion much trouble and irregularity in his disordered bishopric, and a perfect whirlwind of denunciation disturbed the religious atmosphere of German Pennsylvania.

It is not difficult, when one knows the stiff orthodoxy, the bigoted denominationalism, and the wild enthusiasm of German religious life in that period, to understand why, even across seas and in face of crying destitution of any kind of preaching, that of the Moravians stirred up this tempest; but the picture is a painful one, and we gladly turn from it to look at another form of activity which the Moravians alone of the German churches in America developed, the Indian missions.

One of the numerous subjects which engaged the interest of that many-sided man, Zinzendorf, was the endeavor to do good to the Indians of Pennsylvania. Missionary work had been from the first a leading object of the Moravian Church; two years before Count Zinzendorf's arrival a Moravian brother, Christian Henry Rauch, had begun a mission among the Indians at Shekomeko, on the border between the States of New York and Connecticut. After indescribable discouragements and hardship among the filthy, drunken, degraded savages, he and his fellow-workers gathered a little Christian community, and a few converts, the firstlings of the Indian mission, were taken to Pennsylvania to be baptized at the Huguenot settlement of Oley, "in the barn of Mr. Van Dirk (there being no church there)."

The Germans in Colonial Times

Zinzendorf visited the Shekomeko mission during his presence in this country and made some other hard and perilous journeys into the Indians' country. He was probably the first white man to set foot in the lovely and unfortunate Valley of Wyoming. His perils and journeyings were without especial result in the Indian work, which was being carried on by the Moravian brethren with a hopeful, steadfast courage and resolution which must win the admiration of all who know the long, sad, glorious history of Moravian missions among the Indians,—that lengthy story of faithful and self-sacrificing efforts for the red man, constantly harassed and destroyed by the greed and fear of the white men.

Of this unhappy condition the missionaries at Shekomeko soon had experience. As soon as their little work had begun to flourish and expand, it drew upon them the opposition of the authorities of Connecticut and New York, who dragged the brethren hither and yon to hearings and trials, until one of the missionaries died from fatigue and exposure; forbade their preaching; arrested and imprisoned Post and another, who were guilty of the crime of residing among the Mohawk Indians to learn their language; and finally exiled the missionaries on the information of a "clergyman of Dover, who had said they were in league with the Papists."

After being left to themselves for some years, the Indian converts of Shekomeko were removed to Bethlehem, where, after a temporary lodgement was found for them near Bethlehem, at a place expressively called Friedenshütten or the "Tents of Peace," they were at length settled at "Gnadenhütten on the Mahony," not far from the present Mauch Chunk. This was organized as much upon the model of the other church settlements as was possible where the inhabitants were recently converted Indians instead of the pious and energetic children of the fatherland, and in a few years the brethren said, with innocent satisfaction, that it had "become a very regular and pleasant town." At the earnest request of the northern Indians, a blacksmith-shop was established for them at Shamokin (Sunbury); and scattered Indian settlements and families were constantly ministered to by the missionaries.

The accounts of the Indian work are full of interesting details of Indian speech and mode of life and thought which makes them decidedly superior in human interest to the ordinary run of missionary reports, usually a painfully edifying form of literature. One of the converts being exhorted by a Puritan clergyman of Connecticut to Sabbath-keeping with other virtues, naïvely tells the missionary that "as to doing no work on Sunday, that was easy,"—probably having no great desire to work on any day of the week. Another informed a "Dutch clergyman" who had indeed baptized him but given him no other pastoral oversight, that he acted much worse than one who planted Indian corn, "for," he said, "the planter sometimes goes to see whether his corn grows or not." The Indian converts used, for a long time after the death of the missionary who departed during the persecutions of the New York government, to go to wail and weep over his grave in the heart-rending Indian fashion. The visiting of heathen Indians at Gnadenhütten was a grievous trouble and expense, for they could not be sent away empty, however poor their host might be, if the forest reputation for hospitality was to be maintained, and the savage clansmen were often neither safe nor pleasant guests. We shall see how this Indian rite of hospitality without grudging or question was to bring suspicion, ruin, and death upon the Indian towns of Ohio forty years later. But now all was peaceful and "pleasant" in Gnaden-hütten on the Mahanoy.

Life in the other church settlements of the Moravians was also full of interest, energy, and vigor. Its form was a sufficiently strange one, and it is no wonder that outsiders, unacquainted alike with the life and the forms of expression of the Brethren's Unity found it then, and find it still, incomprehensible. The first thing to note is that the early church settlement of Bethlehem was what is known as a pilgrim congregation, that is, the whole community was a strongly organized society for evangelistic work. Many of the brethren and sisters (who, it may be worth while to state, were not celibates, and took no vows) were sent from time to time to make what Friends would call "religious visits" in the surrounding country, or, in Moravian phrase, "received and accepted the appointment to" some Indian Mission. Those of the community not on these expeditions worked for the support of the missionaries and the whole settlement. They did not give up their property to the community, but they did so offer their time and work. When the "fishermen," as Zinzendorf had named the missionaries, returned from a preaching-tour, they might be and were set to burning bricks, splitting rails, mending shoes, or they nursed the sick or "served" the stranger. The brethren established their own postal service between Bethlehem and Philadelphia. The "single brethren" worked the farms, and houses were provided in which they were lodged and fed, under the oversight of a temporal and spiritual head ; the "single sisters" did spinning, and were provided for in the same way. The children, taken from their parents when two years old, were brought up in church schools ; but the present ancient and celebrated Moravian schools had another and later origin. All these divisions of the population, with the married brethren and sisters, were organized into "choirs," which had their own meetings, love-feasts, etc. One peculiarity of Moravian life must be mentioned,—the text-book published for many years by the eldership of the church, in all the various languages in which they have members, with passages of Scripture and hymn verses for every day of the year ; the allusions to the "watchword" for the day are so frequent in Moravian history that it may be worth while to explain this, now a common custom with many pious persons, but first introduced into the Brethren's Unity.

It would not be of value to note the missionary activity of the Brethren,—the places in which they planted churches like other denominations ; only those spots where they were the pioneers are to be mentioned. Besides Bethlehem and Nazareth (which presently returned to the possession of the church through Whitefield's financial embarrassments) they founded settlements at Lititz (Lancaster County) in 1747 ; at Graceham, near the Monocacy settlements of Maryland, about the same time ; at Emaus, near Bethlehem, in the same year as Lititz ; and ten years later was begun the Wachovia or

Salem community in North Carolina. Only Bethlehem had the Economy or church settlement idea in its fullness of detail, although some features of it were found in most or all of the other places named.

The southern society, so far from the parent one in Bethlehem, merits special note. An English nobleman, Lord Granville, having an extensive tract of land in North Carolina, was anxious to fill it with German colonists, and, knowing something of the Moravians and liking what he knew, he offered his land to Zinzendorf, who bought it, and sent Spangenberg and a few other brethren south from Bethlehem to select the especial portion upon which they should found a church settlement.

The province of North Carolina had been left behind in the general advance of American colonization, and of German colonists in particular there had been none in North Carolina since de Graffenried, who died forty years before, had brought his hapless Swiss to begin the settlement of New Berne. The province was a trackless, almost uninhabited pine forest, save for a thin fringe of settlements along the coast. Here Spangenberg and his company wandered about, nearly starving; for their provisions gave out and winter was approaching. Finally, on the Yadkin river they selected the tract to which they gave the name of Wachovia, in memory of a former estate, Wachau, of the Zinzendorf family in Austria.

In October, 1753, a company of twelve single brethren set out from Bethlehem to go, by way of the Valley of Virginia, to the new tract. They took their simple possessions in a six-horse wagon. As they passed along, some of the brethren would get a job of threshing oats from the farmers along the route in order to earn feed for their horses. So they came to their new home, took possession of a deserted log cabin, and kept a love-feast, being much cheered by the "daily word," which was "I know where thou dwellest, even in a desert place," whose appropriateness was enforced as they heard the wolves howling round their cabin that night.

They found some neighbors,—in the pioneer sense of neighborhood,—scattered cabins, containing mostly Pennsylvania German settlers, for the tide of southward emigration from Penn's province had begun to flow. One of the brethren was a doctor and one a tailor, and the gifts of these were both prized, though the tailor was somewhat puzzled when a young frontiersman brought him deerskins instead of linsey-woolsey out of which to fashion his breeches. In the next year a minister was sent them, who is recorded as an accomplished Hebrew scholar,—a dubious qualification for life on the Yadkin, one would think, were it not also recorded that he was "a very humble servant of the Lord, ready to do the meanest service for his brethren, and particularly adapted for such a station in the wilderness." Soon a mill was built, to which people came one hundred miles to have their grain ground, and the settlement became such a resort for any one in need of any kind of temporal or spiritual service that it was very fittingly named Bethabara,—"house of passing;" presently came the Indian wars, and the peaceful brethren were compelled to fortify their settlement, when it became a refuge for the people of the countryside even as far as Virginia.

The Indians, however, were entertained and fed so long as they behaved themselves well, and Bethabara became known among them as the "Dutch Fort, where there are good people and much bread."

On account of this influx of refugees, many of whom desired. to cast in their lot with these "good people," who had fed and sheltered them in their extremity, a new town was laid out by the indefatigable Spangenberg, who had come to look after this Southern outpost of the church, and called "Bethania," and on July 18th, 1759, the first house there was occupied by the accomplished Hebrew scholar and his wife, "the daily word being, 'I will fear no evil, for Thou art with me,' which proved a word of much comfort to them amid the horrors of a cruel war, and the consequent necessity of being on the alert night and day."

Spangenberg and some other brethren daily rode through the woods from Bethabara to the new settlement to see how all went on, the other brethren not a little fearful of Indian ambuscade. But Spangenberg, putting his horse to the gallop, came safely through the forest, the brethren racing after him, and so, in this very unclerical fashion, the daily visit was made. Afterwards, the Indians revealed that they had often attempted to waylay the cavalcade, but could not, "for the Dutchers had big, fat horses, and rode like the devil." One Easter Sunday during the war, a company of militia suddenly arrived just as Spangenberg had finished his sermon, and insisted that he should preach them another in English, with which request the doughty bishop gladly complied.

When the war had been ended for some years, it was

thought time to carry out Zinzendorf's original plan, and found in the centre of the tract the principal settlement, and so, in 1766, Salem was begun. From this centre, Bishop Ettwein not only ministered to his brethren, but extended his labors to the Germans who had begun to found in South Carolina the flourishing settlements on the Congaree, Saluda, and Broad Rivers.

Around Salem a number of little settlements grew up which were at first organized in accordance with the pattern of the famous "Economy" at Bethlehem, but this was given up just previous to the Revolution. Friedberg was formed from Pennsylvania German emigrants; Friedland was to be a "land of peace" for the much-tried emigrants from Broad Bay, in Maine, led there by the Moravian brother Soelle in 1769, arriving, after a shipwreck on the coast of Virginia, "poor, wayworn, and many of them in ill health." Hope was the cheerful name of a village of English people, most of whom had learnt to know and love the brethren while refugees in the troubled times of the Indian war, at the "Dutch Fort, where there were good people and much bread."

CHAPTER XVIII

CONRAD WEISER AND THE FRONTIER WARS

IN 1742 there came to Pennsylvania the man who was to perform for the "dispersed Lutherans of Pennsylvania" the same service of reorganization and shepherding which Schlatter did for the Reformed people and John de Watteville for the Moravians. This was Heinrich Melchior Muhlenberg, affectionately called the "patriarch" of the Lutheran church in America. He was a Saxon by birth,—a man of education, piety, tact, ability, and exhaustless energy. For nearly half a century he poured out all these gifts in the service of his beloved church, and brought it from a condition of formless disorganization, ministered to—where it was served at all—by weak or unworthy men, to a state of vigorous and fruitful growth. Had not the foolish policy of adhering to the German tongue been for a time imposed upon the church, it might have grown from the slip of Muhlenberg's fostering to a vine that should overshadow the land ; its present great numerical increase comes largely from the later emigration of Germans, although the old seats of the church in Pennsylvania, New York, New Jersey, Virginia, and the Carolinas have never been entirely desolate.

Muhlenberg's reports and diaries, sent during his whole service to the Fathers at Halle, that seat of German Pietism from which he and his colleagues were sent out, are an immense fund of the pioneer history of the Lutheran church in this country, and indeed his life and activities touch the history of the province at many points. His journeys and those of his brethren through the country show us where Germans were congregated ; that the circle of settlement had now by the middle of the century reached northward and westward until it touched what Muhlenberg calls "the first blue Mountains,"—North Mountain, the northern wall of the Lebanon and Kittatinny Valleys ; that the western parts of Maryland and Virginia were settled by Germans who had their organized churches ; how it was possible, with considerable hardship, as the patriarch found, to go from the neighborhood of Philadelphia to Kingston on the Hudson, where was another group of Germans anxious to be ministered to, and that even the far-south colonies of Georgia and the Carolinas were interested in and for their brethren in the faith in Pennsylvania.

It is to be deplored that no edition of the Halle Reports is easily obtainable in this country, outside of large historical collections, and that the projects for its republication with historical notes, and its translation with or without these notes have never been carried out to completeness, from lack of encouragement. From its pages can be formed a picture of the provincial life in the German settlements on the frontier,—the scattered log houses in the woods, the bridgeless streams, the little log churches at which a school-master perhaps taught the children on week-days or edified the shepherdless flock on Sundays from a "postil" of some good Lutheran divine. We see the "vagabond shepherds of souls," the unordained men, "who were of no account at home," yet came here, took possession of churches, and vexed Muhlenberg's righteous soul. We see, too, at the house of his father-in-law Conrad Weiser, Indian chiefs on their way to extort presents from the proprietaries that they might "sit quiet," in spite of stealthy French incitements. We have pictures of the sea-voyages,—one hundred days on the ocean, when the supply of water was exhausted, and the passengers gave themselves up to die of thirst. And we see, too, the busy, bustling provincial towns, containing schools and learned men with whom these graduates of German universities held brotherly counsel, their presses teeming with controversial pamphlets,—a tempest in a teapot, lively, if small,—with churches and church quarrels in abundance. It is the time when the New England provincials, aided by a company of the Broad Bay Germans, were taking Louisburg ; when the lilies of France dropped forever from Montreal and Quebec and Fort Duquesne before Bouquet and his Royal American regiment of Germans ; of Braddock's defeat and the Indian massacres, and the " Great Runaway" of frightened pioneers from the frontiers of settlement ; when Dr. Smith was trying to found the German schools, and succeeding in founding the University of Pennsylvania ; when Saur was fulminating against him and the Ephrata brethren were in full tide of prosperity ; when Franklin was writing on frontier defence ; when the Stamp Act was passed and repealed, and the Revolution was preparing.

A character and life of much more general interest than that of the patriarch Muhlenberg, was that of Muhlenberg's father-in-law, "Conrad Weiser, the Interpreter." It is a life which touches the story of the colonial Germans at many points. A child of one of the poor Palatines sent over to New York by Queen Anne, in Pennsylvania attracted by the influences proceding from Ephrata and Bethlehem, concerned in all the Indian negotiations of the province for twenty years, a colonel of provincial militia in the terrible time following Braddock's defeat,—his biography might be the thread upon which to collect the annals of the German settlements in the middle colonies.

His own autobiography tells the story of his early life in the best and simplest manner. After speaking of the Great Exodus, the arrival of the Germans in New York, and their dissatisfaction with Livingston's treatment of them, he says : " Bread was very dear, but the people worked hard for a living, and the old settlers were very kind and did much good to the Germans, though some of a different disposition were not wanting. A chief of the Maqua (Mohawk) nation, named Quaynant, visited my father, and they agreed that I should go with Quaynant into his country to learn the Mohawk language. I accompanied him, and reached the Mohawk country in the latter part of November, and lived with the Indians ; here I suffered much from the excessive cold, for I was but badly clothed, and towards spring also from hunger, for the Indians had nothing to eat. I was frequently obliged to hide from drunken Indians. Towards the end of July, I returned to my father, and had learned the greater part of the Mohawk language. There were always Mohawks among us hunting, so that there was always something for me to do in interpreting, but without pay." After an account of the land troubles at Schoharie and his father's unsuccessful embassy to London, Conrad Weiser continues: "The people got news of the land on Suataro and Tulpehocken in Pennsylvania; many of them united and cut a road from Schochary to the Susquehanna river, carried their goods there, made canoes, floated down the river to the mouth of the Suataro creek, and drove their cattle overland."

Conrad did not come with them, but he and his young wife remained behind, living near Schoharie among the Indians for some years longer. Then he followed his people to Pennsylvania, where he farmed and taught school until, two years after his emigration, an Indian of the Six Nations, Shekellamy, stopped at his house in Tulpehocken and asked Conrad Weiser to go with him to Philadelphia as a volunteer interpreter; Conrad, who seems to have had and retained a sincere friendship for his "comrades"—as he calls them—of the red race, acceded to the request, and gave so much satisfaction that in 1732 he became the official interpreter for the province.

"We have always found Conrad faithful and honest," said the Indians, "he is a good and true man, and has spoken their words and our words,—not his own." He was untiring in his labors; it make one's mind stand aghast to read the mere records of his journeys: to the great council of the Six Nations at Onondago, to Shamokin for the Governors of Maryland and Virginia, as well as his own great province, to Lancaster and the great treaty there in 1744; in the next year we find him in New York "surrounded by chiefs." Then he goes to tell the Indians of John Penn's death, for he has a deep perception of the complexity and importance of Indian etiquette, and is never weary in urging the provincial authorities to conform to it. "It is customary with the Indians," he admonishes the governor, "that let what will happen, the chiefs will not stir to do any service or business when they are in mourning till they have a small present in order to wipe off their tears and comfort their heart."

Weiser went twice with Moravian missionaries to the Indians : once with Zinzendorf to Wyoming, where his timely return probably saved the count's life, for Weiser's knowledge of the Indian character made him justly apprehensive for the good man's safety ; a second time he accompanied Bishop Spangenberg and others to the Great Council Fire to beg from the Six Nations a place of refuge for their exiled Christian Indians. Weiser's ideas of the best form for missionary work to take among these people are original, but he certainly spoke with authority, for no man of his time knew the savage character as he knew it. He advises that "missionaries should take up their abode in the midst of the Indians, and strive to make themselves thorough masters of the language, conform as far as possible to their dress, manners, and customs, yet reprove their vices ; translate the Bible into their own language," and that "the missionaries should study the Indian tunes and melodies, and convey to them the gospel in such melodies in order to make an abiding impression ; and patiently wait for the fruits of their labors."

His views on selling liquor to Indians were vigorously expressed : "If rightly considered, death without judge or jury to any man that carries rum to sell to any Indian town, is the only remedy to prevent that trade, for nothing else will do. It is an abomination before God and man."

Weiser himself was a religious man, a Lutheran in affiliation, though he had a kindlier feeling for the Moravians, especially on their first appearance in Pennsylvania, than most of his church, and although there was a strange interlude in his very common-sense career when he, with many others in his vicinity, fell under the influence of that extraordinary Dunker monk, Beissel, and was even baptized by him into his community. But this was only a passing impression, serving rather to show the inexplicable attraction of the " Magus of Conestoga" than the religious instability of Conrad Weiser.

In 1748 Weiser took his "great journey to the Ohio" to exercise his vast influence upon the western Indians, who were disaffected through the machinations of France ; in the next year he went to New York among his old Indian friends, where he had lived in the first years of his manhood ; in 1750 he was "most of the year from home." In the following years he was in Albany, trying to find out what were the intentions of "Colonel Johnston ;" in "Aughwick," where he heard from an Indian king the latter's poor opinion of the strategy exhibited at Fort Necessity by a Virginia militia officer, one Colonel Washington, who "would by no means take advice from the Indians ; he lay at one place from one full moon to the other, and made no fortification at all but that little thing upon the meadows. He is a good-natured man," said the savage potentate, tolerantly, "but had no experience." All

these toilsome journeys, these wordy and formal negotiations were to be in vain. The Council at Albany,
where Franklin, who was accompanied by Weiser, tried
to unite the English colonists against the encroachments
of the French was equally unavailing.

In the year 1755 the storm broke,—the terrible
"French and Indian War," with its tales of frontier
massacre and frontier defence. The German colonists
from their situation on the outskirts of civilization felt
the full force of it. The frontiers of Pennsylvania had
always enjoyed peace from savage invasion, the German
pioneers notoriously having the friendship and confidence of the Indians beyond that of any other nationality. But after Braddock's defeat, which Weiser dares
only allude to as "the unhappy action last summer,"
when the red men felt their power, and when their
stealthy scouts found (to their surprise) the outposts of
white settlement almost unguarded, they fell upon the
frontiersmen, and butchered, scalped, and, in the phrase
of the time, "captivated" all Europeans alike. The
Germans were settled along the Blue Ridge, and almost
in the centre of this curve of settlement lay Weiser's
home at Tulpehocken ; so he was in the heart of things,
and with his well-known ability and unparalleled knowledge of Indian ways, was naturally selected to take a
prominent part in the defence.

At the beginning of the alarm, Governor Morris
writes him : " I heartily commend your courage and
zeal, and that you may have the greater authority, I
have appointed you a colonel by the commission here-
with. I leave it to your judgment and discretion, which
I know are great, to do what is best for the safety of

the people and service of the Crown." Nobly did Weiser deserve this confidence ; his letters from day to day during those times of terror give us a most lively picture of the border warfare as it affected the Germans.

The first blow fell upon the Moravian mission station at Gnadenhütten on the Mahanoy (the present site of Weissport). Though conscious of their danger, the brethren had made a covenant to remain at the post of duty, and were sitting unsuspectingly at supper when, alarmed by the barking of the dogs, who were always very sensitive to the prowling presence of Indians, a brother threw open the door, and was shot upon the threshold. The Indians shot down several of the missionary family, while others effected their escape to the surrounding woods. The savages then set fire to the cabin, and Brother Senseman, one of the pious laborers, as he cowered in the woods, saw his wife in the midst of the burning house standing with folded hands, as she said, submissively, " 'Tis well, dear Saviour, I expected nothing else."

In a fortnight the whole border was deserted, the loneliest cabins were places of ashes, plunder, and blood, and the terrified people crowded into Nazareth and Bethlehem for refuge. The Whitefield House at the former place was stockaded, and the brethren met in a love-feast " to celebrate the completion of their work,"— rather a curious cause for such a feast. The Rose Inn at Nazareth also sheltered fugitives ; the mill at Friedensthal, where the single brethren furnished an efficient garrison, was stockaded, and from Bethlehem we have the following account : "Your Honor can easily guess at the trouble and consternation we must be in on this occasion in these parts. As to Bethlehem, we have taken all the precautions in our power for our Defence; we have taken all our little Infants from [the school at] Nazareth to Bethlehem for the greater security. Although our gracious King and parliament have been pleased to exempt those among us of tender conscience from bearing arms, yet there are many amongst us who make no scruple of defending themselves against such cruel savages. But, alas, what can we do, having very few arms and little or no ammunition, and we are now, as it were, become the frontiers."

While the "merciless Savages" were invading Lehigh County, other parties were terrorizing the more southerly frontiers of Berks and Lancaster Counties. A month after the massacre at Gnadenhütten of the missionaries, Weiser writes of an attack on the west side of the Susquehanna: "The people here seem to be senseless, and say the Indians will never come this side of the Susquehanna river, but I fear they will." His fears were abundantly justified; four days after he writes the information brought by his sons, who had just "arrived from Shamokin, where they had been to help down their cousin with his family. People are coming away in a great hurry. I pray, sir, don't slight it. The lives of many thousand are in the utmost danger. It is no false alarm. I suppose in a few days not one family will be seen on the other side of the Kittatiny Hills." But he tells another friend bravely that he has sent "to alarm the township in this neighborhood, and to meet me early in the morning to consult what to do, and to make preparations to stand the enemy, with the assistance of the Most High." The next day he details his military measures, the companies and beats into which he had divided the people, and also that "I sent privately for Mr. Kurtz, the Lutheran minister, who came and gave a word of exhortation to the people and made a prayer suitable to the time." A few days after he writes hopefully : "I believe that people in general up here will fight. I had two or three long beards in my company [alluding to the custom of wearing beards as a distinctive mark of the peace sects] one a Mennonite, who declared he would live and die with his neighbors. He had a good gun with him." But a few days, and he writes a "melancholy account" of new outrages. "I must stand my ground," he says, with modest confidence, "or my neighbors will go away." Then he forwards petitions, stops on his way to Philadelphia to appeal for the poor refugees in Reading, and to recommend "a Mr. Christian Bussey, a doctor in this town ; a hearty and very worthy person, has neither wife nor child, and will do all he can,"—which also the valiant doctor did, being a very active officer in frontier defence, along with such Germans as Weitzel, Arndt, and Wetterholt.

The last man named believed himself to be "kugelfest," or magically safe from bullets, but was killed in a tavern where he was passing the night, by Indians exasperated through the false dealing of one of his worthless officers,—a piteous fate for a brave and honorable man.

Many of the German ministers preached and prayed "suitably to the times,"—we find exhortations to enlist in defence of the province delivered in Lischy's pulpit in York County ; and Roth, a minister of Northampton

Town, writes that, " as I was preaching, the people came in such numbers that I was obliged to quit my sermon" and proceed to organize a militia company, and send for " fifty guns, one hundred pounds of powder," and other strengthening of the secular arm.

The German frontiersmen were as well inclined as the oftener praised Scotch-Irish, to "play the man for their people." Sometimes they built a blockhouse, such as Kellar's near Wind Gap, and garrisoned it themselves, sheltering there every night during the harassed winter of 1757–58. Sometimes they built cellars of refuge, and on the door of one of them, the Ulrich fort, was the rude but terribly appropriate verse :

> "So oft die Thür den Angel wendt,
> An deinen Tod, O Mensch, gedenk.—1751."
> " Whene'er this door its hinge doth turn,
> The nearness of thy death then learn."

The Zellers fort near Lebanon was built, under the superintendence of a woman, Christine Zellers, by negro slaves ; and the same woman, once being alone in the fort and seeing some Indians prowling about, stationed herself at a cellar window with an axe, and killed three, as they successively put their heads in to reconnoitre. It was upon the frontier of Lebanon County that Regina Hartman and her sister were captured ; but this pathetic tale belongs rather to the history of Bouquet's treaty of Muskingum.

Muhlenberg has preserved us the sad story of the massacre of some of his parishioners, the Reichelsdorfer family, who had purchased land on the frontiers of Berks County, but abandoned it when the war with the Indians broke out. The father and two daughters had gone out to this plantation to bring in some wheat; the girls were naturally impressed with their danger, and on the evening before their intended return to the settlements they spoke of a presentiment of approaching death, and sang with their father the familiar funeral hymn, "Wer weiss wie nahe mir mein Ende?"—"Who knows how near my end may be?" On the next day the father, while putting the horses to the wagon to take them home, was suddenly attacked by Indians. Giving himself up for dead, he ejaculated, "Lord Jesus, I am thine, living and dying," and the savages, awed by the sacred name, which they recognized, paused for a moment. Reichelsdorfer rushed through the woods to the nearest house for help, but when he arrived there he heard the Indians at their murderous work. Running back, he discovered his house in ashes, the body of one of his daughters consumed; but the other, though scalped and mangled by the tomahawk, was still alive, told him "all the circumstances of the dreadful scene," and then begged him to stoop that "she might give him a parting kiss, and then go to her dear Saviour."

But to return to Weiser, whom we find in 1756 posting soldiers, attending councils, and sending troops to protect harvesters. Armstrong's capture of Kittaning gave the people rest from their enemies this year, but in 1757 the same frightful alarms recur. Weiser attended a council at Easton, in July, and remarks cheerfully that "the Indians are altogether good-humored, and Teedyuscing [the mighty Delaware chief] behaves very well, and I have not seen him quite drunk since I came to this town." But in October he must inform the Governor that "it is certain that the enemy are numerous on our frontiers, and the people are coming away very fast;" and a few days after, "It has now come so far that murder is committed almost every day . . . so fly with my family I cannot do, I must stay if they all go;" yet he was at this time "in a low state of health,"—the beginning of his last sickness.

But in the next year we find him collecting "fifty-six good, strong wagons" for General Forbes's expedition to Fort Duquesne, and wishing "May the Most High prosper our labor with success;" and seeing the Governor discourteous in those ticklish times to a delegation of his Indian friends in Philadelphia, he writes with all his old-time vigor :

"I will say that he does not act the part of a well-wisher to his majesty's people. You may let him know so. Here is my hand to my saying so.
"I am, sir
"A loyal subject and a well-wisher to my country,
"CONRAD WEISER."

There passed a strong, heroic soul away when Conrad Weiser was laid to rest on his farm at Womelsdorf, where the Indians came to mourn at his grave for many years after. "We are at a great loss," they said, pathetically, at one of the conferences at Easton, "we sit in darkness by the death of Conrad Weiser; since his death we cannot so well understand each other." And, indeed, few white men have ever understood, not simply the Indian language, but the savage character, as did this friend and "comrade" and valiant fighter of the Indian.

The Germans in Colonial Times

During the period of Weiser's failing health, the provincial authorities cast about them for some one to take his place in the negotiations with the savages, and in some way heard of the qualifications of Christian Frederick Post, who was accordingly charged with the difficult and dangerous embassy to the tribes "on Ohio," which then meant the Allegheny affluent of the present stream as well. Post was a Moravian, and had been in the mission at Shekomeko, where he married a baptized Indian woman. At this time he was in Bethlehem, and on account of his friendly relations with the Indians, through his labors among them and his marriage into their tribe, it was thought that he might be able to persuade the western Indians not to add their forays to the French endeavors to hold "New France" in America.

He started in July; "proceeded as far as Germantown, where I found all the Indians drunk," he says, calmly; and after this hopeful beginning, decided to go by a more northerly route than the one usually followed, which was in general the subsequent National Road, as made by Braddock and afterwards by Forbes. Post concluded, as he expressed it, "to go through the inhabitants," or settled parts of the country; but he writes, "It gave me great pain to observe many plantations deserted and laid waste, and I could not but reflect on the distress the poor owners must be drove to, who once lived in plenty, and I prayed the Lord to restore peace and prosperity to the distressed."

His own distresses and dangers might have occupied a less unselfish mind; he notes simply how his party "slept upon the side of the mountain without fire for fear of the enemy;" how they "saw three scalps on a bush;

to one of them there remained some long, white hair ;" how " the wolves made a terrible music this night." They arrived at Kuskuskee, the Indian town about fifteen miles from Fort Duquesne, and after interminable negotiations and speeches, and a visit to the French fort, Post succeeded in " prevailing on the Indians to withdraw from the French interest."

He started homeward, his Indian guides in great terror, for they knew that a party was out after them : using all their Indian craft, they eluded the pursuers, and arrived safely in Fort Augusta, now Sunbury. One of Post's guides afterwards informed the Moravian that he had sold his life to the French, but was unfortunately prevented from keeping his engagement to kill him,—a circumstance which does not seem to have astounded Post, nor much moved him. He possessed in full the courageous faithfulness of the Moravian missionary, and told the Indians, very simply, " If I die in the undertaking, it will be as much for the Indians as for the English. I am resolved to go forward, taking my life in my hands, as one ready to part with it for your good."

So, in a few weeks, Post again plunged into the wilderness to persuade his savage friends to keep quiet in their towns, and " in consequence thereof," he writes, proudly, " the French were obliged to abandon the whole Ohio Country to General Forbes after destroying with their own hands their strong fort of Duquesne." Post returned with the victorious army from what, as soon as he has heard of its capture from the French, he scrupulously calls " Pittsburg." He had his share of hardship, to which, as a soldier of the cross, he was as well inured as any of the military men about him. On December 25, he notes, "the people in the camp prepared for a Christmas frolic, but I kept Christmas in the woods by myself,"—we may believe with many longing thoughts of the Christmas vigils and festivities of the Moravian Bethlehem; it is good to know that he returned safely there, having rendered such brave service to the province and its people.

We have seen how in North Carolina the Moravian brethren of the "Dutch Fort" offered a place of refuge to all the inhabitants of the frontier, entertaining refugees from as far as Virginia. It must have been only from the more southern portions of this province that the fort at Bethabara offered refuge, for we know that the settlers of the northerly part of the Valley of Virginia stood their ground through eleven years of savage and desolating warfare, gathering into the little groups of log cabins, dignified by the name of forts, whenever there was an alarm, and going out to their farming labors under guard when it could not be done in safety in any other way. The cal annalists, Kercheval and Doddridge, have prese ed a most vivid and detailed picture of the life in these times of what was more commonly called, in the South, "Braddock's War," when the people were "forted," as the expression ran. We know that since the days of Jost Heit's "trek" to Winchester, twenty-five years before, this valley had been filled with German pioneers, and this agrees with the frequent occurrence of Teutonic names, more or less disguised, among those of the heroes of these stirring border tales.

Doddridge describes a scene which must have found

its counterpart in many a German settler's cabin in those days. "I well remember, when a little boy, the family were sometimes waked at the dead of night by an express with a report that the Indians were at hand. The express came softly to the door or back window, and by a gentle tapping, waked the family; this was easily done, as an habitual fear made us ever watchful and sensible to the slightest alarm. The whole family were instantly in motion, my father seized his gun, my mother waked and dressed the children as well as she could; and being myself the oldest of the children, I had to take my share of the burthens to be carried to the fort. There was no possibility of catching a horse in the night to aid us in removing to the fort; besides the little children, we caught up what articles of clothing and provisions we could get hold of in the dark, for we durst not light a candle or even stir the fire. All this was done with the utmost despatch and the silence of death; the greatest care was taken not to waken the youngest child; to the rest it was enough to say 'Indian,' and not a whimper was heard afterwards. Thus it often happened that the whole number of families belonging to a fort, who were in the evening at their homes, were all in their little fortress before the dawn of the next morning. In the course of the next day, their household furniture was brought in by parties of the men under arms."

One German pioneer woman was not warned by such prosaic means as an "express;" she told her husband the night before an Indian attack that she could see the savages on the Massanutten Mountain, two miles away, around a fire cooking supper and preparing for their dark night's work, but was laughed at as superstitious for her warning, which proved true the next day.

These women were certainly not easily alarmed, nor did they lose their courage under the most frightful circumstances. Two families going to take refuge in a fort were attacked by the savages, and the husbands both killed at the first fire ; the newly made widows, seizing their dead husbands' guns, defended themselves and their orphans and brought them safely to the fort.

The house of an aged Mennonite preacher was attacked, the old man shot dead in his door-way, and his sons also slaughtered ; his eldest daughter, Elizabeth, caught up her little sister in her arms, and shut herself in the barn ; her Indian pursuer running back to the house for live coals with which to set fire to her refuge and thus drive her out, the Mennonite girl slipped out, forded a river, and escaped safely to a neighbor's, clasping tightly her little sister.

One old German, George Sigler, was the sole guardian of a party of women and little children on their way to the fort at Woodstock, when they were attacked. After wounding one Indian, the old man clubbed his gun and fought with desperation. Meanwhile, the women and children made their escape safely to the fort. Sigler, wounded and bleeding, continued the fight till he dropped from loss of blood, having saved his helpless charges by the sacrifice of his own life.

When the savages attacked and murdered the whole family of a man named Miller, save one little girl who escaped to warn the neighbors, the men who ran thither with their rifles at the first alarm found, on the threshold of the cabin which held the bleeding bodies of the murdered pioneers, a large German Bible; the Indians had attempted to burn it, but the closely bound book had resisted the flame, and but a few pages were consumed; this half-burnt and bloody relic is still preserved.

Some of these people were led away into captivity, and had to see their children and feeble ones slaughtered before their eyes when they could not keep up with their lithe, vigorous captors. Yet some captives taken young and adopted into the tribe were happy to remain among the Indians: of these were such men as Lewis Bingaman, who, captured when a boy near New Germantown, lived to be a great chief among his adopted people. Some years after Indian outrages had ceased, and the border had rest from its enemies, a worthless young white man committed the unprovoked murder of an Indian. Decoying the young chief away on pretence of hunting, he got behind him, shot him, robbed him of his rifle, hunting dress, and ornaments, and came home to boast of his cowardly deed. A few days after a German of the neighborhood met Lewis Bingaman, the German boy who had become an Indian warrior. Bingaman told him that he had come in at the head of thirty warriors to revenge the murder of his comrade, and urged him not to warn the murderer, for if the savage revenge was balked, they would exercise it, Indian fashion, upon all the whites, not excepting women and children. The German kept silence, thinking the English murderer deserved his punishment. Bingaman decoyed him into the Massanutten Mountain on the same pretext which he had used to his Indian victim, and the murderer was never seen again. His fate in the revengeful hands of the white savage may be best left to the imagination.

The settlements of the Palatines in Western New York, which had made the Mohawk a German stream for forty miles of its course, were naturally exposed to the inroads of the Indians, yet it was not their warlike neighbors, the Six Nations, who took the initiative in the attack. Weiser's arguments and representations to his "comrades" of the "Six Council Fires" had some effect, and the confederacy took part only half-heartedly and partially in the French and Indian War. When Onontio sent them ambassadors, money, and a commander, they went upon the war-path with savage alacrity, but they had no further plan than the Indian one of a foray; after dealing one of their terrible stealthy blows they would retire, quarrel over the spoil, and wait to see whether Onas or Onontio * would offer them the best terms, to decide whether it should be peace or war.

But when they took up the hatchet they were, if unreliable, very terrible allies, and so the French Captain Bellêtre found them when he came in 1757 to lead the Indians against the little settlement of German Flats (now called Herkimer, after its most prominent man, and its valiant defender at this and other times of stress). Nicholas Herkimer was the son of a Palatine emigrant, the lieutenant of the local militia, the possessor of a large, fine, and (best of all) defensible house, which served as a fort to the vicinity; what was most im-

---

* "Onas" was the Indian name for Mr. Penn and hence for the Pennsylvania government, and "Onontio" their designation for the French.

portant, he was a man of inexhaustible courage and resource, a tower of strength to the neighborhood.

Bellêtre's foray took the little settlement entirely by surprise. The news of an intended French attack, given them by a friendly Indian, was incredible to the settlers of German Flats, who, like most of their countrymen, had lived in friendship with their wild neighbors. Bellêtre fell upon them on a dark November night; his Indians butchered and scalped nearly half the people—men, women, and children indiscriminately—after a short but brave resistance, and took more than one hundred prisoners with him to Canada, besides a quantity of plunder, which, although the French captain exaggerated it, was really quite large, for the Palatines were known to be rich for frontier farmers. Herkimer's fort they did not venture to attack.

In the next spring the French returned, but found that Nicholas Herkimer had made such effective preparations for defence that they inflicted less damage and terror than in their previous attempt. They fell upon a company of settlers on their way under escort of Herkimer's militia to a place of safety, but were beaten off by the guards; the settlement suffered again, but again Herkimer's fortified house was untouched.

With the conclusion of peace, the Germans of the Mohawk country held a festival of thanksgiving—a sort of Peace Jubilee—in their churches, from the unfortunate village of German Flats to the old seats of the Palatines at Schoharie and the Camps; and we may be sure it was a heartfelt thanksgiving that was offered up by the pioneers.

CHAPTER XIX

THE "ROYAL AMERICAN" REGIMENT

THE military qualities of the German frontiersmen were so distinguished that they attracted the attention of the British Parliament, which in 1755, the year of Braddock's defeat, ordered a regiment raised among the German and Swiss settlers of Maryland and Pennsylvania. "As they were all zealous Protestants and, in general, strong, hardy men, accustomed to the climate, it was judged that a regiment of good and faithful soldiers might be raised out of them, particularly proper to oppose the French ; but to this end it was necessary to appoint some officers who understood military discipline, and could speak the German language." Proceeding on this principle, by the advice of the English minister to the Low Countries, some Swiss officers in the service of the Dutch republic were selected, and, among others, Henry Bouquet was made lieutenant-colonel of the new organization.

The selection was marvellously fortunate. Bouquet was a native of Berne, a man of unusual resourcefulness, courage, and ability, of high principles and cultivated mind, the greatest possible antithesis to the British soldier of the type of Braddock, or Loudon, Bouquet's titular superior. In the regiment were enrolled such German officers as Weissenfels, subsequently distinguished in the Continental army, and we have noted that the Rev.

The "Royal American" Regiment

Michael Schlatter found a place in it. as chaplain after the termination of his ministerial work in Philadelphia.

Bouquet came to America in 1756, and spent that winter in Philadelphia. He made friends among the best people of the town, and a feeling, perhaps tenderer than friendship, arose between him and a Philadelphia girl, the grand daughter of Chief-Justice Shippen, Miss Anne Willing. When in the next summer the Royal Americans formed part of Forbes's victorious forces at the taking of Fort Duquesne, it is to this "Dear Nancy" that Bouquet "has the satisfaction to announce the agreeable news of the conquest of this terrible fort. The French," he cries, exultantly, "seized with a panic at our approach, have destroyed themselves—that nest of pirates which has so long harbored the murderers and destructors of our people. The glory of our success must, after God, be allowed to our General, who kept such a number of Indians idle and procured a peace from those inveterate enemies, more necessary and beneficial than the driving of the French from the Ohio."

We know that the young Swiss's generous enthusiasm for his commander, though amply justified, was a little misplaced, and that it was the self-sacrificing Moravian missionary Post whose efforts kept the Indians quiet. After Forbes's return to Philadelphia and death, Bouquet succeeded to the command of the new Fort Pitt, and his men built the block-house which is the only existing remnant of the fort, and proudly placed upon it the name of their honored commander.

For the next seven years the Germans of the new regiment had the distasteful task of performing garrison duty in the long chain of scattered forts, or block-houses, which extended from Philadelphia to Fort Pitt, Sandusky, and Detroit; they were "military hermits" in the recesses of the forest, and the commander and his men found the isolation of the frontier very hard to bear. Near Fort Ligonier, where Bouquet was stationed, there was a German family, the Byerlys; the wife was a Swiss woman, Beatrice Gulden, from Bouquet's native canton of Berne, and with his countrywoman the Swiss officer would talk amid the wilds of Western Pennsylvania of their far-away mountain home.

Some battalions of the regiment were more fortunate, if it can be said to be fortune which sent some of them to participate in the campaign of Acadia, with its heartless deportation of the poor people; others were part of the expedition against Crown Point, and the mere fact that they held their ground in their rude intrenchment, defeating the Frenchmen by their unerring borderers' rifles, made it, in the words of Parkman, "an achievement of arms, which in that day of failures was greeted both in England and America as a signal victory." A battalion of the Royal Americans was also among the unhappy garrison of Fort William Henry, which having won by brave defence a capitulation with the honors of war, was assailed by Montcalm's Indians, and its members shot and scalped without mercy. In 1758 these German soldiers helped to take Louisburg from the French; in the next year they were with Prideaux at the taking of Niagara, and—far prouder deed—they were with Wolfe at Quebec. In the first assault at Montmorency "the ill-timed impetuosity of the Royal Americans proved the ruin of the plan;" but their gallant leader must have overlooked a fault so soldierly, for it is from Quebec that the regiment dates the right to its present motto,—"*celer et audax.*" It was these German soldiers who saw what the dying French general rejoiced that he would not live to see,—the surrender of Quebec ; and they were among the first English garrisons of Canada, when, in the next year, that province finally surrendered to the English. Forerunners of the English-speaking race everywhere, we find them in 1762 in Havana, where to-day other American regiments, not royal, form the garrison of that Morro Castle which the English built during their occupation of Cuba at this time.

It was the year after (1763) that there burst upon the western country the fearful surprise of Pontiac's conspiracy. The military hermits in their little posts were cut off, killed, or captured. At Fort Bedford a garrison of twelve Royal Americans held the forest post. " I should be very glad," wrote the commandant, guardedly, "to see some troops come to my assistance. A fort with five bastions cannot be guarded, much less defended, with twelve men, but I hope God will protect us." The small garrison of Fort Le Bœuf—a dozen men, six of whose names show their German descent—held their little fort until it was set on fire by burning arrows, and then cut their way out and marvellously escaped to Fort Pitt. Fort Pitt, gallantly held by Ecuyer, of the Royal Americans, was the only western post remaining except the besieged Detroit.

Bouquet, who was in Philadelphia, promptly started for the relief of these hard-pressed garrisons. He had but a handful of men, described in terms now sadly familiar to us, as "just landed from the West Indies in a very emaciated condition." But their leader's indomitable courage triumphed over everything. He took his little handful of yellow-faced invalids, plunged into the wilderness, reached and relieved Bedford, then Ligonier, and pressed on to Fort Pitt.

At a place (which Bouquet called Edge Hill, but which is commonly known as Bushy Run) about twenty-six miles from the fort he was suddenly attacked by Indians, as Braddock had been. But they had a very different man to deal with from that brave and pig-headed martinet. He knew and did not despise the Indian methods of warfare, but neither was he terrified by them. He was friendly with the savages, having, it is said, adopted an Indian boy, but he understood perfectly how to meet the new conditions of war in the woods by the use of frontiersmen's methods, and the suggestions in Smith's account of his campaign, "how to form and discipline a corps of rangers," which probably emanated from Bouquet himself, show how admirable an Indian fighter he was.

Forming a rude fortification with wagons and flour-bags, in which shelter he put the wounded, Bouquet sustained all the afternoon a galling attack from yelling, abusive, invisible savages ; yet they could not drive him from his position. That night he wrote to his general, Amherst, the letter of a brave man in the very presence of death. "We expect to begin at daybreak. Whatever our fate may be, I thought it necessary to give your Excellency this early information that you may at all events take such measures as you think proper with the provinces for their own safety and for the relief of Fort Pitt. The situation of the wounded is truly deplorable. The conduct of the officers is much above my praises."

But on that dreaded next day Bouquet executed a clever *ruse de guerre*, by which he drew the Indians into a trap and completely defeated them; then destroying the provisions, etc., which his weakened force could no longer carry, he made litters for the wounded, and brought his command safely into Fort Pitt. The savages were too thoroughly cowed by their overwhelming defeat by this handful of white men in the savages' chosen fighting-ground of the forest to attempt anything against Fort Pitt. Pontiac's war was ended and the frontiers were safe.

The wild, enthusiastic gratitude which Bouquet's wonderful fight evoked has almost passed from knowledge now; few, even of those who are acquainted with the dismal story of Braddock's ambuscade and defeat, which brought on the horrors of the French and Indian War, know of Bouquet's ambuscade and victory, which crushed Pontiac's conspiracy and gave Eastern Pennsylvania and Virginia final rest from savage warfare. Bouquet's name and fame are alike overlaid with dust. Yet he and his regiment of Germans acted a brave part in their time, and have deserved better of their country than the oblivion which has fallen upon them.

The Swiss colonel received the thanks of the provincial legislatures of Pennsylvania and Virginia. He was promoted to a brigadier-generalship. He was naturalized, evidently expecting to settle upon the tract quaintly called "Long Meadow enlarged," which he had bought among the German settlements of Frederick County, Maryland. One of his captains writes him from

The Germans in Colonial Times

Lancaster of the general joy over his honors: "You can scarcely imagine how this place rings with the news of your promotion, for the townspeople and German farmers stop us in the street to ask if it is true that the King has made Colonel Bouquet a General: and when they are told it is true, they march off with great joy. So you see the old proverb is wrong for once which says that he that prospers is envied, for sure I am that all the people are more pleased with the news of your promotion than they would be if the government would take off the stamp duty,"—certainly a strong comparison, when we remember that the captain alluded to the hated Stamp Act.

Bouquet was not the man to grow slothful in his honors. His humanity and his soldierly sagacity were alike interested in forcing the Indians to restore the prisoners whom they had taken during the long course of those nine years of border hostilities. So by a daring yet well-guarded march to the Indian towns on the Muskingum, and by a mingling of severity and adroitness, he induced the Indians to deliver up their white captives, who were brought to Carlisle for identification and return to their homes. Among the redeemed prisoners was that Regina Hartman whose true story, told simply by Muhlenberg, is far more affecting than in its dressed-up form of fiction.

As a little nine-year-old child upon the frontiers of Lebanon County, her father had taught her the sweet hymns of the Fatherland. The Indians fell upon their cabin while the mother and one son were away at mill, murdered the father and son at home, and took the little girls, Barbara and Regina, captive. The description of the long march through the rough and pathless wilderness with another strange child tied upon her back, the separation from her sister, the captivity to an "old she-wolf" of an Indian who forced the German child into the wintry woods for firewood and food from roots and tree-bark, the hunger, cold, and nakedness,—all have the affecting strength of truth. At first the poor child was stupefied by her misery ; then she began to recollect the teachings of her pious home, and often, taking her little nursling with her, the two children would kneel in the lonely woods, repeating the hymns and prayers which Regina had learnt. So nine years passed ; then " the wise and brave Colonel Bouquet" freed them and brought them to Carlisle, whither all those who had lost relatives or friends by Indian captivity were bidden to come and identify them. But no one knew the eighteen-year-old maiden, clad in the rude dress which the kindly soldiers of Fort Pitt had given from their own poor wardrobes. As Regina and her little foster-child stood bewildered, an old widowed woman in the crowd began to repeat the hymn of the wilderness :

> " Allein und doch nicht ganz alleine,
>   Bin ich in meiner Einsamkeit,
>   Denn wie ich ganz verlassen scheine,
>   Vertreibt mir Jesus selbst die Zeit.
>   Ich bin bei Ihm und Er bei mir,
>   Ich komm mir gar nicht einsam für.''

> " Alone yet not alone am I,
>   Though in this solitude so drear,
>   I feel my Jesus always nigh,
>   He comes my lonely hours to cheer ;
>   I am with him and he with me,
>   I cannot solitary be.''

Regina sprang out from the line, repeated the hymn and her German prayers, with which she had so often solaced her slavery in the Indian camp, and then threw herself upon her old mother's neck. Soon after she and her mother visited Muhlenberg ; Regina had insisted that her hymn told her of a book through which God spoke with men, and she wished to have it. When Muhlenberg gave her a Bible and desired her to try and read something from it, she opened it at a passage in Tobit and read "in a clearly beautiful and moving manner :" "When he was made captive . . . even in his captivity, (he) forsook not the way of truth." As no one came to claim the little foster-child, it was thought that her parents had been murdered by the savages when she was taken, so the poor widow and her recovered child took her into their own humble home. It is sad to say that the other daughter, Barbara, was never restored.

Shortly after his victorious return from the West, General Bouquet was ordered to Pensacola, where, in the midst of life, with "honor, love, obedience, troops of friends," he fell a victim to fever, and died within nine days after reaching his station. He left his plantation in Maryland to the brother of his "dear Nancy." The very place of his burial has been destroyed. Thus perished in his prime a gallant, noble, and talented man ; but it was not until he had done his work in freeing the frontiers from the terrors of Indian invasion with the aid of his gallant Germans of the "Royal American Regiment."

CHAPTER XX

THE REDEMPTIONERS

FOR some years a system had been growing up for enabling poor immigrants to pay their passage by "serving"—as it was called—for a certain length of time in the new land, thus giving their labor in exchange for their passage money. Such arrangements we find occasionally from about the date of the founding of Germantown ; but the class of " redemptioners," as they were known to the law, did not become large enough to attract notice until the middle of the eighteenth century.

When the first large bodies of immigrants arrived in Pennsylvania they excited the fears of the provincial authorities, and laws were passed requiring them to have their names registered and to take the oath of allegiance. By compliance with this law, the names of thirty thousand German, Swiss, and other European emigrants have been preserved for the information of their descendants, although, owing to the adoption by the English clerks of the maxim that "anything would do for the name of a Dutchman," the appellations are wonderfully disguised and disfigured.

After several outbreaks of alarm on the part of the English government lest the Germans should prove bad citizens, it was recognized that the superior prosperity of Pennsylvania was owing largely to their thrift and industry ; that they were steady, hard-working laborers, enterprising merchants, well-trained artisans, and, on occasion, good fighters; and the provinces generally tried to stimulate rather than discourage the Teutonic influx.

Unfortunately, the management of the emigration fell largely into the hands of conscienceless speculators, of whom Waldo, of Maine, the Zauberbühlers, of South Carolina, and Livingston, of New York, are the types. In Pennsylvania, on the contrary, there was no organized attempt to exploit the German immigration, and so it took its way towards Penn's province in overwhelming preponderance.

The opportunity to make money out of them was too good to be lost, and if the Quakers would not embrace it, a few ship-captains in Rotterdam did. The Stedmans, an English firm owning many of the vessels which sailed from the ports of the Low Countries, obtained a bad eminence in the traffic, which by the middle of the century rivalled the horrors of the slave-trade in its callous cruelty. Of this we have much testimony, and from eye-witnesses.

Although the emigration agents pictured the journey as an easy and cheap one, the poor pilgrims found it in reality to cost far more than had been estimated. The long journey down the Rhine, the passing of its innumerable custom-houses, and the (often prearranged) detention at Rotterdam until the ship sailed, were designed to exhaust their means and leave them in debt to the shippers. The poor people, with German thrift, brought their great chests on board filled with dried fruits, bacon, liquor, and medicines, as well as clothing and money. But these were intentionally stowed in other vessels, so that the emigrants, deprived of their own provisions, were compelled to buy them from the captain, thus increasing their debt. On these crowded, foul ships, during the long voyage (three months was the usual time), with poor and insufficient food, the death-rate was frightful. In the years 1750 and 1755 Saur notes that two thousand corpses were thrown into the sea. On the ship on which Heinrich Keppele, the first president of the German Society, emigrated, two hundred and fifty persons died.

Gottlieb Mittelberger, a school-master and organist of Würtemberg, came over in 1750, and on his return, after living four years in New Providence, Pennsylvania, he wrote an account of his travels. He says "the most important occasion for publishing this little book was the wretched and grievous condition of those who travel from Germany to this new land and the outrageous and merciless proceeding of the Dutch man-dealers and their man-stealing emissaries,—I mean the so-called Newlanders." He, as well as Muhlenberg, describes the tactics of these detested traffickers, how they delude the poor Germans with glowing descriptions of the "Elysian fields which seed themselves without toil or trouble," and tell the people "he that goes as a servant becomes a master, as a maid becomes 'your ladyship;' the peasant is a nobleman, the artisan a baron." Mittelberger declares that his countrymen in Pennsylvania implored him "with tears and uplifted hands to make this misery and sorrow known in Germany, so that not only the common people, but even princes and lords, might learn how they had fared, to prevent other innocent souls from leaving their fatherland, persuaded

217

thereto by the Newlanders, and from being sold into a like slavery."

What this slavery is he goes on to describe: "The sale of human beings on the ship is carried on thus: every day Englishmen, Dutchmen, and High German people come from the city of Philadelphia and other places, go on board the newly arrived ship, and select among the healthy persons such as they deem suitable for their business, and bargain with them how long they will serve for their passage money. When they have come to an agreement, adult people bind themselves in writing to serve three, four, five, or six years for the amount due from them, according to their strength and age. But very young people must serve until they are twenty-one years old. When one has served his term he is entitled to a new suit of clothes at parting,"—called the "freedom suit,"—"and if it has been so stipulated, a man gets in addition a horse, a woman a cow." We can see that to young, strong, single persons the arrangement would be a favorable one, enabling them to learn the ways of the new country and to be assured of a support during their first years in the unfamiliar surroundings.

But Muhlenberg, speaking from the stand-point of a clergyman often appealed to by the distressed, gives a sad picture of the fate of those unable to serve. "Old married people, widows, and the feeble no one will have. If they have healthy children, the freight of the old people is put upon them, and the children must serve the longer, are the harder to sell, and are scattered far from one another; see their old parents and their brothers and sisters seldom or never, and forget their mother tongue. The old people, meanwhile, freed in such wise from the ship, are poor, naked, and distressed, look as tho' they had come from the grave, go about in the town begging from the Germans,—for the English mostly shut their doors upon them, fearing infection."

And the organist Mittelberger goes on to describe the conditions of life in Pennsylvania in homely but vigorous words: "Work and labor in this new and wild land are very hard and many a one, who came here in his old age, must work hard to his end for his bread. Work here mostly consists in felling oak trees and as they say here 'clearing' large tracts of forest. . . . Stumps of oak trees are in America certainly as hard as in Germany. . . . People are very foolish if they believe that roasted pigeons will fly into their mouths in America without their working for them."

He returns again and again to the lies and deceptions of the Newlanders, of which he had had personal experience. "When these men-thieves persuade persons of rank such as nobles, learned or skilful persons, who cannot pay their passage and cannot give security, these are treated just like ordinary poor persons. And when they are released at last from the ship they must serve their lords and masters, by whom they have been bought, like common day laborers. Their rank, skill and learning avails them nothing, for here none but laborers and mechanics are wanted. But the worst is that such people, who are not accustomed to work, are treated to blows and cuffs like cattle till they have learnt the hard work. Many a one, on finding himself thus shamefully deceived has shortened his own life." The "Hallesche Nachrichten" casually mentions the finding of a suicide's body: "He arrived a few days since from London or Amsterdam, could not pay his passage and probably was too proud to serve for a time, which it is suspected was the cause of his suicide." Mittelberger mentions the case of a noble lady who, with her two daughters and a son, came to Philadelphia, intrusting her means to a Newlander: "this villian remained behind with the money; in consequence of which this lady found herself in such want and distress that her two daughters were compelled to serve. In the following spring this poor lady sent her son to Holland to search for the embezzler of her money; but nothing had been heard of him as yet, and it was even rumored that the young gentleman had died during his voyage." And we find Pastor Kunze imparting to the Fathers in Halle "an idea which had occurred to him" of a way to obtain an assistant pastor as follows: "If I had say £20 I would buy the first German student who came to these shores owing his freight, put him in my upstairs room, begin a little Latin school, teach in the mornings myself and let my servant teach the rest of the time and be paid by a small fee." On this wise the benevolent and business-like clergyman became possessed of a collegian, out of whom he made, in course of time, a minister.

That persons of the better and upper classes were not infrequently among the redemptioners may be the reason why no possible stigma attached to the condition; although other classes of the population, the negro slaves and the convict servants, approached them in condition, *they* were regarded as degraded, while the redemptioners soon paid their debts, bought land for themselves, and were on an equality with the rest of the emigrants who had had enough money on their arrival to pay their passage. The women among the redemptioners very often married their masters or masters' sons ; the traditions of almost every Pennsylvania German family contain examples of this. One of the signers of the Declaration of Independence, Charles Thornton, had been a redemptioner, as were the parents of the Revolutionary general, Sullivan. These must have been among the Irish redemptioners, for this nationality supplied a few as well as the German. Many members of the Virginia House of Burgesses had been "servants" before they ruled others as legislators. The condition is much more repugnant to our ideas of personal liberty than it was to those of our forefathers, as are also the tone and expression of the numerous advertisements announcing the arrival of emigrant ships, and offering servants for sale.

Here are specimens : "The ship Boston, Mathew Carr, Master, is to-day arrived from Rotterdam with several hundred Germans, among whom are all sorts of artisans, day laborers, and young persons, both men and women as well as boys and girls. Those who are desirous of providing themselves with such persons, are desired to communicate with David Rundle, Front Street." The people are described and praised in terms of salable commodities ; they are "fresh and healthy;" there are "nice children" in another load ; the trades and abilities of the emigrants are exhaustively catalogued. In the advertisements of the sale of service, it was really the service, not the person of the servants, that was offered, but the advertisers were by no means careful to avoid this expression. Miller's "Staatsbote," a year after the repeal of the Stamp Act, contains the following : " For sale, the time of a German bound girl. She is a strong, fresh and healthy person, not more than twenty-five years old, came into the country last autumn and is sold for no fault, but because she does not suit the service she is in. She is acquainted with all kinds of farm work, would probably be good in a tavern. She has still five years to serve." Another is " a pious and Godfearing girl with a special fondness for outdoor work." A succinct notice offers " A Dutch apprentice lad ; can work well." One trusts that servants of such virtues and abilities found masters as good. But this was, as Muhlenberg says, " according to the characteristics of the buyers and what the providence or permission of God has decreed."

It is easy to see how the whole system, both of transportation and serving, gave abundant opportunity for dishonest and cruel treatment. The Germans resident in Philadelphia made several endeavors to have some sort of inspection of vessels established, but the governor was unwilling to interfere with the profit of the rich and unscrupulous European merchants ; it was alleged that he had some pecuniary interest in not disturbing the traffic.

At length, in 1764, a particularly shocking instance of sickness and need on board the ships which arrived in the autumn of that year was brought to the notice of the public through a letter in the " Staatsbote," probably written by Pastor Helmuth. He describes the pest-house as " a veritable Tophet, a land of the living dead, a vault full of living corpses, where nothing but their sighs and tears showed that the souls were still in their wasted bodies. The stench and the revulsion of body as well as mind, yes the feelings of humanity, forbade me to carry out my intention of speaking or praying with them, not to mention that for this there was neither place nor opportunity. . . . God, who has promised eternal life to those who feed Him in those who are an-hungered, clothe Him in the naked and visit Him in the sick, will incline the hearts of those who have the means, to take this opportunity of showing that they are not unworthy of temporal and eternal goods." The editor of the "Staatsbote" adds the information that before this appeal was printed, money, clothing, and food had been spontaneously sent to the sufferers.

The generous Germans who had given this help informally saw the great need of an organization of persons which should make it its business to look after their distressed fellow-countrymen, and so, "on Second Christmas, 1764, in the Lutheran schoolhouse in Cherry Street," was formed the "Deutsche Gesellschaft," still existing in an honorable and vigorous old age. The meeting arranged for the relief of such cases of destitution among their country-people as might occur, and for protection of the redemptioners in making their contracts, and sent a translation of their rules and a petition against the abuses suffered by the German emigrants to Governor John Penn, and then, in the words always used at the end of the minutes, "the Society parted from each other in love and friendship."

In 1765 a law was passed by the Assembly doing away with many of the abuses, modifying others, and in general so bettering the lot of the poor emigrants that the Society was justified in reprinting it as a pamphlet, with the proud title, "The First Fruits of the German Society." And through the years we find in the records of the Society homely notes of how it interfered to protect a little German boy from an unkind master, how the aged president of the Society went in person to deal with the oppressors of a widow, how they paid a German woman "to cure the hand" of an emigrant, furnished bedding and clothing, food and mediicine for the living, and buried the dead.

The example of the Germans in Philadelphia was followed by those in other cities, and German societies were formed in New York, Baltimore, and Charleston. In all these cities were many Germans, and the same conditions obtained to some degree.

In the province of New York we hear little of redemptioners; yet we occasionally meet with allusions which prove that the relation was not unknown there, although it was not so frequent as in Pennsylvania. One of these is the story of Lady Johnson, the wife of the powerful Indian agent in the Mohawk Valley. She was a redemptioner, Catharine Weissenfels, serving in the family of two brothers named Phillips. Johnson, not then Sir William, saw the blooming, pretty German girl, and fell in love with her. A neighbor, presently inquiring of one of the Phillips brothers what had become of their maid, was told, "Johnson, the d—d Irishman, came the other day and threatened to horsewhip me and steal her if I would not sell her. I thought £5 better than a flogging and took it, and he's got the gal." Thus Catharine Weissenfels passed to Johnson. She bore him three children; for the German girl was the mother of his heir, Sir John, and her daughters were married to General Clause and to Sir William's nephew, Sir Guy. When she lay dying of consumption she begged him to marry her, and at least legitimate her children; bolstered up on her death-bed the ceremony was performed, and so for a few days the dying Palatine woman was Lady Johnson in the eyes of the church and the world. Perhaps her lord's roving heart returned to her in his last days, for he willed to be buried "beside his beloved wife Catharine," and when, late in the nineteenth century, his dust was disturbed there was found among it a slender gold ring, bearing the date of their belated marriage, which he had taken from Catharine's dead finger.

The name of one New York redemptioner has become famous in later times as the first man to resist successfully the endeavors of a royal governor to curb the freedom of the press. One of the poor little Palatine children who was brought a penniless orphan to the province of New York in 1710 was John Peter Zenger, the thirteen-year-old son of Magdalena Zenger, a Palatine widow. As we know, Governor Hunter took those children and apprenticed them to citizens of the province without much regard to the feelings or desires of the poor families to which they belonged; so Weiser's two sons were taken from him and given first to one master and then to another, until little Frederick died shortly after his apprenticeship.

But the young Zenger found a good master, kind and upright; he was given into the hands of William Bradford, the printer, and from him learned not only the art and mystery of typography, but the higher art of living

15   225

a brave and upright life. After the Palatine boy's term of apprenticeship was over, he became his master's partner ; but in 1733 he set up a press, and in the same year a paper of his own.

This paper was designed to support the people's side in the disputes between the royal governor and his loving subjects. This purpose Zenger carried out with such fearless exposition of the governor's misdeeds that he was made the object of all sorts of persecutions in order to silence him. The governor ordered copies of Zenger's paper burnt by the hangman, which that official refused to do, and "delivered them into the hands of his own negroe and ordered him to put them into the fire which he did ;" the governor commanded the aldermen to attend this *auto-da-fé*, whereat they "forbade all the members of this Corporation to pay any obedience to it."

Finally, in 1735, the governor succeeded in having Zenger tried for libel, for making what strike the modern reader as very moderate remarks upon the ursurpations of the royal representative. The young German printer would probably have fallen a victim to the hatred and strength of the ruling powers, had he not been defended by Andrew Hamilton, of Philadelphia, at that time the most celebrated lawyer in the colonies, in a speech which is even yet very good reading for its wit, its adroitness, its clarity, and its rare and restrained eloquence.

"I am truly very unequal to such an undertaking on any account," said Hamilton, "and you see I labor under the weight of many years and am borne down with great infirmities of body ; yet old and weak as I am, I

should think it my duty, if required, to go to the utmost part of the land, where my service could be of
any use in assisting to quench the flame of persecution
set on foot by the Government to deprive a people of
the right of remonstrating (and complaining too) of
the arbitrary attempts of men in power. . . . The
question before you, gentlemen of the jury, is not of
small or private concern : it is not the cause of a poor
printer of New York alone which you are now trying ;
it may in its consequences affect every free man that
lives under a British government on the Main of
America. . . . It is the best cause, it is the cause of
Liberty !''

It is hardly necessary to say that Zenger, who seems
to have been universally liked and honored as the representative of that cause of which Hamilton spoke so
solemnly, was acquitted when " the jury in a small time
returned," says Zenger, " upon which there were three
Huzzas in the Hall, which was crowded with people,
and the next day I was discharged from my Imprisonment." The poor Palatine apprentice lad and the persecuted printer lived to be an honored citizen of New
York, where he died ten years after this trial.

In the province of Maryland, most of the German
emigrants entered through Pennsylvania, coming to the
port of Philadelphia, and so there was little need for
the work of a German society until in the early years
of the nineteenth century, when one was founded.
There were, however, a few German redemptioners in
Maryland.

In South Carolina we know they were quite numerous,
and, from occasional complaints to the Council of the

province, that they had to encounter the same treatment from avaricious or cruel ship-masters as had their brethren of Pennsylvania. Thus, on one occasion the records of the Council tell us that "a considerable number of Protestant Palatines have been on board the St. Andrews, Capt. Brown commanding, these twenty-six weeks past and there is yet no likelihood of them to get free of her, because there is none yet who have purchased their service," so they beg the government to pay their passage money for them, which advance they will repay. But a few pages farther, Captain Brown's unhappy "freights" complain "that last Friday they were the whole day without any sustenance and had been the like for several days before." The captain, being called to account for his passengers' involuntary fasting, said coolly that "if they had asked him for food in their language, he would not have understood them." One poor old woman, widowed during the long voyage, and whom, on account of her age, no one would buy, was released by Oglethorpe and given a home in the Salzburgers' orphan house.

It seems that Orangeburg and Saxe Gotha in particular received a large part of the increase of population which came to them in the years between 1744 and 1750 through the influx of redemptioners.

One Southern redemptioner had a romantic family history. There was, during the Peasants' War in the time of Luther, a Count of Helfenstein, who, with his wife and child, was butchered by the maddened peasants. Some of his family escaped from the slaughter; but so poor did his descendants become that when, in the eighteenth century, Frederick Helfenstein desired

to emigrate to America, he had not the means to pay
his passage, and he and his wife "served" as redemptioners in Savannah to make up the sum. He afterwards
became wealthy, though the British dragoons quartered
upon him during the Revolution plundered him unspar-
ingly, his greatest offence being that he had two sons in
the patriot army. These sons, serving under Wayne in
a Pennsylvania regiment, thus came to the middle colonies, and the northern branch of the Helfenstein family
is thought to originate from these exiled soldiers of independence.

CHAPTER XXI

THE GERMANS AS PIONEERS

WHEN the French and Indian War was ended, the Germans rapidly filled up the counties of Pennsylvania west of the Kittatinny Mountains. This country had been claimed by the Indians, and was not opened to white settlement until the treaty of Albany in 1754. The government of the Penns, always scrupulously just in its dealing with the old forest friends of Onas, did not permit encroachment on the Indians' lands, and frequently ejected the Irish pioneers who had squatted on land not yet opened to settlement, burning their cabins and forcing them away. But as soon as white men could justly enter, a number of Germans took up land there, within the present limits of Perry County, the first deed being given to John Pfautz, after whom the valley of that name is called.

That Germans were the first settlers of Schuylkill County is proved by the names of the pioneers, Orwig and Jaeger. Even in the northerly region of Bradford they came first ; two families of the Schoharie people, following in 1770 the trail of the Tulpehocken emigration, found the country so much to their liking that they "sought no further."

As soon as the savage hostilities had ceased, Dunkers entered that part of Bedford County now called Blair, and from the time of Forbes's victorious march upon Fort Duquesne dates the German settlement of Somerset, now a very Teutonic district. In 1769 Berlin was begun by some Mennonites, who, in laying out the town, charged all the lots with a ground-rent of "a Spanish milled dollar" for the benefit of churches and schools. When at the end of the Revolution the Indians fell upon and destroyed Hanna's-town, the earliest capital of Westmoreland County, they were first discovered by "the reapers in Michael Huffnagle's field," so evidently there were German residents west of the present limits of Somerset. The pioneers of the latter district were so alarmed by the destruction of Hanna's-town, which was the next settlement to the west of them, that they abandoned their homes and did not return until the troublous times were over.

Everywhere along the Pennsylvanian frontier, as well as in Maryland, Virginia, the Carolinas, and the new country of Kentucky, we find the Germans, either as pioneers, as the first permanent settlers, or as following or intermingling with the Scotch-Irish, who are commonly but mistakenly credited with being always and everywhere the pioneers.

The Germans were pioneers in many other directions than in that of settling the wilderness: the reader of local history is struck with the numerous cases in which a man of this race led a colony, laid out a town, or in some other way showed himself capable of organizing and directing the pioneering of other men. It was very commonly the case, in the earlier half of the eighteenth century at least, that the German emigrants came in an organized body, bringing pastor, school-teacher, and sometimes physician with them.

In business life we see arising among the Germans

merchants like the generous and patriotic Michael Kalteisen, of Charleston, or the honest baker Ludwig.   The
Teutons were pioneers in many lines of manufacture,—
notably, most of the early iron-masters of Pennsylvania
were of this nationality.   In the South, too, Governor
Spotswood, the "Tubal-Cain of Virginia," used his
German settlers in this work.   The first German iron-
master was the Mennonite Kurtz, who built a furnace in
1726 at Octorara in Lancaster County.   The same
county saw the rise—and fall—of the famous "Baron"
Stiegel, who came to Manheim in the latter half of the
eighteenth century, no one knows whence, but with
plenty of money.   He bought the Elizabeth furnace,
which remained a hundred years in use ; laid out the
town of Manheim, and gave a lot to the Lutherans for a
church building at the nominal rental of one red rose in
June paid to him or his heirs ; he was the first maker of
flint glass in Pennsylvania.   He had two "castles,"
whose furniture was the wonder of the time ; he is said
to have entertained George Washington at one of his
residences, to have had a band to play and a cannon
whose firing announced his arrival, and in general lived
at such a pace that the Revolution and his extravagance
combined reduced him to bankruptcy and to teaching
his former workmen's children for a livelihood.   He lies
in an unknown grave.   But the ceremony of paying the
red rose to his heirs has recently been revived, and now
the "Feast of Roses" in Manheim every June is one of
the most interesting and picturesque fêtes observed in
our country.   The woollen manufactures of Germantown
were soon famous, and the name of the town is still the
designation of a particular kind of worsted.   The pottery

The Germans as Pioneers

of the Pennsylvania Germans was well known and good, though its decorations and mottoes did not reach a very high æsthetic level. The Germans were the earliest makers of musical instruments ; the first organ built in the United States was made some time previous to 1737 by Matthias Zimmerman, a carpenter and joiner, of Philadelphia. Harttafel, Klein, who built the first organ for Bethlehem, and the famous Moravian family of organ-builders, the Tannebergers, some of whose instruments are still in use, flourished from 1740 to 1770. Adam Geib, who "came to New York in 1760 and began business on a very unpretentious scale," built the old organ of Grace Church, and his sons were among the earliest piano-makers of America.

In paper-making and type-founding they were the first and best of American manufacturers in their time. The productions of the German press challenge comparison with anything else done in colonial America. A phenomenon, rather strange in consideration of the Teutonic view of woman's sphere, is the fact that two of the earliest woman printers of America were German women. The female portion of Zenger's family had helped him in his business ; and in 1746–48, after his death, his widow Cathrine carried on a printing and publishing business "at the Printing Office in Stone Street, where Advertisements are taken in and all persons may be supplied with this Paper,"—as her imprint announces. A few years before the Revolution, "an energetic business woman," the widow of Nicholas Hasselbach, conducted in Baltimore the printing-office bequeathed by her husband. The attempt to make glass at New Germantown in Massachusetts was, however, a failure, as was the wine-making in various parts of the country, and, ultimately, the silk manufacture at Ebenezer. Everywhere, however, we see the German colonists pursuing the plainer tasks of civilization successfully; they built churches, schools, and mills wherever they went, and supported religion and education in their own tongue earnestly.

But it was as farmers that these colonists won the admiration of such aliens as the Philadelphia physician, Benjamin Rush. He commends their substantial farm buildings, their good judgment of land, their care of their stock, their well-built fences, their economy in burning wood in stoves instead of the large, wasteful fireplaces, and their gardens, which gave them a healthful abundance of vegetables. Dr. Rush speaks, too, of the fine, large horses which pulled the Conestoga wagons. The commendations which he bestows on the farmers he extends to the mechanics of the race, and he speaks well of the peaceable, frugal, honest dispositions of the kind and friendly people. His whole little book shows a knowledge and comprehension of his strange fellow-citizens which is refreshing to meet amid the mass of ignorant and biassed misjudgment which has disfigured much that has been written before and since about the Pennsylvania Germans.

CHAPTER XXII

THE GERMANS IN THE REVOLUTION

No one who has seen the activity and vigor of the life among the German settlers in the colonial period will be surprised that in the event which is generally accepted as marking the close of that period—the Revolutionary War—they took an important part. In those communities where the Germans, few in number, had been assimilated, and, as it were, lost, in the English population around them, the citizens of German descent stood side by side with those of Anglo-Saxon blood in resistance to the British. But in the settlements which were as yet German, where they had their own language, schools, churches, ministers, newspaper and press, we find organizations purely German taking part in the struggle, and the Teutonic element accorded a representation in proportion to its numbers, influence, and patriotism. So, glancing at the smaller settlements, literally "from Maine to Georgia," as the older phrase ran, we find the Germans everywhere stirred and affected by the birth-throes of the new nationality.

At the little town of Waldoboro, or Broad Bay, a German is chosen clerk of the Committee of Correspondence; another is the first man in the place to display the American flag, the Stars and Stripes, when the new ensign is adopted; and the names, prominent in the early annals of the hard-tried little colony, of Ludwig and Ulmer, reappear at the head of the numerous militia companies, which, as the phrase ran, "performed a tour of duty." Ludwig had been at Crown Point during the French and Indian War, and he put his military experience again at the service of his country. These militiamen were chiefly employed in guarding the coasts of hundred-harbored Maine against the depredations of British cruisers, but they were not successful in preventing the sufferings which the colonists endured from the destruction of crops and property. Of these evils of war the Waldoboro people endured their full share, and we have the records, no less pathetic because of their homeliness, of how the Counce family were without bread or potatoes for forty days, and kept an involuntary Lent by supporting life upon the fish they caught, or how one of the Lermonds was favored in that his crop of rye ripened unusually early, how he threshed it out upon a flat rock, and sold it by the peck to his starving neighbors.

And far away in North Carolina the brethren of the Wachovia tract were experiencing the difficulties of keeping true to their non-resistant principles when the country was aflame with tumult, hatred, and patriotism around them. The Regulators before the battle of the Alamance insisted that the brethren ought to divide their harvests with them ; militiamen and the Tories and British troops of Cornwallis alike made the church settlements what the brethren patiently and euphemistically called "rather expensive visits ;" the Provincial Assembly tried to meet at peaceful Salem and "failed for want of a quorum ;" until, on the Fourth of July, 1783, "the solemn Thanksgiving Day of the restoration of peace was celebrated with great joy and gladness of heart and with especial gratitude to the Lord, for all his mercies and providential preservation during these trying times."

In Charleston, Michael Kalteisen, a prosperous merchant, organized a German military company which afterwards became the ancient and honorable German Fusiliers, who served through the Revolution with energy and distinction.

In Georgia, most of the Salzburgers in Ebenezer took the side of the colonies, and a number of their names are found on the honorable roll of the Georgia Provincial Congress which met in Savannah in 1775. Their names are also found upon another roll in which are written those whom General Prevost proscribed for their loyalty. We find "Adam Treutlen, rebel governor," and a number of "rebel counsellors, colonels," and other insurgents obnoxious to the Royalists. When, in 1779, Prevost made his descent on Georgia and took Savannah, he established a post at Ebenezer. One of the Salzburger pastors, Triebner, an earnest loyalist, offered to guide the British soldiers to his parish, where they dug a redoubt, still to be traced, around the church, took the building for a hospital and finally desecrated it into a stable, shot at mark on the weather-vane which bore Luther's swan, and desolated and harried the neighborhood. The farm-house of Rabenhorst, the other pastor, was among those burnt, and the redemptioner Helfenstein, whose romantic history has been given, was the especial object of attack because he had two sons in the patriot army. When at length the British retired from Georgia at the close of the war, Triebner went with them, which was doubtless prudent, for he must have found it hard to face the wrath of his patriot parishioners when they came back to the site of their ruined village home. Pastor Triebner was almost an isolated instance among the German clergy of adhesion to the royal cause; yet in the neighboring city of Savannah we have the most glaring instance of a clergyman of fine reputation and brilliant talents who ruined himself by his misplaced loyalty.

This was the Rev. John Joachim Zubly, a clergyman of St. Gall, in Switzerland. He arrived in Georgia in 1746, and after a varied ministry—first at the valiant little colony of Frederica, whence he was driven by the Spanish attack upon the place, then in South Carolina—he settled in Savannah, where his talents, learning, and attractive character gave him a great reputation and enabled him to build up a large congregation. At the outbreak of the resistance to England he took the patriot side; he preached an eloquent sermon before the Provincial Congress on the alarming state of American affairs, based on the text, "So speak ye, and so do, as they that shall be judged by the law of liberty," which was published in Philadelphia and republished in London. He was a delegate both to the Provincial Congress of Georgia and to that in Philadelphia, and his position, ability, and patriotism gave him great influence. Yet, when the actual fact of independence was in sight, Dr. Zubly became terrified. He wrote to Sir James Wright, Royal Governor of Georgia, warning him of the plans of Congress. This correspondence, which could not but be considered treasonable, was discovered, and Zubly fled, leaving a letter in which he said, "I am off for Georgia greatly indisposed." On reaching home he openly took sides with the Tories, was banished from the city, and part of his property confiscated. He returned after his royal friends re-established their government, and was at his post of ministerial duty during the siege of the city. He died in Savannah in 1781, "broken in heart and broken in fortune," yet loved and pitied by many who remained faithful to him to the end of a career which had almost led him to the distinction of a signer of the Declaration, yet had so fatally and sadly failed. The beautiful church of the "Independent Presbyterians" in Savannah, a faithful reproduction of the old colonial structure, contains an affectionate tablet to his memory,—that of a gifted, godly, yet misguided man.

In this glance at the scattered German settlements we have omitted the central colonies of New York, Pennsylvania, Maryland, and Virginia, where the Germans had their chief homes, where they were wealthy, numerous, and prominent. Did they here show the same characteristics of these smaller companies of their nationality? We may answer unhesitatingly, yes. "The Germans who composed a large part of the inhabitants of the Province [of Pennsylvania]," says Bancroft, "were all on the side of liberty." As Pennsylvania was the keystone, intellectually and morally as well as geographically, of the German colonies, we may see in its record an epitome of them all. The provinces of New York on the north and of Maryland and Virginia on the south were more of frontier settlements,—at least in their German portions ; they were, in the excellent phrase of one of our historians, "the rear-guard of the Revolution ;" from the southern provinces went out those hardy German pioneers who explored and settled Kentucky and Tennessee, who filled the ranks of Clarke when he took "the Illinois country" for the United States, who rushed to the defeat of Ferguson at King's Mountain, but not, we are proud to say, those fierce borderers who " left none to mourn for Logan" or who slaughtered the Christian Indian women and children of Gnadenhütten.

The record of the Germans of Pennsylvania is not of frontier warfare but of service in council and field, and the Teutonic servants of our infant country were many and faithful and valorous. German names are numerous in all the committees and conventions which preceded or organized the Revolution. We find them on the county committees of correspondence, of observation, of safety, in the two provincial conventions in Philadelphia, and among the associators.

The German press teemed with pamphlets, sermons, and addresses : one of the most notable of these was the "Address" of the vestries of the Reformed and Lutheran churches and the officials of the German Society to their fellow-countrymen in New York and North Carolina. It is a very clear, well-written, and temperate recital of the causes and course of the Revolution up to the time of the pamphlet's appearance, 1775. The Pennsylvanian Germans, it says, are associating in militia companies for the cause of liberty, raising rifle corps, subscribing money. In the midst of this patriotic ardor, they are shocked to learn that the Germans of Tryon County (Western New York) and of North Carolina " appear to be unfriendly to the common cause ;" but they excuse it by the influence of the Johnson family in the Mohawk Valley and by the distance of the frontier settlements from sources of information. They urge their brethren to read the English papers, and promise to forward to them what news the more favored Germans of Philadelphia may receive. To the pamphlet (a publication of the press of Heinrich Miller) are appended the addresses of the Continental Congress to the people, to the inhabitants of Great Britain, and to King George III.

Steiner and Cist republished Paine's " Common Sense," and were the original publishers of his " Crisis ;" afterwards, it was from their press that there issued the little stoutly bound duodecimo with its blue paper covers, Baron Steuben's " Rules for the order and discipline of the troops of the United States." But this was four years after the Germans of Philadelphia had addressed their brethren to the north and south of them, and three years after we read in the yellowed files of Miller's " Staatsbote" succeeding assurance of the safety of " Captain Burr," taken at Quebec, and followed by news of Howe's landing (" not universally believed"), the item set forth in the boldest antique type that the office could boast :

" Philadelphia, den 5 July. **Gestern hat der achtbare Congress dieses vesten Landes die vereinigten Colonien freye und unabhängige Staaten erkläret.** Die Declaration in Englisch ist gesetzt in der Presse : sie ist datirt den 4ten July, 1776, und wird heut oder morgen in druck erscheinen."

As the " Staatsbote" was the only Philadelphia paper which appeared on Friday, and the Declaration was adopted on Thursday, it was thus through the columns of a Pennsylvania-German paper that the first news of independence was published.

The Germans in Colonial Times

The German pulpits were neither silent nor uncertain in all these crises of new national life : many pastors preached to the soldiers when they left, encouraging them to their duty, as did Gobrecht, of York County. Helfenstein, of Lancaster, addressed departing soldiers of his patriotic town from the text, "If the Son shall make you free, ye shall be free indeed,"—when he had to be accompanied home by a guard, so great was the excitement ; and also from the words, "If God be for us, who can be against us?" The German soldiers of the War of Independence had apparently no doubt that God was for them, if we may believe the tradition that they marched into battle singing a verse which evinced more patriotic than poetic fire :

'England's Georgel, Kaiser, König,
Ist für Gott und uns zu wenig."

A Montgomery County pastor got himself into trouble at the beginning of the war by preaching from the sufficiently pointed text, "Better is a poor and a wise child than an old and foolish king, who will no more be admonished." Helfenstein also improved the opportunity, when the captive Hessians were marched through his city, of addressing to them a discourse from the text, "Ye have sold yourselves for nought ; and ye shall be redeemed without money," which, not unnaturally, "gave great offence among the captives."

Perhaps owing to this outspoken patriotism, the Germans, their ministers, property, and churches seemed the especial objects of British destruction and spoliation. When Pastor Weyberg was released from the prison into which he had been cast because of his eloquent addresses to the American soldiers, he preached to his congregation from the sadly appropriate text, "O God, the heathen are come into thine inheritance; thy holy temple have they defiled." The house of the venerable Schlatter was plundered, he was imprisoned, and supported there by his courageous young daughter, Rachel, who, though but a girl of fourteen, used to ride into the city from Germantown with food and comforts for her father; the reason for this severity towards the retired minister was probably that he had two sons in the Continental army, one of whom—imprisoned like his father—subsequently died from the sufferings of his incarceration. We have mentioned that Pastor Nevelling, of New Jersey, was so valued by the British that a reward was offered for his apprehension. The sons of the patriarch Muhlenberg were obliged to flee from their congregations,—Frederick from New York and Ernest from Philadelphia. It was during Ernest's enforced exile in the country that he began those botanical studies which have made his name famous. The Germantown pastor was also an exile from his home.

Meanwhile, in the country districts, the Germans of the different counties were well represented upon various Revolutionary "Committees." German names are common in the committees of Lancaster, Berks, Bucks, York, Northampton, Bedford, and Northumberland Counties.

We find the committeemen engaged upon the most various duties. They directed the formation of the associators or minute-men in the earlier part of the war; they took up collections for the relief of the poor of Boston during the siege; they looked to the provision of powder and guns, of "Camp kettles and frying pans for the militia." They forbade the selling of tea and the holding of dancing-schools, not considering it a time to dance. They cited before them people who had "been so wicked and abandoned as to speak disrespectfully of the Honorable the Continental Congress." Captain Hambright, the Pennsylvania-German chairman of the Northumberland County Committee, asks "the good people of their townships to spare from each family as many blankets as they can for the use of the militia and Flying Camp;" and also (with a canniness more suggestive of a Scot than a German) directed that the committee should look after "women and children whose husbands are now in actual service and who are in real distress and need of relief." York, being a frontier county, discouraged "the consumption of gunpowder so necessary to our Indian trade and to the hunters of this province, but for the most useful purposes." The committees also examined whether a captain had "hid himself behind an old barn in the battle on Long Island," or why another did not march with his company, the reply "being in no wise satisfactory." Nothing brings before one so vividly the real men and women of the War for Independence as the perusal of these old minutes, homely, full of quaint detail, but showing the development of that character—resourceful, vigorous, undaunted—which we now call American. To this new nationality the Germans of colonial times certainly contributed their share.

When it was a question of deeds, not words, of fighting in the field instead of passing resolutions in committee meetings, many Germans entered the army. The most picturesque of the early Revolutionary bodies were the riflemen of the frontier, and among these, whether recruited in Virginia, Maryland, or Pennsylvania, we find a number of Teutonic names.

The enthusiasm in Pennsylvania was so great that a number in excess of its quota was raised and accepted. Of the nine Pennsylvania companies four had German captains ; and we have a letter from the York County Committee of Safety speaking of the enthusiasm evinced in recruiting : "The company are beyond the number fixed for this county and as Gen. Gates tho't it improper to discharge any, we have sent them all. P.S. The company began their march the nearest road to Boston this day."

They arrived fresh and untired, much astonishing the New Englanders. "They are remarkably stout and hardy men," writes Thacher, "many of them exceeding six feet in height. They are dressed in white frocks and rifle shirts. These men are remarkable for the accuracy of their aim, striking a mark with great certainty at two hundred yards distance." They remained in Cambridge, the *bête noire* of the British soldiers, who "are so amazingly terrified by our riflemen that they will not stir beyond their lines."

In July three companies of them were sent on the unfortunate expedition to Canada with Arnold. A young German-speaking volunteer, John Joseph Henry, followed the troops to Canada ; "nothing," writes Colonel Hand, "but a perfect loose to his feelings will ever tame his rambling desire." Poor Henry was most effectually tamed by the sufferings, starvation, failure, capture, and imprisonment which he underwent, and from the effects of which he suffered during the remnant of his life. Many of the riflemen died in Quebec; some enlisted in the British army, in order to get a chance to escape, and many of them succeeded in the enterprise; the rest were finally exchanged. Hendricks, the gallant young commander of one of the Cumberland County companies, was killed in the attempted assault of Quebec, and his admiring enemies buried him by the side of General Montgomery. The remaining companies of the riflemen, when their term of enlistment expired, had become so valuable to Washington— "they are indeed a very useful corps," he wrote to Congress—that they were reorganized and became the First Regiment of the Pennsylvania Line.

Early in the war it was "resolved to form a German Regiment," which was carried out, and it performed long and valiant service at Trenton, at Princeton, at the Brandywine, at Germantown, endured the hardships of Valley Forge, and marched with Sullivan in his expedition in 1779 to the country of the Six Nations.

There were Germans in almost all the Pennsylvanian regiments of the line, especially in the Second, Third, Fifth, Sixth, and Eighth, and many of these organizations were commanded by German officers.

The Legion which was raised by the French nobleman, Armand de la Rouerie, who threw himself into our War for Independence to forget a luckless love affair, contained many Germans: after the deplored death of Pulaski, *his* Legion, also somewhat Teutonic in its complexion, was incorporated with Armand's. This organization seems to have been a general refuge for unlucky Germans: when de Heer, who had recruited dragoons in the Pennsylvania-German districts in 1777, was captured in the Jerseys, the fragments of his command were also taken into the French officer's Legion. De Heer was an officer of Frederick the Great, and his dragoons were Washington's provost guard.

Among the Pennsylvanian Germans who served their province and the Revolution well are two men, utterly different in character, history, and service, yet alike in one thing,—their honest and perfect devotion to the cause of liberty : these are the philosopher Rittenhouse, and the "baker-in-chief for the army," Christoph Ludwig.

Rittenhouse, a descendant of the first Mennonite preacher of America, the quiet, studious scientist who jested during the French and Indian War that "if the enemy raided his neighborhood he would probably be slain making a telescope as was Archimedes tracing geometrical figures," left his peaceful, honored life, his calculations, and his instruments, to be the engineer of the Committee of Safety, and in this capacity he was called upon "to arrange for casting cannon, to view a site for a Continental powder mill, to conduct experiments for rifling cannon and musket balls, fix upon a method of fastening the chain for the protection of the river, superintend the manufacture of saltpetre and locate a magazine for military stores"—on the peaceful banks of the Wissahickon !

He issued burning addresses to the citizens when the enemy was advancing on Philadelphia ; he was a member of the State Assembly and drafted the new State Constitution ; he was the first treasurer under this instrument, succeeding another Pennsylvanian German, Michael Hillegas. He subsequently fixed the boundaries of the province and was the first director of the United States Mint. A Tory poet, much grieved at this political activity of the man of science, wrote pathetically,—

" A paltry statesman Rittenhouse became."

But to most Americans there will appear nothing paltry in the spectacle of this first scientist of Penn's province laying his time, his talents, and his feeble strength at the feet of that cause of "our country" of which the descendant of the non-resistant Mennonites wrote so warmly.

The other name which we have mentioned is much less known, yet Christoph Ludwig—"the Governor of Letitia Court"—was a prominent figure in his day. An old soldier, a sailor, a wide traveller, he finally settled down in the little Philadelphia court to his trade of confectioner and baker, probably in the expectation of a quiet evening to an eventful life. But when the first mutterings of the Revolutionary storm were heard the old soldier of Frederick the Great could not remain quiet. We find him as active on all the Revolutionary conventions and committees as he had been in the benevolences of the German Society, of which he was one of the most energetic members. In 1776 an advertisement in the "Staatsbote" tells us that "Christoph Ludwig of Letitia Court seeks a man who understands the making of powder." Once when a proposition to raise money by subscription for arms was about to be defeated in the convention, a loud voice was heard to say in a strong German accent, " Mr. President, I am only a poor ginger-bread baker, but put me down for two hundred pounds ;" this closed the debate. He was a volunteer in the Flying Camp, serving without pay or rations. He lost an eye in the service. We have a picture of the old man, when a party of mutinous militia was about to leave for home, kneeling bareheaded before them and beseeching them with strong, homely words to stay and fight for the common defence. There is reason to believe that he went on a secret mission to the Hessians in the British camp, to whom he portrayed in glowing colors the happiness and prosperity of the patriot Germans of Pennsylvania.

In 1777 Ludwig was appointed "Director of Baking in the Armies of the United States," but when the proposition was made that he should furnish the army with a pound of bread for each pound of flour delivered him, as had been the practice of former army bakers, he refused. "No," he said, "Christoph Ludwig does not want to get rich by the war ; he has money enough ;" and he explained that one hundred pounds of flour should give one hundred and thirty-five pounds of bread by the increase in weight of the water,—a fact to which "the committee were strangers," although Ludwig's rascally predecessors had not been. No wonder that Washington's favorite name for him was "honest friend," and that a certificate of Washington's appreciation of him was one of Ludwig's greatest treasures in his old age.

When the British plundered other German patriots they did not overlook the baker-general of the Continental army ; but Ludwig, when he returned to his desolated house, would not run into debt to replace anything, and slept for six weeks in soldierly fashion between blankets rather than borrow money to buy sheets. During the yellow fever epidemic of 1797 the old man of nearly fourscore worked as a journeyman at the bakeoven to provide " bread for the poor in that period of awful distress."

Shortly before his death some one wished to sell him a life of Washington, then lately deceased. " No," said the general's honest friend, " I am travelling fast to meet him. I shall hear all about it from his own mouth." And in a few months the old soldier, sailor, baker, and patriot passed to meet his old commander.

He left his money to various religious and benevolent institutions, but most of it for the free education of poor children, and even yet the Ludwick Institute keeps green the memory of Washington's " honest friend," the baker-general of the Revolution.

A Pennsylvania-German woman, whose brave deeds in the Revolutionary War are better known than the fact of her Teutonic blood, is the heroine of Monmouth whom we call by the soldier's nickname of " Moll Pitcher." She was a servant in the family of Dr. Irvine, of Carlisle, and her maiden name was Maria Ludwig,— of course, no relative of the redoubtable Christoph. She was married to a man named Heis, or Hays, and when her employer went to the war Hays also enlisted. " Mollie," as she was called, stayed behind in some anxiety, particularly after a friend, with the kind thoughtfulness which distinguishes some friendship, came and told her of a dream of some misfortune to Mollie's husband. A few days after, when Mollie's washing was just finished and still hung wet upon the line, a man came riding up to tell her of her husband's sickness.

The Germans in the Revolution

Taking her clothes, still wet, and making them into a
bundle, Mollie jumped up, pillion fashion, behind the messenger, and went off to nurse her husband. Once with
the army she found much to do for other sick soldiers,
and remained in camp, attending to the wounded and
carrying water to them in battle : the men used to say,
"Here comes Moll with her pitcher," and so arose her
sobriquet.

Her heroism at the battle of Monmouth, when she
helped to serve the gun at which her husband had just
fallen wounded, is famous. For this the husband was
promoted, and, after the war, the brave woman herself
was given the pension and brevet rank of a captain.
The wife of Alexander Hamilton used to speak of her
recollection of Moll as "a little freckle-faced Irish lass,"
in which, except as to Mollie's nationality, she was probably correct. One of "Moll Pitcher's" grandchildren
described her as a short, thick-set woman with blue eyes,
reddish hair, and strong, masculine features ; she added
that the heroine of Monmouth was much feared by her
grandchildren for her rough, brusque ways ; and that
she had learnt one thing in the army,—she swore like a
trooper.

Care for the suffering Revolutionary soldiers on a
larger scale than that of "Moll with her pitcher" was
given by other Pennsylvanian Germans. The hospitals
of the Revolutionary army during the campaigns in the
Middle States were almost all located in German settlements, and the inhabitants showed much kindness to
the unfortunate soldiers, who suffered terribly, not only
from wounds but from "camp fever" (typhus), and the
conditions summed up by the Medical Director-General,

Dr. Shippen, as "the want of clothing and covering to keep the soldiers clean and warm,—articles not at that time procurable in the country : partly from an army being composed of raw men, unused to camp life and undisciplined, exposed to great hardships and from the sick being removed great distances in open wagons."

There were hospitals at Bethlehem, Lititz, Ephrata, Easton, Allentown, Reading, and Lancaster,—all of them German centres. The Moravian towns were selected because of the large community buildings—the Brethren's and Sister's Houses and the like—in these places ; the same fact probably led to the selection of Ephrata ; Bethabara, the Moravian settlement in North Carolina, also had a hospital.

We have few details of any of these establishments except of Bethlehem, Lititz, and Ephrata. To Bethlehem were removed the sick of the army during the retreat through the Jerseys, but the greatest number of these sufferers were sent to Easton and •Allentown. They arrived in Bethlehem in a pitiable condition of suffering and neglect ; two soldiers died in the wagons while waiting to be taken into the buildings set apart for their reception. The good Moravians gave them food and clothing, provided coffins and a burial-place for the dead, and Bishop Ettwein was constant in his ministrations to them. During the occupation of Bethlehem by the sick, he lost a little son from fever, the infection being brought by his father from the soldiers' bedsides. After the battles of Brandywine and Germantown the Moravian settlement was again filled with wounded soldiers ; Lafayette was nursed here, after his wound at Brandywine, by Mrs. Boeckel and her daughter

The Germans in the Revolution

Liesel. It is not known how many of the soldiers died in the Bethlehem hospitals during the various times when the community houses were so used: the mortality was so fearful that the number of deaths was kept secret; it is thought to have been about five hundred.

The hospital at Lititz was filled with typhus patients, and they infected those who cared for them. Their two surgeons died shortly after the patients were brought to Lititz; five of the Moravian single brethren, who had volunteered as nurses, fell victims to their benevolence, as did the assistant pastor, Schmick, who had come safely through the perils of an Indian mission to die in this peaceful pastorate, a sacrifice to his patriotic devotion.

The community of Ephrata showed equal kindness and unselfishness; they received after the battle of Brandywine about five hundred sick soldiers into their town, relinquished to them two of their largest cloister buildings, Kedar and Zion, gave them food and maintenance while sick, and buried them when they died, as a great number—about two hundred—did. The plot of ground where the soldiers are buried is still known, though neglected and overgrown with brambles; the project to erect a monument over the remains of these soldiers of the Revolution was never carried out.

It was very natural that the cloister of Ephrata should take a leading and liberal part in the care of these suffering soldiers. Miller, the successor of Beissel, was prior at that time, a learned and large-minded man, esteemed by all who knew him, and a friend and correspondent of Washington. The legend of Miller's successful endeavor to save a Tory's life may be but a legend, yet it shows the estimate of his character held by those who knew him that such a story could have grown up about him. The tale is that a certain Michael Wittmann had been an enemy and reviler of Miller for years. During the Revolution Wittmann, who was a virulent Tory, was arrested and sentenced to death. Miller walked from the monastery at Ephrata to Washington's head-quarters in order to beg Wittmann's life, which Washington refused. "Renegades must suffer," said the general, "otherwise I should be very glad to release your friend." "Friend!" exclaimed Miller; "he has spit upon and reviled me, he is my bitterest enemy." "What, can you ask for the pardon of your enemy?" said Washington. "Jesus did as much for me," answered the good man. Washington then placed the Tory's pardon in the prior's hands, saying, "My dear friend, I thank you for this example of Christian charity."

The German portions of the colony of Maryland, mostly embraced in Frederick County, being in near neighborhood to Pennsylvania and largely settled from that State, show much the same traits in the Revolutionary struggle as we have seen in Penn's province to the north of them.

The "Maryland Journal" says, "On the second of July, 1774, about eight hundred of the principal inhabitants of the upper part of Frederick County assembled at Elizabeth Town" (which we will remember was the name by which Jonathan Hager desired his town to be known) and after passing a number of resolutions "they proceeded to shew their disapprobation of Lord North's Conduct by Hanging and burning his Effigy after which a subscription was opened for the relief of the poor of

Boston." And a receipt signed by Christopher Edelin
shows how the poor Germans of the musically named
settlement of Linganore gave out of their poverty to
their brethren of Boston suffering in the common cause.
"John Chrisman 10 s., Jacob Hosler 2 s., Peter Kemp
5 s.," run the sums and names through a long list.

Among the men of the Revolutionary committees of
Frederick County we find such names as that of Edelin,
just mentioned ; of Thomas Schley ; of Jonathan Hager,
the founder of Hagerstown ; of Ludwig Weltner, later
colonel of the German Battalion ; and of Christian Orndorff, afterwards a major in the Sixth Maryland Regiment.

Hager had been elected to the General Assembly of
the province a few years before, but had been declared
ineligible because not a native-born subject, which proceeding was criticised by the governor and his council
as "unprecedented." Hager, however, was not disabled
from taking an active part in the Revolutionary movement up to the time of his sudden accidental death. He
left two children : the daughter, Rosina, wedded General
Daniel Hiester, of Reading, one of four brothers who
served in the Revolution ; and the son was an officer in
the Revolutionary army, and married Mary Madeline,
the beautiful daughter of the wealthy and patriotic
Major Christian Orndorff. It is said that General Gates,
happening, when entertained one day at the hospitable
house of her father, to catch sight of the young girl as
she stood in front of a mirror examining the effect of a
new cap, was so charmed by her loveliness that he wished
to make her his wife, but the capricious beauty refused
to marry "a man old enough to be her father," as she

said ; and certainly she showed sound judgment when she preferred young Hager to the pinchbeck hero of Saratoga.

The Frederick County committees attended to the usual business of such Revolutionary organizations, raising money and men, buying "powder and Lead," and calling to account persons who "refused to associate." In the course of these investigations they caught a bigger fish than usually came to the net of the backwoodsmen,—that is, Dr. John Connolly, who was endeavoring, at the instigation of Lord Dunmore, to raise the Indians on the frontier and invade the "back settlements." We may imagine the feelings of the members of a frontier committee in laying hands upon a man engaged in such an enterprise. Connolly was rendered harmless by being retained as a prisoner to the end of the war, certainly a great service done by the Frederick County committee.

Two of the rifle companies sent to Cambridge were raised in Frederick County, though, as no rolls have been preserved, we cannot tell how many of the rank and file were Germans. Shortly after this organization was formed it was proposed to raise in Maryland, as had been done in Pennsylvania, a German regiment, which, commanded by Colonel Weltner, was largely recruited in Frederick County. Subsequently the remnants of the riflemen and the German regiment were both incorporated into the Eighth Regiment of the Maryland Line. Pulaski recruited his Legion largely in Baltimore, and we know that there were many Germans in it. While the Polish nobleman was in Baltimore, he paid a visit to Bethlehem, where Lafayette was lying wounded, and it was then that there occurred the incident of the preparation of Pulaski's banner by the sisters of Bethlehem which Longfellow has embalmed in his beautiful and wildly inaccurate poem.

There were also many Maryland Germans in the unlucky organization of the Flying Camp, most of whom were captured at Fort Washington and succumbed to the hardships and cruelties of British prisons. One sergeant, Lawrence Everheart, when he saw the inevitable capture of the fort, ran to the river, got into a boat, and made his escape almost miraculously from the doomed post. He lived to fight many another day, for, returning with the remnants of the Flying Camp to his home, he enlisted at Frederick in the regiment of Colonel Washington, and followed that daring cavalry-man through his various engagements until, being sent to reconnoitre Tarleton's position before the battle of the Cowpens, Everheart was wounded and captured; he was taken before the British leader, who asked anxiously if Washington and Morgan would fight him. "They will," answered Everheart, "if they can keep together two hundred men." Taken as a prisoner to the field, one of his captors, finding that the prisoner was likely to be recaptured, shot him in the head, but did not wound him seriously. Everheart rejoined his leader, Washington, who, dashing on with his usual impetuosity, was set upon by Tarleton himself, and only saved from injury by Everheart's disabling Tarleton's sword-arm. The German sergeant recovered from his wounds and lived to be an honored veteran in his Maryland home, and there received his old commander whose life he had saved, when the two soldiers rushed into each other's arms with tears. Everheart finally became a Methodist preacher,—a strange ending to the career of the fiery, daring dragoon.

The Germans of the Mohawk Valley and of all that portion of the present State of New York which was known in Revolutionary times as Tryon County had a terrible phase of the Revolutionary struggle to encounter : that resulting from the policy of England in employing against her rebellious subjects the barbarous assistance of the Indians. We have seen the Valley scourged with the whip of the French and Indian War, but in the Revolutionary struggle it was chastised with scorpions.

As soon as the Revolution threatened, the inhabitants of the Mohawk Valley German settlements formed a committee, and later their militia organization was completed, with Nicholas Herkimer, their defender in the previous war, as colonel of the first battalion and other Germans at the head of the remaining three. They sent few, if any, of their soldiers to serve in any distant campaign ; it was evident from the first that the battle was to be fought out on their own land and was to be a combat to the death for house and home.

It was not until the summer of 1777 that the unhappy Valley knew the full terror of an Indian and Tory invasion. Meanwhile, the Schoharie people had tried to secure the Indians' neutrality ; they held a council with them, at which a woman, Mrs. Richtmeyer, was the interpreter, and secured from them promises—which the Schoharie people themselves did not trust—of peaceable behavior. So when the first news reached the German settlements on the Mohawk that St. Leger, with a large force

The Germans in the Revolution

of Indians and the even more hated Tory regiment of
Johnson's Greens, was marching to besiege Fort Stanwix,
desolate the Valley, and form a triumphant junction with
Burgoyne, Herkimer and his fellow-militiamen knew
what to expect. They were alarmed, like sensible men;
but Herkimer, at least, was too brave and steady to be
terrified.

Yet of one of the most terrible phases of civil war
he and his fellow-countrymen of the other settlement
had bitter knowledge. One of the awful signs of the
last times is to be that a man's foes shall be those of his
own household. In Schoharie this was sadly true in
those days; there the Revolution set brother against
brother and father against son. And in Herkimer's own
family we see the same dreadful result of civil dissension.
According to one tradition, his own wife had fled to the
Tories in Canada. A brother, appointed in the first
Revolutionary uprising to be one of the colonels of militia, subsequently had his property confiscated for disloyalty. His sister, Elizabeth Schuyler, had a son
whose deficiency of intellect did not excuse the fact
that he was in correspondence with the enemy. Another
sister was the wife of Dominie Rosencrantz, who was
thought more than lukewarm in the cause of liberty.
His niece, Gertrude, though the widow of an officer
killed by Brant's Indians in a gallantly vain attempt to
carry despatches from Fort Plain to Cherry Valley, was
suspected of having assisted her son by her second marriage in his flight to Canada. On the other hand, we
shall see Bell, the husband of Catharine Herkimer,
though suffering from a wound which disabled him for
life, yet bringing his wounded brother-in-law from the

field of Oriskany. There were some Germans, though they were everywhere exceptions, who chose the king's side and won rank and such credit as could be gained from their adherence : such was General Daniel Clause, a German of the Mohawk Valley who married one of Catharine Weissenfels's children, yet a follower of Johnson and an officer in the British army.

Against these bloodthirsty foes in front and these traitors in the rear Herkimer called to arms the militia of the Valley. It was a *levée en masse*. "Whereas," says Herkimer's proclamation, "it appears certain that the enemy, about two thousand strong, Christians and savages, are arrived at Oswego with the intention to invade our frontiers . . . as soon as the enemy approaches every male person, being in health, from sixteen to sixty years of age, in this our county shall . . . march to oppose the enemy with vigor as true patriots for the just defence of their country. And those above sixty years of age shall assemble armed at the places where women and children will be gathered together, not doubting that the Almighty power upon our humble prayers and sincere trust in him will then graciously succor our arms in battle, for our just cause."

So the little force was collected, and on the morning of August 4, 1777, marched to the relief of Fort Stanwix, then beleaguered by St. Leger's Indians and Tories. Herkimer had sent the runner Adam Helmer to the fort with news of his approach, and had appointed a signal—a cannon shot—which was to tell him when to attack the besiegers in their rear. But his men were too impatient to await this ; they urged their general to press forward. In vain the elder man, an experienced

The Germans in the Revolution

Indian fighter, counselled caution, and told them that their small company—there were but eight hundred of them—and the hard-pressed garrison of the fort were all that stood between their homes and utter destruction. "I, indeed, have no one to mourn for me," said the childless man, "but I am as the father of you all." The militia—rashly brave and insubordinate, as was the wont of these frontier levies—would not listen to their gray-haired leader: finally the dissension rose so high that men taunted Herkimer with the Toryism of some of his family and called the defender of the Valley a coward. Herkimer was forced to give way; but he prophesied, only too truly as the event proved, that those who had been loudest in their taunts would be the first to run.

The little band plunged into the woods. Crossing a causeway thrown up in a dark ravine, crowded together upon the narrow path, the Indian war-whoop was heard, and everywhere the trees broke into rifle-fire; they had been ambushed like Braddock, like Bouquet. The rear-guard, who had dared the others to advance, turned and fled; it is some satisfaction to know that almost all of these loud-mouthed cowards were slaughtered in their flight. The rest of the frontiersmen gathered into circles about Herkimer, who was already wounded; some "took trees," as the backwoods phrase was, and when the Indians, waiting until a gun was discharged, rushed in to tomahawk the soldier while he loaded, Herkimer directed that two men take a tree and one fire while the other load. The brave general's leg was shattered, but he ordered his saddle placed against a tree, and sat there calmly directing the fight. Some of his men urged him to withdraw to a less exposed position. "No," he answered; "I want to look the enemy in the face." Presently he took from his pocket pipe, tobacco, and flint, and composedly lit his pipe.

At noon reinforcements reached the British, the Tory regiment of Johnson's Greens. But instead of causing the Germans to give up the fight against such fearful odds, this filled them with a Berserker rage that was unconquerable. These were their traitorous fellow-townsmen, who had taken up arms against their own flesh and blood. The infuriated men could not wait to fire; they clubbed their muskets, they choked the Tories to death with their bare hands, they fought hand to hand with knives. Before this fury of hatred and despair the Indians raised their retreating cry of "Oo-nah," and the British soldiers fled, leaving their dead on the field. But the brave farmers had lost frightfully; many officers were killed, some captured; their loss amounted to one-fourth of the number engaged; whole families were dead on the field. A mournful ballad made upon the fight of Oriskany deplores:

> "Brave Herkimer, our general's dead
> And Colonel Cox is slain,
> And many more and valiant men
> We ne'er shall see again."

Some of the fighters took immediate revenge for the death of their friends. Thus, Henry Diefendorf lay dying, shot through the lungs; he begged for water, and one of his comrades stamped a little hole in the ground and, collecting the rain which fell during part of the battle, gave a drink to the dying man. When he had expired, the friend cried with an oath, "I'll have a life for that one," and shot a large Indian lurking behind a tree. One of the men, Adam Franks, grew hungry during the long fight, so he composedly sat down with true German placidity, took some food from his knapsack, and having refreshed himself, dashed forward, crying, "Jetzt d'rauf auf die Kerl'."

The remnant of the Valley's defenders returned, bringing with them their wounded general; he was taken to his home and his leg unskilfully amputated. In a few days he began to sink. "I am going to follow my leg," he said. He wrote a report of the battle, made his will, and taking his well-used German Bible, began to read the 38th Psalm. "O Lord, rebuke me not in thy wrath : neither chasten me in thy hot displeasure. . . . My lovers and my friends stand aloof from my sore; and my kinsmen stand afar off. They also that seek after my life lay snares for me. . . . In thee, O Lord, do I hope : thou wilt hear, O Lord my God." So, brave, pious, and unafraid, the defender of the Mohawk Valley passed away.

Nicholas Herkimer is described by one who knew him as a thick-set, stout man, "not above six feet in height," with dark hair prematurely gray. He was not the illiterate man he is sometimes represented, but well read in the Bible (which gave strength to his last hours) and in the history of the Reformation. We have seen how sorely he was tried by the defection of those near to him, in what a horror of sudden surprise and battle he met his death, and with what a calm courage he fronted it. He remains forever a simply heroic figure of the German pioneer.

Though the stubborn fight of Oriskany had saved the

Valley for the time, had destroyed Burgoyne's plans and led to the first success of the war, the surrender of Saratoga, it was but a temporary remission that was purchased by all this heroism and loss. In the next year, 1778, Brant, the pitiless Indian leader, the representative of the powerful Johnson interest, and the pious translator of the Book of Common Prayer into the Mohawk dialect, appeared in his first-named character when he attacked and burnt the little settlement of Andrustown near German Flats, the most westerly of the settlements; he caught and killed all but one of the runners sent out to get intelligence of his movements. The one who escaped was the adroit and fleet-footed Helmer, whom we shall see again and again repeating his successful escape of this time. One German settler, in despair, shut himself into his log cabin, and was there burnt alive; his bones were found twenty years after, gathered up and buried, by a Connecticut settler who came to this frontier after the Revolution was over.

Schoharie, which had been less exposed than the western settlements, had been able to send militia and provision to the assistance of General Gates; some of the patroon Stephen van Rensselaer's German tenants, being asked to send what they could spare, stripped themselves of provisions to supply the army. When the patroon next visited his estates, he greatly surprised these Germans by giving them deeds for their lands as a mark of his admiration of their generosity; they had not expected, nor thought that they had deserved, any reward.

The Schoharie people, though they sent re-enforcements to Gates, did not neglect their own defence: they had early ordered that the inhabitants should bring their rifles to church with them ; they now built forts, arranged signals to tell of an Indian invasion, and prepared for defence. The women and children were to be gathered into these forts, and one gallant girl, Mary Hagedorn, refused to go into the cellar of the fort on an alarm. "I will take a spear," she said, "which I can use as well as any man, and help defend the fort." The captain, Hager, understood her spirit. "Then take a spear, Mary," he said, "and be ready at the pickets to repel an attack."

To tell all the incidents of the pioneers' defence would fill a book : some by their pathos, their courage, or their interest, may be added to the story. Such is the tale of Catherine Merckley's death. She was accounted the most beautiful girl in the Schoharie settlements. She was betrothed to a young pioneer, who had given her a pair of silver shoe-buckles as a betrothal gift ; they were to be married in a fortnight. The Indians attacked her on her return from a visit at a neighbor's ; she fell from her horse mortally wounded, and died clasping her hands over the wound. The Indian who scalped her said as he looked at her beautiful, dead face, "She was too handsome a paleface to kill." The next day her lover and some other men of the settlement laid her uncoffined body in a grave : the silver buckles, his gift, were still upon her feet.

A quaint old ballad begins :

> "A story, a story,
> Unto you I will tell
> About a brave hero,
> His name was Christian Schell."

The Germans in Colonial Times

This hero lived at Schellsbush, a short distance from Fort Dayton near the present Herkimer. His home, a strong block-house well adapted to resist Indian forays, was attacked by a number of savages under the lead of a Scotch Tory, Captain McDonald. Schell, his four sons, and his wife composed the garrison ; two of his children, twin boys, were captured before they could take refuge in the house. After vain attempts to set fire to the block-house, Captain McDonald fell wounded at the door. Schell instantly dragged him inside, where he served the double purpose of a hostage and a fresh supply of ammunition, which was taken from his person. Schell's wife loaded the guns while the men fired, and when a desperate attack was made upon the house and the enemy thrust their guns through the loop-holes,—

> " she spoiled
> Five guns as I am told
> With nothing but a chopping axe,
> Which shows that she was bold."

In a pause of the fight, she raised the verse of Luther's hymn,—

> " Und wenn die Welt voll Teufel wär
> Und wollt uns gar verschlingen
> So fürchten wir uns nicht so sehr
> Es muss uns doch gelingen."

The men joined in, and the brave words of the Marseillaise of the Reformation rang through the American forest. Presently the attacking party drew off, with the loss of about twenty of their number at the hands of this one family of six German pioneers. It is sad to have to record that brave Schell and one of his sons were ambushed the next year in their cornfield by Indians, and mortally wounded. When Schell lay dying, his neighbor, Hartmann, who had been with him in the fatal attack, came from the death-chamber, and being questioned how the hero was, answered, we may believe with tears as well as bitterness, "He's going to die, and he's praying for the 'poor Indians.'" Thus died Christian Schell, the hero of Schellsbush, and a Christian in deed as in name.

While the Germans of the Mohawk Valley were fighting and suffering in defence of their homes, and those of Pennsylvania and Maryland were aiding the cause with men, money, and counsel, other frontier communities took a different part in the struggle for freedom. The Germans of Virginia, most of them living in the Shenandoah Valley, took a place between the two akin to their geographical station.

The first stirring of the Revolutionary tide lifted them also into the current of the larger national life. By an odd coincidence, a Shenandoah Valley lad was present and consenting at the Boston Tea Party. Jacob Bumgardner had accompanied his father with his team and wagon to distant Boston, and when the mysterious stir of the enterprise filled the streets the boy followed the crowd, and even went into the hold of the vessel and helped to fasten the tea-chests to the rope that they might be drawn up for destruction. In order that the matter might be kept secret the disguised "Indians" were probably glad to use the help of a stranger. This participant in the Boston Tea Party afterwards became a Revolutionary soldier.

When the riflemen were called out the frontiersmen

of Frederick County, Virginia, formed the first company from the South which reached the camp at Cambridge. They rendezvoused at Morgan's Spring, near Shepherdstown, on June 17, 1775,—"not a man was missing." After a prayer invoking the blessing of God on their enterprise, they started, not before all had "solemnly agreed that as many of them as might be alive on that day fifty years should meet again at Morgan's Spring;" they shouldered their rifles and, as one of them expressed it, "made a bee line for Boston." On that day fifty years there were but four of the Virginia riflemen living : the two Bedinger brothers, Henry, of Virginia, and George Michael, of Kentucky ; Lauck, of Winchester, and Hulse, of Wheeling,—names which prove the German complexion of the corps.

The tireless fellows, " armed with tomahawk and rifles, dressed in hunting shirts and moccasins, and seeming to walk light and easy and not with less spirit than in the first hour of their march," reached Boston on the 10th of August, having made the march of six hundred miles in fifty-four days. As they approached the camp of Cambridge, Washington, who was making a reconnoissance, came galloping up, and when the captain reported his company "from the right bank of the Potomac, general," the stately Virginian threw himself from his horse and shook hands with each man of the Virginia company, while tears of joy rolled down his resolute face.

The riflemen served through the siege of Boston, and were then embodied in an organization which was captured at Fort Washington ; most of the prisoners were retained in captivity until the end of the war. The

The Germans in the Revolution

indefatigable Henry Bedinger, on his release, having made his way home with two fellow-soldiers by the grotesque system of "ride and tie," with a horse which their combined finances had purchased for the journey, re-entered the army in hopes of assisting at another siege, that of Yorktown, which unfortunately ended before the former rifleman could reach the front.

Morgan's riflemen also contained some of the Shenandoah Valley Germans ; six of them formed what was known as the "Dutch Mess," and although they went through many battles they all survived the war, and several lived to be very old. Morgan's men were sent on the unlucky expedition to Quebec, and one hundred of the men with their leader were captured there.

Another famous German regiment from Virginia was the Eighth, of which Peter Muhlenburg, a son of the Lutheran patriarch, was colonel, Abraham Bowman, lieutenant-colonel, and one of the Helfenstines a major. The story of Peter Muhlenberg is well known, at least the dramatic incident, better authenticated than most such, of how he ended his sermon in the little church at Woodstock with the statement, "that in the language of holy writ, there was a time for all things,—a time to pray and a time to preach,—but those times have passed away ; there is a time to fight and the time to fight is here." And giving the benediction he descended the pulpit, threw off the gown forever, and ordered the drums beat at the church door, where he enrolled that day three hundred Germans of the valley in his regiment. The organization took a severe but honorable part in the Revolutionary struggle. General Muhlenberg, as he afterwards became, was the trusted friend of Greene, saved the day at Brandywine, led the re-enforcements which took the last of the British works at Yorktown, and was a valiant, active, honorable soldier.

Another German, of noble blood, Baron Gerhard von der Wieden, is concealed under the plain appellation of General Weedon, who commanded a Virginia regiment in Muhlenberg's brigade.

There were many Germans in Augusta County, Virginia, which tract at the beginning of the Revolutionary period liberally included the present West Virginia, Kentucky, and most of the western country so far as settled. Bancroft has noted how these pioneers gave out of their poverty to the relief of the people of Boston, bringing their gifts through the pathless wilderness. There were many Revolutionary soldiers later from among these people.

A quaint story of these frontier regions at the end of the war tells how a young officer of the Continental army, Lieutenant Brooke, had been ordered to bring a detachment of troops through the mountains to join Lafayette. The lameness of his horse stopped him at a wayside blacksmith-shop, where they spoke only German ; the young lieutenant's regimentals exposed him to the suspicion of being a British officer, nothing but hunting shirts having been seen in that region before. He was detained as a prisoner until some one was found who could read his English commission and let him pass on.

Among the foreign officers who came to our aid in our war for independence were two Germans who are well known by name to all Americans, though neither ever attained to the popular worship accorded the best example of their class,—the French nobleman Lafayette. These Germans are Steuben and Kalb.

The Germans in the Revolution

The character and services of Steuben are the best known and the most important. He was the descendant of a military family; he had served long and honorably under Frederick the Great, and was a man of middle age when he came to offer his sword to the Americans. Landing at Portsmouth in the latter part of the year 1777, he travelled across the colonies to see Washington at Valley Forge and Congress in its refuge at York. Passing through "Baron" Stiegel's little town of Manheim in Pennsylvania, the old officer of the great Frederick was delighted to see his general's picture serving as the tavern sign, as, indeed, might be seen in many other parts of the colonies, for the "King of Prussia" was a very favorite tavern emblem. At Lancaster—then the largest inland town in the United States—the German population invited him to a ball, and were very proud of the Prussian officer's distinguished manners and the brilliant star of the order "pour la Fidélité" with which he dazzled their unaccustomed eyes.

Arriving at Valley Forge, Steuben found a scene of misery, confusion, and mismanagement which might have daunted a courage less stout. The descriptions of the camp have a sad familiarity to our ears, even in this end of the century after: the commissary and quartermaster's departments, we are told, were in a useless confusion; there was no inspector-general, the person appointed to it by popular influence being Conway of "cabal" fame, who had never performed its duties; there were no hospital nor medical stores, and men sickened and died for lack of care.

Steuben found the Continental army "in want of provisions, of clothing, of fodder for our horses, in short, of everything." The very officers were in rags. The disciple of Frederick the Great saw "officers mounting guard in a sort of dressing-gown, made of a blanket or old woollen bed-cover." His aids shared their rations with the starving sentry at their door. He once invited a party of young officers to dine with him on condition that none should come "that had on a whole pair of breeches." The guests clubbed their rations and "we feasted sumptuously," says young Duponceau, "on tough beefsteak and potatoes with hickory-nuts for dessert." The Baron called his gay, brave, young guests his "sans-culottes," and in this way originated the nickname which was to come into such terrible prominence in another and later revolution. And all this privation and suffering was in a country not so totally exhausted by war but that its resources might have availed to feed and shelter its troops, had not the miserable political jealousies which ruled the fallen Continental Congress been allowed to interfere.

Baron Steuben gave up in despair the attempt to introduce a better system in place of these abuses and turned his energy and talents to the task of disciplining the army. By a happy mixture of tact, energy, enthusiasm, and capacity, he succeeded during the miserable winter of Valley Forge in bringing out of the untrained militia—not, indeed, a Prussian army, but, what was more to the purpose, an American one, which in the next year took the fortress of Stony Point after a brilliant and desperate assault without a shot, at the point of the bayonet,—a weapon which the Continental soldier had previously known only as a good thing upon which to stick meat in order to cook it.

The Germans in the Revolution

Steuben labored like a drill-sergeant in the personal instruction of the troops, and we have a ludicrous description of how the baron, unable to speak English, would begin to swear in German, then in French, then in both languages together. When he had exhausted his artillery of foreign oaths he would call to his aids : "Viens, mon ami Walker, mon cher Duponceau, come and swear for me in English, je ne puis plus, I can curse dem no more—dese fellows will not do what I bid dem." The men laughed, the needed interpretation was made, and presently the movement was faultlessly executed.

In spite of these hard words, which broke no bones, the soldiers loved the bluff old soldier, and so many children were named in his honor that he jokingly said, when urged to lay aside his title in the republican enthusiasm of the French Revolution, that it would be of no use, there were too many "Baron Steubens" in existence.

He was called pre-eminently "The Baron." A woman once came to him to ask permission to name her child for him ; "What will you call him?" asked Steuben, who had a profusion of Christian names. "Why, to be sure," said the woman, "I'll call him 'Baron.'"

He acquired one namesake under singular circumstances. Inspecting a Connecticut regiment one day, Baron Steuben found a fine soldierly sergeant named Jonathan Arnold. The Baron, who had sat on the court which unwillingly condemned the hapless André and had the utmost detestation of "the wretch who drew him to death," advised the man to change his name. "But what name shall I take?" said Arnold. "Any name you please ; take mine," cried the baron, "mine is at your service." So Jonathan Arnold duly became Jonathan Steuben, and under that appellation fought well, and returning to his Connecticut home after the war, married and had a son, whom he named, after his own patriotic godfather, Frederick William. To him Baron Steuben willed a farm, and Frederick William Steuben of Connecticut was a good soldier in the war of 1812, dying in the service. The adoption of English names by Germans is a lamentably frequent thing, but the taking of this German name by a Connecticut Yankee is unique, both in its occurrence and its reasons.

Towards the end of the war, when Steuben was sent South to assist Gates in his contest with Cornwallis, he found the same disorganization, suffering, and peculation rife out of which he had brought order at Valley Forge. He had the happiness to see his "Rules for the Order and Discipline of the Army of the United States," the famous "Blue Book," which he wrote with such pains and difficulties, adopted as the regulations of the victorious Continental army ; to see his adaptation of the American riflemen's skirmishing tactics studied, applauded, and adopted by Frederick the Great, his own former teacher in the art of war ; and to know himself beloved and honored by the country and the army which he had helped to create and to save.

The other German soldier whom we have mentioned with Steuben is a much less sympathetic figure than the bluff, passionate, warm-hearted old baron. He, too, claimed to be a nobleman, and called himself and was called Baron De Kalb. But the cold fact of history is that he was the son of a Bayreuth yeoman, who left his peasant home at Hüttersdorf in the elevated capacity of a waiter, and, after a score or so of years, reappeared, a lieutenant in the French army, " M. Jean de Kalb, son of the Seigneur de Huettersdorf." He had assumed the nobility, without which his military career would have been forever barred to him ; and we must not be too severe upon a frequent and perhaps innocent deception.

His succeeding career is of a piece with this rather dubious beginning. After the passage of the Stamp Act, he was sent by Choiseul to America on secret service to discover the extent of the disaffection of England's colonies and how far it could be used in the French minister's attempt to crush England's colonial power, as that of the French had been crushed at Quebec. De Kalb (to give him his chosen name), travelled for six months over the American colonies, but reported to his master that the disaffection was not yet so extreme as to impel the colonies to actual rebellion, and so Choiseul's project of fomenting and assisting it was dropped.

For eight years De Kalb had no more connection with America, until, in the year of the Declaration of Independence, he joined the expedition of Lafayette to put his sword at the service of the cause of liberty. The older soldier was to be the head of the expedition and his promised commission to antedate that of the young Lafayette.

The two men were utterly different in their characters, motives, and intentions. De Kalb's biographer says well that Lafayette's ship, the Victory, "brought over the last of the condottieri and the last of the knights-errant." Yet De Kalb, though a mere and a typical soldier of fortune, served his temporary country well and faithfully, even when sorely tried by the jealous and

meddling Congress, the undisciplined militia, and the un-
civil native American officers. He regarded Washington
as weak, a judgment in which he probably stands alone
among the men who served under the patient, undaunted
resolute Virginian. But if he could not appreciate "this
imperial man," he at least understood the situation well
enough to be convinced of the impracticability of the
ridiculous plan which he had come to carry out—that
of making the Duc de Broglie commander-in-chief of
the patriot armies. The duke had been certain that
"a military and political leader is wanted," and equally
convinced that he was fitted to be that leader. The
French volunteers soon gave up this idea.

De Kalb served and suffered bravely in the long,
wearisome struggle against not only the British enemy,
but the supineness of the people, the wrong-headedness
of Congress, and the wretched provision for the army;
and he crowned his service by a hero's death in the terrible defeat when Gates's army was cut to pieces at
Camden. That thinly plated hero "rode rapidly away"
when the troops first broke, but the foreign soldier led
charge after charge against the unbroken British army
until he fell, a mortally wounded prisoner, pierced by
eleven bullets.

In person and character Kalb was a type of the
peasant race from which he sprang: fair and tall, vigorous even in advanced life, temperate and self-restrained,
devoted to his wife and family, capable of enormous
work, and, although but a soldier of fortune, faithful unto
death to the colors and the country which he was
serving.

CHAPTER XXIII

"THE REAR-GUARD OF THE REVOLUTION"

AT the same time that frontiersmen were helping the
cause of the sea-board colonies, they were engaged upon
an enterprise daring and strenuous enough to have, of
itself, furnished an outlet for less plentiful energies. It
gives one a fresh conception of the strength of this
young giant of the West when one sees the people of
the East building a nation, raising an army, fighting a
revolution ; and knows that at the same time, to the
westward, the same nationality was passing the barrier
of the wilderness, struggling with stealthy Indians and
British soldiers, and conquering from both their possessions in the Mississippi Valley.

Among these pioneers of Kentucky and Tennessee,
these pathfinders of the Wilderness Trace, and backwoodsmen led by Clark into " the Illinois country," there
were many Germans. In fact, it would be strange were
it otherwise, for " the West" of those days was reached
through the Shenandoah Valley, and its hunters, pioneers, and permanent settlers came from the Valley of
Virginia and the mountains of the Carolinas—both sections containing many men of Teutonic race.

Among the men who early wandered over Kentucky
and Tennessee, before any permanent settlement was
attempted, we find the names of George Jäger, Michael

Stoner, Caspar Mansker, Isaac and Abram Hite, and John
and Abraham Bowman.

It was Jäger who first fired the imagination of Simon
Kenton by a description of the wonderfully rich country
of " the cane brakes"—Kentucky. Jäger had been taken
prisoner by the Indians when a child, and had spent
years living in their villages and hunting with them ; on
many of these expeditions he had been upon buffalo
hunts in Kentucky, and he described the richness of the
country and the abundance of game in such glowing
terms that Kenton with Strader—probably another German—went down the Ohio in search of this hunter's
paradise. They did not find any country answering to
Jäger's description, and were beginning to doubt his
word, when they were attacked by Indians, Strader was
killed and the other two fled in panic from " the dark
and bloody ground." Kenton subsequently returned
alone, and discovered Jäger's Elysium on the banks of
the Licking.

Michael Stoner, (really Steiner) was also among the
many daring hunters and guides who camped and hunted
in Kentucky years before there was any thought of permanent settlement there. As early as 1767 he was with
Harrod,—afterwards the founder of Harrodsburg,—and
they went as far south as the future site of Nashville.
In 1774 Governor Dunmore sent him with Daniel Boone,
to find, and bring out to safety and civilization, a party
of surveyors deep in the western wilderness at the " Falls
of the Ohio," which we now call Louisville. Stoner and
Boone made the journey of eight hundred miles through
the wilderness in sixty-two days, and brought the pioneers of the rod and chain home without harm. In the

next year, while the Eastern colonies were seething with revolt and the first blood of the Revolution was shed, Michael Stoner was "making a crop of corn" in the new, rich land.

Casper Mansker, the third of the German pioneers I have just named, had a much longer and more interesting connection with the winning of the West. He was with the famous "Long Hunters," who left the Holston settlements in the backwoods of the province of North Carolina in 1769 and were so fascinated by the wilderness, its novelty, its dangers, and its hunting, that some of the party did not return for a year, and hence got their picturesque name. Caspar Mansker (whose name is usually disguised as "Mansco," while his "station" was called simply Caspar's) led one division of this large party back over the mountains with a drove of horses which was being taken, through the Indian towns, to Georgia. He went back and forth over the Cumberland mountains many times. He was the first white man to navigate the Cumberland river, descending the stream in 1770 by means of a canoe. We hear frequently that "Captain Mansco" has "bro't out a party," for which duty of guard and escort he was paid in what was known as "guard certificates,"—orders which passed as currency in the wilds of Tennessee. When on this duty he would not allow any one to march in advance, "to take away the scent from him," as he expressed it. He had well-grounded confidence in his ability to detect Indian snares : "I can see pote sides and pehind, too," he used to say ; yet he was once "gobbled up" by an Indian hunter,—not captured, but decoyed into range by the imitation of the wild turkey's call. Mansker de-tected the imposition in time to kill the Indian, though he averred that *he* would not have done so, it was the act of his pet rifle, his "Nancy," as he called her; when the Indian came in range, "Nancy wanted to speak to him," and spoke with fatal effect. Of this gun he was almost as fond as he was of his "gute alte frau." Like Sergeant Everheart, who saved Colonel Washington's life in the hand-to-hand conflict with Tarleton, Mansker in his old days became an ardent and earnest Methodist.

Among the names signed to the Compact of Government when the backwoods commonwealth was formed at Nashville in 1780 are several German ones; the bearers we find, as we pursue the history of early Tennessee, meeting with tragic fates sometimes. Besides Mansker— who, indeed, lived to a green old age, owning one of the best mills in the settlement—we find Coonrod, crushed by a falling tree on the site of Nashville, and Jacob Stump, killed by Indians in his field, while his father, "old Fred Stump," just escaped with his life by running; "By sure, I did run dat time," the old German was wont to say, looking back upon his experience. He was a rival of Mansker in the milling business in later and more peaceful times.

Abram and Isaac Hite were surveyors, early settlers, and explorers of those times; Abram was one of the party who, in 1774, cut down the first trees on the present site of Cincinnati. Isaac was one of the surveying party brought home by Stoner and Boone; he led a company of adventurers to Harrod's station in 1774; he "raised corn" in the country, and sat in the Transylvania legislature which met under the elm-tree in 1775, and—not contented with the too-peaceful life of Harrod's station—he went with an exploring party south as far as Bowling Green. He and "Abram Hite, Jr.," were part of the garrison of Harrodsburg in the winter of 1777–78, and he went with the second expedition to Maryland after powder and (more courageous than the first) brought it across the wilderness to the garrison.

It is probable that the Hites were descendants of that Jost Heit who led the Pennsylvania Germans into the Valley of Virginia; the Bowmans we know descended from Heit's son-in-law, who was one of that patriarchal train who had come a generation before to settle what was then the wilderness; and the wandering foot must have been an inheritance of the race.

John Bowman was one of the captains sent East to recruit men for Clark's expedition to the Illinois; another captain whose name shows his race was Leonard Helm; but, indeed, a large proportion of this expedition was probably drawn from the Germans of the Valley, for Governor Patrick Henry feared the weakening of the sea-board people in their Revolutionary struggle by recruiting many men among them, and specially ordered that the companies be raised west of the Blue Ridge.

We know the story of how Clark and his backwoodsmen surprised and captured the British posts. Captain Bowman received the surrender of Cahokia, and Captain Helm was put in command of the captured Vincennes, which was soon taken by the British and Helm retained as a prisoner. Most of his tiny garrison had been cut off, and resistance was impossible; but the heroic story of his marching out, accompanied by one soldier, with

the honors of war on account of his brave defence, has
not much authority, and we must surrender the tale as
reluctantly as Helm did the fort.

Bowman was the commander of one of the companies which the undaunted Clark took on his terrible
march to reconquer Vincennes, and it is to him that we
owe the best account, his contemporary "journal" of
the expedition. His jottings picture it all to us better
than the lengthy descriptions of formal historians: "The
road very bad from the immense quantity of rain that
had fallen. The men much fatigued." "Marched all
day thro' rain and water. Our provisions began to be
short." "Many of the men much cast down, particularly the volunteers." "Camp very quiet but hungry;
some almost in despair." "Our pilots say we cannot
get along—that it is impossible." "Heard the morning
and evening guns from the fort. No provisions yet.
Lord, help us!'" "Set off to cross the Horse-Shoe
plain about four miles long all covered with water breast
high. Here we expected some of our brave men must
certainly perish, having froze in the night and so long
fasting. Having no other resource than wading this
plain or rather lake of waters we plunged into it with
courage. Never were men so animated with the thought
of avenging the wrongs done the back settlements as
this small army was." And never surely did a handful
of frozen, starving men make so glorious a conquest as
this, when Post St. Vincents and the whole British possession of the Northwest Territory fell before them.

We have a whimsical picture of the captive Helm
comfortably drinking apple-toddy with the commandant
when Clark's half-perished heroes began to fire upon

the post, a picture perhaps not exact, but certainly well invented, for the gallant Helm was fond of the pleasures of the table.

Soon after, we see him free and in arms again, on an expedition to intercept stores for what Bowman calls phonetically Omi (by which he means Aux Miami, the present site of Fort Wayne), which is brilliantly successful. "He took seven boats loaded with provisions," writes Bowman, who was disabled from active service now by an accidental explosion of powder in firing the thirteen guns which announced the cession of the fort to the Americans. Presently Bowman notes that Helm is left to command the town in all civil matters, and that "the boats are run out of sight" with the prisoners for Kaskaskia—"God send a good and safe passage," prays the pious Bowman.

When Bowman returned to Kentucky we do not know ; some time after we find him in command of the expedition against the Indian town of Old Chillicothe, where he was thought to have shown "torpor" in attacking the strong and well-defended place. Boone says, guardedly, that the expedition turned out "not to the advantage of Colonel Bowman's party," which was attacked on its retreat, and only enabled to get off by the exertions of Major Bedinger and a few other determined men, who dashed into the bushes on horse back, scoured the woods in every direction, and cut down as many of the Indians as they could overtake.

This Major George Michael Bedinger, who, having "been in the war to the eastward," had been appointed adjutant of the Chillicothe expedition, might be taken as a typical figure of the later pioneer and settler of Kentucky. Born in Pennsylvania, taken to Virginia as a child, he grew up on the border. At the house of his widowed mother was held the first gathering of Stephenson's riflemen. His elder brother, Henry, was a sergeant in the company which George Michael also joined. He was at the siege of Boston and also at Fort Washington, where he was taken prisoner but—more fortunate than his brother—was soon exchanged.

Meanwhile, a third of the widow Bedinger's sons, Daniel, a lad of sixteen, had run away to join the patriot army, and was also a prisoner, taken at Brandywine. When the British evacuated Philadelphia, George Michael went there and found the boy Daniel, apparently dying, on a pile of straw in a deserted British hospital. "Michael knelt by the side of the poor emaciated boy, took him in his arms, and carried him to a house where he could procure some comforts in the way of food. He got an arm-chair and some leather straps, put Daniel in the chair, swung him by the strap on his back, and carried him some miles into the country to a farmhouse. Daniel was very impatient to travel, and left before he was well able to walk, while Michael walked by his side with his arm around him to support him. Thus they travelled from Philadelphia to Shepherdstown."

Soon after, George Michael emigrated to Kentucky, and we find him with a party of ten others from his old neighborhood "improving land" on the Licking. He had been in Kentucky but a few months when he was called to go on the expedition to Chillicothe ; three years after, at the disastrous rout of the Blue Licks, Major Bedinger is said to have again "borne himself gallantly as a brave and efficient officer." He lived to marry one of the Clay family, be the proprietor of the famous Blue Licks, and die there full of years and honors.

To mention all the German pioneers whose deeds and names are recorded would fill a book in itself. German names are abundant on the rolls of service of the militia companies, particularly those of Bowman and Holder; we hear that in Woodford County, there was "quite a respectable number of families from Germany." Tradition has preserved the speech of a Mrs. Coffman, whose nationality shows through the disguised spelling; when informed that the Indians had killed her husband, the bereaved widow asserted that "she would rather have lost her best cow than her old man."

More heroic figures are the backwoodsmen Crist and Crepps, who, attacked with thirteen others,—one a woman,—while on a salt-making expedition, managed to defend their boat until half their men were killed; then the two left the boat, but Crepps fell mortally wounded soon after. He was found and brought into a fort to die, while the rough backwoodsmen, never prone to enthusiasm, lamented over the "tall, fair, handsome man, kind, brave, and enterprising, the lion of the fight," exposing himself with cool courage in the vain hope of saving the others.

Crist, his companion, dragged himself through the woods; he could not walk, a bullet had crushed the bones of his heel. He bound his moccasons on his knees and crawled on. At night he came to an Indian camp-fire, but was not seen, and crept through a little "branch" or stream that he might leave no trace. His clothes were torn to rags, his wounded leg was so stiff

285

and swollen that he could only drag it after him. After four days of such crawling, with no food and but little water, he came in sight of Bullitt's Lick. He called for help, but a passing negro thought it an alarm of approaching Indians and rushed away. The white men at the Lick were more clear-headed; they came out to search the woods, found Crist, unable to lift a hand, and carried him to the settlement. "His recovery," says the chronicler, "was slow and doubtful, it was a year before he was a man again;" but he lived to be old and hale.

One more type of the German pioneer must be mentioned—the fierce, implacable, unscrupulous Indian fighter, the terror of the red men, and the darling of the rougher element on the border, Lewis Wetzel. He had once been wounded and taken prisoner, with a younger brother, by the Indians, but he soon escaped, showing a coolness and daring at his early age—he was but fourteen—which many older men might envy. His father was afterwards killed by the Indians, and he and a brother vowed that thereafter so long as they lived they would kill every Indian they could. They fulfilled this pious engagement nobly; it is said that Lewis Wetzel took more scalps than the two armies of St. Clair and Braddock put together.

Lewis would go hunting Indians as other men hunt game; both he and his brother killed Indians who came to treat under promise of safe-conduct. He slaughtered the savages under any circumstances of barbarity, treachery, and personal danger; yet withal he was so admired that when an American general arrested him for one of his murders, a plot was formed to assassinate the arresting officer, the whole country was in a flame, and petitions for his release poured in. He is described as a man of powerful frame, with piercing black eyes, and hair which, when he unbound it, fell to his knees. It will be recollected that Kenton's opponent in his early fight had such hair, and that Kenton gained the victory over him by winding the man's locks about a tree and thrashing him—as Kenton thought, to death— in this Absalom-like posture.

The frontiers of North Carolina contained many Germans, mostly emigrants from Pennsylvania. Here partisan warfare, with its barbarities and cruelties, its assassination and satisfaction of private grudges under color of a public cause, raged in all its shamefulness.

At the time after Charleston had fallen, when Cornwallis was overrunning the State and many of the most determined patriots—men like Pickens and Hayne— were reduced to " take British protection," as it was then called, many of the more peaceable and simple-minded Germans of the frontier did likewise. A large proportion of the Tories attacked by the Whig militia at Ramsour's Mills in 1780 were of this class and unarmed, yet they made a stand against the militia, who scattered after the first few volleys and could not be brought together.

The wife of Christian Reinhardt had left her house at the beginning of the skirmish and taken refuge in a neighboring canebrake. Here a frightened deer came, looked for a moment at the cowering woman and her little children and dashed off. When the fight was over, Mrs. Reinhardt returned to her home, to find the house, the stables, and even the smoke-house filled with the dead and wounded. She gave so freely of her sheets and blankets as winding-sheets for the dead that in a short time she had no linen left.

The Toryism of the residents about Ramsour's Mills must have been assumed only under stress of circumstances, for when Cornwallis afterwards marched through the locality his Hessians fraternized with the Germans there to such disastrous effect that many of the mercenaries deserted from the British service.

Mecklenburg County, though its inhabitants were mostly Scotch-Irish, had a few Germans, and the name of one, John Phifer (Pfeifer), is among the signers of the famous, if rather dubious, " Mecklenburg Declaration." Phifer was afterwards a minute-man, and a member of the Provincial Conventions of 1775 and 1776, but died early.

Another German, Frederick Hambright, brought as a child from Germany and afterwards emigrating to North Carolina after a residence in Virginia, traces for us the course of most of the Germans populating the old North State. He left relatives in Pennsylvania, where we have seen John Hambright vigorously administering the affairs of the Northumberland County Committee of Safety. Frederick Hambright was also one of the Associators of Tryon—afterwards Lincoln—County, in his new home, with such other Germans or Swiss as the Forneys, Seitz, and many unmistakable names. He performed many "tours of duty" as a militiaman, and sat also in the Provincial Convention of 1775.

When in 1780 the call was issued for the gathering of the bordermen to take Ferguson at King's Mountain, such a man as Hambright could not be missing, and ac-

cordingly he and his son John marched to meet the
"over-mountain men." By the departure of their
colonel Hambright would have succeeded to the command, but on account of his age—he was then over
fifty—it was thought best to appoint a younger man.
But the Pennsylvanian German cared too much for the
cause to be angered by the slight, and when subsequently
this officer was killed he took the command which was
his by right.

On the way to attack the British, the intelligence was
brought in that Ferguson was to be known by the richness of his uniform, but that he had on a checked shirt
over it. The German frontiersman instantly called the
attention of his "South Fork boys" to this. "Well,
poys," he said, in his German accent, "when you see
dat man mit a pig shirt on over his clothes, you may
know him who he is;" and they did know him, and with
their unerring Deckhard rifles (made in Pennsylvania-
German Lancaster and esteemed the best rifle on the
frontier) they brought down the British officer.

During one of the gallant charges with which the
English turned back the steady climbing of the riflemen
up the mountain—only to have them return, take trees,
and resume the attack—Hambright was wounded in the
thigh; he would not speak of it, but when it was discovered by his men and they urged him to leave the
field, he answered that "he knew he was wounded, but
he was not sick or faint; he could still ride very well,
and he deemed it his duty to fight on till the battle was
over." When he was taken from his horse after the
battle, the blood had filled his boot. He remained per-
manently lame from the injury. Afterwards he said he

had been afraid that if he had given up, his men would have neglected " to load and fire as often as they should ; they might have stopped fighting to care for him,"— which was not what the resolute old man would have approved. He left a numerous posterity to inherit his fame, being the father of twenty-two children ; he lived to ninety years of age, an elder in the Shiloh Presbyterian Church—peaceful name !

One of Hambright's soldiers, Abram Forney, a Swiss, after the fight saved the life of a Tory neighbor who besought him earnestly to "get him out of this bull-pen," promising faithful service to the patriot cause,—which promise he redeemed, for he fought well at Guilford Courthouse in the next year. Forney, who belonged to an earnestly patriotic family and had much Tory plundering to revenge, being at Guilford Courthouse himself, found his term of enlistment expired before the battle, but could not refrain from staying " to see the shooting-match," as he expressed it.

They were a resolute, hard-fighting, hard-hitting set of men—these mountaineers of the wilderness ; but in spite of their lack of discipline, their Indian-like uselessness for a regular campaign, and their many other failings, one cannot but admire the cool courage of men to whom a battle was "a shooting-match," or who, wounded and bleeding, " deemed it their duty to fight on."

The last incident of Revolutionary history which affects the Germans is one in which they were the victims and not the aggressors : the massacre of the Moravian converts at Gnadenhütten. Among the militia, fierce and lawless, who did this shameful thing there were no Germans. They were Scotch-Irish borderers from Western

"The Rear-Guard of the Revolution"

Pennsylvania who were urged to it by indiscriminating hatred of all Indians, whether or not they had done the white men harm.

The Indian missions of the Moravian church in the Tuscarawas Valley of Ohio were prosperous and beautiful villages, the wonder and admiration of both white and native visitors ; they had churches and schools, comfortable log houses, good plantations, and farm-yards filled with cattle and poultry. During the whole course of the Revolutionary War, the Moravian missionaries, with the help of the " national assistants" or converted Indian helpers, had succeeded in keeping their converts from taking part in hostilities on either side, the Brethren's Unity having, like the Friends, a testimony against war. But renegade Moravian Indians may have taken part in border forays, though they were expelled from the church when this was known ; and the dangerous laws of Indian hospitality made it incumbent upon the people of Gnadenhütten to entertain all comers, whether war parties bound for the settlements or Brodhead's American troops on their way against the savage Indians. Often the missionaries succeeded in turning back these war parties ; Zeisberger and Heckewelder also sent early intelligence to Fort Pitt of any projected Indian forays, and often saved the frontiers by this means, but these communications were necessarily confidential, known only to the commanding officers at the fort, and therefore did nothing to allay the popular distrust.

There was suspicion on the border that the Christian towns of the Tuscarawas were "half-way houses" for their hated assailants, and when, in the spring of 1782, a family of Scotch settlers were murdered, a company of

Western Pennsylvania militia, led by Colonel Williamson, was raised to revenge this deed upon its supposed authors, the Moravian converts.

The winter before, the Hurons and other heathen tribes had descended upon Gnadenhütten and taken away all its inhabitants as prisoners to the British garrison at Detroit. After a miserable winter a remnant of the Christian Indians, plundered and poor, had obtained permission to return to the villages of Gnadenhütten and Salem to make a crop and to gather together their household utensils, farming implements, and all the property which they had hidden when the Hurons took them away into captivity.

The day was set for the Moravian Indians' departure northward, when the war-party which had just done the massacre came through the town, selling the property of their victims (after the Indian custom) while camped a mile from Gnadenhütten. The one captive whom they had taken alive urged the Moravian Indians to flee ; he was sure, he said, that the party would be tracked to that place and the Christian Indians involved in indiscriminate revenge. But the people decided, after a council, to remain until they could gather together their property, "relying, in the event of the appearance of American militia, on their innocence and their common religion."

It proved a vain reliance. Williamson's party reached the settlement and announced that they had come to guard the Indians into safety at Fort Pitt. The national assistant at Salem, John Martin, hastened to his town with the news ; there old Israel, a former chief, brought out his sacred belts of wampum, which he had received when a chief and which pledged the faith and friendship

of the Americans, and reassured by the sight of these
sacred tokens Martin and his people consented to go
with the party to Fort Pitt.   Martin, delighted with the
kindness of the militia commander, opened his heart to
him, telling of the hopes of the converts that they might
have a church school in their new place of refuge;
"they would send to Bethlehem for teachers and ministers," he said; "did not the colonel think it a good
plan?" Colonel Williamson approved it, and his men, to
whom it was mentioned, "praised the Indians for their
piety."

The Salem people were brought in under guard; they
gave their new friends their guns "for safe keeping"
and acquiesced in the burning of their houses " to prevent war parties from harboring there;" besides, they
said, joyfully, had not the Christian American soldiers
promised them a much better town where they were
going? Those Indians who spoke English rejoiced in
"the opportunity to glorify their God," and preached to
the militia. "Truly you are good Christians!" remarked
the militiamen. The Indian boys, of whom there were
many in the settlement,—for the harvesting party had
consisted, after Indian custom, mainly of women and
children,—frolicked with some of the half-grown boys
of the frontier levy and taught them how to make bows
and arrows.

As the Salem people came to the bank of the stream
opposite Gnadenhütten, the militia seized and bound
them, and forcing them across the river, they found the
rest of the Indians there under guard, imprisoned in
two houses. A rude sort of trial was then held,—or
rather a tumultuous discussion,—in which the militia

accused the Indians of having taken part in the war and plundered the settlements. Some articles, of those sold by the marauding party, were found in the Indians' possession, and this was thought a proof of guilt. The Indians defended themselves against the charges, but in vain.

Finally, Williamson—whose fault was, as Doddridge says, "a too easy compliance with popular opinion and popular prejudice"—made an attempt to save the prisoners by asking a vote on the question whether the Christian Indians should be taken to Fort Pitt or put to death ; only eighteen of his ninety men voted to spare their lives. Opinion was divided as to the mode of execution, whether to shut them in the houses and burn them alive, or tomahawk and scalp them ; the last was chosen in order that the scalps might be trophies of the campaign.

The Indians, after solemnly protesting their innocence, only asked time to prepare for death. They passed the night in prayer and the singing of hymns (which some of their murderers mistook for the warriors' death chant), and in the morning were led out in couples from the two houses which the American militia had nicknamed, with a ferocious pleasantry, "the slaughter-houses." The Indian, Abraham, whose long, flowing hair promised "a fine scalp," was the first to be dragged out by a rope, killed, and his coveted scalp secured.

When the men and boys were all killed, the work went on with the women and children ; one of the women, Christiana, who had been taught at Bethlehem, spoke English well, and was an educated and refined woman, fell on her knees to Williamson and begged for her life; "I cannot help you," he said, coldly, turning away. Two boys escaped, one to die afterwards from the results of his scalping wound. In all there perished twenty-nine men, twenty-seven women, and thirty-four children, twelve of them babies.

This deed was not done in the heat of passion, nor after innumerable provocations had been given by a daily slaughter such as reigned at that time on the Kentucky border; it was performed in cold blood, after its subjects had been promised safe-conduct, disarmed, and deceived by those who pretended to be friends, protectors, and fellow-Christians.

The militiamen returned to Western Pennsylvania boasting much of their deed. But no one since has felt any inclination to boast of the shameful and treacherous action of these borderers. It is a misfortune that it counts as Revolutionary service, and that a few of the names of the men who did it, with which Doddridge refused "to stain his page," are preserved among the rolls of the Pennsylvanian soldiers of the Revolution.

The contemporaries of the murderers of Gnadenhütten viewed the deed much as we do after the lapse of a century. The reverend annalist of the border just quoted calls it "an atrocious and unqualified murder;" Colonel James Smith, who had suffered many things in Indian captivity and was a brave and determined Indian fighter, named it "an act of barbarity equal to anything I ever knew to be committed by the savages themselves except the burning of prisoners,"—and, as we have seen, Williamson's men considered this method of killing, but relinquished it in order to get scalps. Stover, who escaped from the wreck of the Crawford expedition after unimaginable exertions and sufferings, said, in his simple "Narrative," "I am far from approving the Moravian slaughter;" and after speaking of the few wild Indians (possibly six in number) who were caught and involved in the general destruction, Stover continued, "But the putting to death of the women and children who sang hymns at their execution must be considered as unjustifiable, inexcusable homicide, and the colonel who commanded the party, and who is said perseveringly, contrary to the remonstrance of officers present, to have enjoined the perpetration of the act, is a disgrace to the State of Pennsylvania." Colonel Gibson, who commanded at Fort Pitt, wrote of "the late horrid Massacre perpetrated at the Towns on Muskingum, By a set of men, the most savage Miscreants that ever degraded human nature." It is a relief to turn from these furious denunciations, wrung from brave frontiersmen by the horror of the deed, to the words of the heathen Indians concerning the same slaughter : "We sought to compel our Christian countrymen to return to the wild sins in which we live ; but the great Manitou loved them too well ; he saw our schemes ; he saw their pious lives ; he took them."

We have traced the annals of the colonial Germans from the peaceful idyls of Germantown and the Rosicrucians beside the Wissahickon, through the Great Exodus of the "poor Palatines ;" we have seen the kindly province of Penn filling with "defenceless" Mennonites, the outlawed Schwenkfelder, the Dunkers and their strange fanatic outgrowth, the Ephrata cloister. And later we have seen such sturdy pioneers as Jost Heit and Schley and Conrad Weiser, such saints and confessors as the exiled Salzburgers and the hopeful, fearless Moravians ; men like Post at the Indian council-fires, or Bouquet and his Royal Americans at Bushy Run breaking victoriously through the ring of yelling savages. We have learnt the strange or pathetic adventures of the poor redemptioners, seen the industry of the German farmers, heard the clatter of the German press and the quaint comments of Saur and Miller on passing events. And, last of all, we have traced the part of the Germans in the Revolution—from that lad of the Shenandoah Valley who was a guest at the Boston Tea Party, and the border riflemen who " began their march the nearest road to Boston this day," to Peter Muhlenberg leading the final assault on the British lines at Yorktown, the pioneers of Kentucky and Tennessee, the men of Clark's march to Vincennes, and the riflemen of King's Mountain. In these days—when a mistaken emphasis is put upon the purely English descent of the American people—it may be well to know that there were other than English strains in that which was to be the American nation ; and that besides Hollander and Huguenot, Swede and Creole, there were Germans who bore a manful part, who dared and suffered, fought and wrought in the making of the new Nation.

CHRONOLOGICAL TABLE OF THE GERMAN COLONIAL EMIGRATION

1683. Arrival of the Germantown colonists in the "Concord," October 6 (16).

1684. The Labadists in Maryland.

1694. Community of " Das Weib in der Wüste."

1702. Settlement on the Skippack, Montgomery County, Pennsylvania.

1708. Kocherthal's colony at Newburg on the Hudson.

1709. The Great Exodus.

1709–10. Colony of Palatines settle in Ireland.

1710. Settlement of Newbern, North Carolina, under de Graffenried.

1710. Palatine colony in New York. Settlement at Oley, Berks County, Pennsylvania.

1712. Flight of the Palatines to Schoharie. Newbern colonists go to Germanna, Virginia.

1713. First record of Germans in German Valley, New Jersey.

1718. First emigration of the Dunkers.

1719. Law's colony on the Mississippi.

1720. Conrad Beissel arrives in Pennsylvania.

1723. Flight of Schoharie colonists to Tulpehocken.

1729. Quitopahilla (Lebanon County) settlement.

1730. Beginning of community at Ephrata.

1731. "Conewago settlements" of York County, Pennsylvania.

1732. Purryeburg, South Carolina. Jost Heit's colony enters the Shenandoah Valley. Weiser made Indian interpreter for province of Pennsylvania.

1733. Emigration of the Schwenkfelder.

1734. First emigration of the Salzburgers to Georgia.

1735. Settlement of Orangeburg District, South Carolina. Arrival of Schley's colony at Monocacy (Frederick), Maryland. The Zenger trial.

1736. Frederica, Georgia. "Great Embarkation" of the Salzburgers. First Moravian emigration to Georgia.

1737. Saxe-Gotha, South Carolina.

1738. Christopher Dock's school. Foundation of Saur's press.

1739. Jonathan Hager founds Elizabeth (Hager's) Town.

1740? First Settlement of Broad Bay (Waldoboro), Maine. Moravians begin settlement in Pennsylvania.

Chronological Table

1741. Arrival of Zinzendorf. Founding of Bethlehem.
1742. Arrival of Muhlenberg. Zauberbühler brings colonists to Broad Bay.
1743. Nazareth, Pennsylvania.
1745. Arrival of Schlatter. Beginning of Ephrata press. First edition of Saur's "Germantown Bible." German Schools controversy.
1746. Moravian settlement at Graceham, Maryland.
1747. Bellêtre's invasion of the Mohawk Valley.
1748. Bellêtre's second invasion. Ephrata press prints the "Martyr-book."
1749. New Germantown (Braintree), Massachusetts.
1750. Beginning of Pennsylvania-German emigration to North Carolina.
1753. Frankfort (Dresden), Maine. Moravians begin settlement on the Wachovia tract, North Carolina.
1755. Braddock's defeat; beginning of the French and Indian War.
1756. Fryeburg, Maine.
1757. Death of the Eckerlins. Capture of Fort Duquesne.
1758. Death of the elder Saur. Post's journeys.
1760. Death of Conrad Weiser. New Germantown (Braintree) colonists go to Broad Bay. Foundation of Heinrich Miller's press.
1763. Stümpel's colonists. Bouquet at Bushy Run.
1764. The younger Saur begins "Geistliches Magazien."
1765. Founding of the Deutsche Gesellschaft in Philadelphia.
1766. Deutsche Gesellschaft in Charleston, South Carolina.
1768. Death of Beissel.
1769–70. Caspar Mansker and the "Long Hunters."
1770. Jäger in Kentucky. First emigration of Broad Bay Moravians to North Carolina.
1772. Moravians found Gnadenhütten in Ohio.
1773. Second emigration from Broad Bay to North Carolina.
1774–75. Germans delegates to Provincial Conventions.
1775. Germans on Revolutionary Committees and as Associators. Collections for the poor of Boston. Riflemen from Virginia, Maryland, and Pennsylvania.
1776. Muhlenberg throws off the gown.
1777. Christoph Ludwig appointed Superintendent of Baking in the Continental army. Battle of Oriskany. Arrival of Steuben.
1778. Muhlenberg at Brandywine. "Moll Pitcher" at Monmouth. Clark's expedition against Vincennes.
1779. Publication of Steuben's "Rules."
1780. Death of De Kalb at Camden. King's Mountain.
1782. Battle of the Blue Licks. Gnadenhütten massacre.
1783. End of the Revolutionary War and of the Colonial period.

LIST OF WORKS CONSULTED

I. GENERAL SUBJECTS.

Der Deutsche Pionier. Cincinnati, 1869–85.

Deutsch-americanisches Magazin. H. A. Ratterman, editor. Cincinnati, 1886.

Goebel: Geschichte des christlichen Lebens in westphal-rheinischen Pfalz. Coblenz, 3 vols., 1852–1862.

Hallesche Nachrichten. Halle a. S., 1787.

The same, partially republished, with notes by W. J. Mann and W. Germann. Allentown and Halle, 1886–92.

The same, partially translated by J. Oswald. Philadelphia, 1880–82.

The same, partially translated by Schaeffer. Reading, 1882.

Löher: Die Deutschen in America. Göttingen, 1855.

Pennsylvania German Society; Proceedings and Addresses. 1891–98.

Pennypacker: Historical and Biographical Sketches. Philadelphia, 1883.

Schlosser: Geschichte des 18ten Jahrhunderts.

The same, translated by D. Davison. London, 1843–52.

Seidensticker: Bilder aus der deutsch-pennsylvanischen Geschichte. New York, 1885.

Seidensticker: Geschichte der Deutsche Gesellschaft. Philadelphia, 1876.

Walton and Brumbaugh : Stones of Pennsylvania. American Book Company. New York, Cincinnati, and Chicago, 1877.

II. SPECIAL SUBJECTS.

Alice Morse Earle : Newspaper Women of Colonial Times. Independent, August 15, 1895.

C. W. Butterfield: History of the Girtys. Cincinnati, 1890.

Rupp : History of Berks County, Pennsylvania. Lancaster, 1844.

Kercheval : History of the Valley of Virginia. Winchester, 1833.

Doddridge : Notes on the Settlement and Indian Wars of the Western Parts of Virginia and Pennsylvania. Wellsburgh, 1824.

Proceedings of the Society for History of Germans in Maryland. 1887.

Scharf: History of Western Maryland. Philadelphia, 1882.

List of Works Consulted

Scharf: History of Maryland. Baltimore, 1879.

McMahon: Historical View of the Government of Maryland. Baltimore, 1831.

Dictionary of National Biography. New York and London, 1892—arts. Law of Lauriston and Oglethorpe.

Bernheim: History of German settlements and of Lutheran Church in North and South Carolina. Philadelphia, 1872.

Memorial of Jean Pierre Pury in behalf of the colonization of South Carolina. London, 1724; reprinted, Augusta, Georgia, 1880.

Mills (?): Atlas of South Carolina. 1826.

Howard M. Jenkins: The Schwenkfelder. Reprinted from "Friends' Quarterly Examiner," London, 1896.

Stevens: History of Georgia. New York, 1847–59.

Hewatt: Historical Account of Colonies of South Carolina and Georgia. London, 1779.

Historical Collections of South Carolina. New York, 1836.

Dalcho: History of Episcopal Church in South Carolina. Charleston, 1820.

Howe: History of Presbyterian Church in South Carolina. Columbia, 1870.

Whitney (Edson L.): Government of Colony of South Carolina: (J. H. U. studies). Baltimore, 1895.

Mills: Statistics of South Carolina. Charleston, 1826.

Egle: History of Pennsylvania. Harrisburg, 1876.

William Gilmore Sims: History of South Carolina (contains Mitchell's map, 1844). Charleston, 1842.

Joseph Williamson: Bibliography of Maine. Portland, 1896.

Maine Historical Collections, Vols. V. and VI.

John W. Jordan: Moravian Mission at Broad Bay, Maine. Bethlehem, 1891.

Williamson: History of Maine. Hallowell, 1832.

Eaton: Annals of Warren [Maine]. Hallowell, 1851; (second edition, enlarged) 1877.

Pattee: History of Braintree [Massachusetts]. Quincy, 1878.

Holmes: American Annals. Cambridge, Massachusetts, 1805.

J. G. Holland: History of Western Massachusetts. Springfield, 1855.

C. Heydrick: Genealogical Record of the Descendants of the Schwenkfelder. Manayunk (Pennsylvania), 1879.

Kurtz (translated by J. Robertson Nicoll): Church History. New York and London.

Barclay: Religious Societies of the Commonwealth. London, 1876.

——: Kaspar v. Schwenkfeld and die Schwenkfelder. Lauban, 1860.

The Germans in Colonial Times

Sydney George Fisher: Making of Pennsylvania. Philadelphia, 1896.

Journals of Von Reck and Boltzius. London, 1734.

Urlsperger: Ausführliche Nachrichten von den Salzburgischen Emigranten. Halle, 1735.

Henry E. Jacobs: History of the Lutheran Church in the United States. (Vol. IV. of American Church History Series.) New York, 1893.

Strobel: History of the Salzburgers. Baltimore, 1855.

Hazelius: History of the American Lutheran Church. Zanesville, 1846.

Jones: Dead Towns of Georgia. (In Georgia Historical Collections, Vol. IV.) Savannah, 1878.

W. J. Mann: Life of H. M. Muhlenberg. Philadelphia, 1887.

M. L. Stoever: Life and Times of Muhlenberg. Philadelphia, 1883.

[Helmuth]: Denkmal der Liebe u. Achtung. Philadelphia, 1788.

C. Z. Weiser: Life of Conrad Weiser. Reading, 1876.

W. L Montgomery: Lecture on the Life and Times of Conrad Weiser. Reading, n. d.

C. Fr. Post: Journals. (Reprinted in Rupp's History of Western Pennsylvania. Pittsburg and Harrisburg, 1846.)

Kapp: Die Deutschen im Staate New York. New York, 1868.

Pritts: Border Warfare. Abingdon, Virginia, 1849.

Frontier Forts of Pennsylvania. Printed by the State, 1896.

Williamson: History of North Carolina. Philadelphia, 1812.

Ramsay: History of South Carolina. Charleston, 1809.

Rev. William Smith: Historical Account of Bouquet's expedition against Ohio Indians. (Republished in Ohio Valley Historical Series. Cincinnati, 1868.)

Cort: Colonel Henry Bouquet and his Campaigns. Lancaster, Pennsylvania, 1883.

Seidenstücker: First Century of German Printing in America. Philadelphia, 1893.

Harbaugh: Life of Michael Schlatter. Philadelphia, 1857.

H. W. Smith; Life and Correspondence of Rev. William Smith. Philadelphia, 1889.

L. T. Reichel: Early History of Moravians in North America (Vol. III. of Moravian Historical Society Transactions). Nazareth, Pennsylvania, 1888.

Concise History of Unitas Fratrum. London, 1862.

De Schweinitz: Moravian Manual. Bethlehem, 1869.

E. H. Reichel, editor: Historical Sketch of Church and Missions of the Moravians. Bethlehem, 1848.

L. T. Reichel: Moravians in North Carolina. Salem, North Carolina, 1857.

List of Works Consulted

Loskiel: History of Missions of the United Brethren to the Indians. Translated by C. I. Latrobe. London, 1794.

J. G. Rosengarten: German Soldier in the Wars of the United States. Second edition, Philadelphia, 1890.

Parkman: Conspiracy of Pontiac. Boston, 1855.

Rupp: Thirty Thousand Names of German Emigrants. Philadelphia, 1876.

G. Mittleberger: Journey to Pennsylvania. Translated by C. T. Eben. Philadelphia, 1898.

Bruce: Economic History of Virginia in the Seventeenth Century. New York and London, 1896.

T. F. Chambers: Early Germans of New Jersey. Dover, 1895.

E. K. Martin: The Mennonites. Philadelphia, 1883.

J. F. Sachse: German Pietists of Provincial Pennsylvania. Philadelphia, 1895.

M. D. Learned: Pennsylvania-German Dialect. Baltimore, 1889.

Rupp: History of Dauphin County, etc. Lancaster, 1846.

R. E. Thompson; German Mystics as American Colonists. In Penn Monthly for August and September, 1871.

Bancroft: History of the United States. New York, 1888.

John Esten Cooke: Virginia (in American Commonwealths Series). Boston, 1883.

Waddell: Annals of Augusta County, Virginia, Richmond, 1886.

McSherry: History of Maryland. Baltimore, 1849.

Case of the German emigrants settled in the British Colonies of Pennsylvania and the back parts of Maryland, Virginia, etc. London, 1754.

Burk, continued by Jones and Girardin: History of Virginia. Petersburg, Virginia, 1804–16.

Jefferson: Notes on State of Virginia. Boston, 1802; new edition, 1853.

Charles B. Coale: Life and Adventures of Wilburn Waters, embracing the history of Southwestern Virginia. Richmond, 1878.

Benton: History of Herkimer County and Upper Mohawk Valley. Albany, 1856.

William W. Campbell: Annals of Tryon County, New York. New York, 1831.

Simms: Frontiersmen of New York. Albany, 1882–83.

Shaler: Kentucky (in American Commonwealths Series). Boston, 1888.

Roosevelt: Winning of the West. Vols. I. and II. New York and London, 1889.

Kapp: Life of Frederick William von Steuben. New York, 1859.

The Germans in Colonial Times

[Von Steuben] : Regulations for the Order and Discipline of the Troops of the United States. Philadelphia, 1779.

Kapp: Leben des Generals Johann Kalb. Stuttgart, 1862.

Charles Goepp: translation of the same. Privately printed. New York, 1870.

The same. New York (Holt & Co.), 1884.

Linn and Egle : Pennsylvania in the Revolution. Printed by the State, 1890–95.

Schreiben des Evangelischen Lutherischen und Reformirten Kirchen-raths wie auch den Beamten der Teutschen Gesellschaft an die Teutschen Einwohner der Provinzen von New York und Nord Carolina. Philadelphia, 1775.

J. H. Dubbs: Historic Manual of the (German) Reformed Church. Lancaster, 1885.

Lee and Agnew: Historical Record of the City of Savannah. Savannah, 1869.

Ramsay: Annals of Tennessee. Philadelphia, 1853.

Haywood : History of Tennessee. Nashville, 1891 (reprint of edition of 1823).

Putnam: History of Middle Tennessee. Nashville, 1859.

Centenary of Kentucky. Louisville, 1892.

Filson: Discovery, Settlement, and present State of Kentucky. London, 1793.

Green: Historic Families of Kentucky. Cincinnati, 1889.

Collins: Historical Sketches of Kentucky. Maysville (Kentucky), 1847.

H. Marshall: History of Kentucky. Frankfort (Kentucky), 1824.

Mann Butler: History of Kentucky. Louisville, 1834.

Allen: History of Kentucky. Louisville, 1872.

Lewis Collins, revised by R. H. Collins: History of Kentucky. Covington (Kentucky), 1878.

Speed: The Wilderness Road. Louisville, 1886.

Morehead : Settlement of Kentucky. Frankfort (Kentucky), 1840.

[Benjamin Rush] : Life and Character of Christopher Ludwick. Republished in report of Philadelphia Charity Schools. Philadelphia, 1860.

Hildeburn : A Century of Printing ; the Issues of the Press in Pennsylvania, 1685–1784. Philadelphia, 1885–86.

Chronicon Ephratense (translated by J. Max Hark). Lancaster, 1889.

Sanford H. Cobb : The Story of the Palatines. New York, 1897.

Abel Stevens : History of the Methodist Episcopal Church in the United States. New York, 1864.

Henry A. Muhlenberg: Life of General Peter Muhlenberg. Philadelphia, 1849.

List of Works Consulted

Henry Cabot Lodge : The Story of the Revolution. New York, 1898.

J. C. Stöver: Kurzte Nachricht von einer Evangelisch-Lutherischen Deutschen Gemeinde in Virginien. Hannover, 1737.

M. V. Smith: Governors of Virginia. Washington, 1893.

Norris: History of the Lower (Shenandoah) Valley. Chicago, 1890.

Fiske: Old Virginia and her Neighbors. Boston, 1897.

R. A. Brock, editor : Official Letters of Governor Alexander Spotswood. Richmond, 1882–85.

J. H. Wheeler: Historical Sketches of North Carolina. Philadelphia, 1851.

William Henry Foote : Sketches of North Carolina. New York, 1846.

C. L. Hunter: Sketches of Western North Carolina. Raleigh, 1877.

J. Hanno Deiler : Zur Geschichte der deutschen Kirchen-Gemeinde im Staate Louisiana. New Orleans, 1894.

Gayarré : History of Louisiana. New York, 1854.

Edmund de Schweinitz : Life and Times of David Zeisberger. Philadelphia, 1870.

Narratives of the Perils and Sufferings of John Slover and Dr. Knight. Cincinnati, 1867 ; reprinted from Nashville edition of 1843.

The Tryal of John Peter Zenger of New York, Printer ; who was lately tried & acquitted for printing & publishing a libel against the Government. Second edition. London, 1738.

David Schenck : North Carolina : 1780–81. Raleigh, 1889.

Lyman C. Draper : King's Mountain and its Heroes. Cincinnati, 1881.

Benjamin Rush: Manners of the German Inhabitants of Pennsylvania. (Republished from edition of 1789, with notes by I. D. Rupp.) 1875.

Cecil B. Hartley : Life of Lewis Wetzel ; also of Kenton and other Heroes of the West. Philadelphia, 1860.

James Adair: History of the American Indians. London, 1775.

Clark's Campaign in the Illinois ; containing Bowman's Journal. (Ohio Valley History Series, No. 3.) Cincinnati, 1860.

Hawks, Swain, and Graham : Revolutionary History of North Carolina. Raleigh and New York, 1843.

INDEX

✌✌

Alamance, 236
Albany, 54, 85, 190, 191, 236
Allegheny River, 198
Allentown, 252
Anabaptists, 27, 93, 164
André, 273
Andrustown, 264
Anne, Queen, 59, 63, 67, 68, 71, 186
Armand, 246
Armbrusters, 164-165
Armistead, 7
Arndt, 194
Arnold, 245
Arnold, Jonathan (see Steuben, Jonathan), 273, 274
Aughwick, 190
Aux Miami, 283

Baden, 21, 69
Baltimore, 224, 233, 256
Bancroft, 239, 270
Bayreuth, 274
Bedinger, David, 284
Bedinger, Geo. Michael, 268, 283-285
Bedinger, Henry, 268, 269, 284
Beissel, 99, 100-104, 152-154, 163, 164, 190, 253
Bell, 259
Bellêtre, 204
Berlin, 231
Berne, 72, 95, 122, 206
Bethabara, 181, 182, 200, 252
Bethania, 182
Bethlehem, 166, 173, 174, 176, 178-180, 183, 187, 192, 193, 198, 200, 252, 253, 256, 257, 293, 294
Biloxi, New, 91
Bingaman, 203
Blue Licks, 284, 285
Blue Ridge, 191, 281
"Blutige Schauplatz" ("Martyr-Book"), 164
Boeckels, 252

Boehme, 13, 42, 43, 47
Bohemia Manor, 39, 40, 41, 42
Bohemian Brethren, 168
Böhler, 171, 172
Bolzius, 126, 144, 149, 152
Boone, Daniel, 278, 280, 283
Boston, 100, 132, 133, 138, 155, 158, 243, 245, 255, 267, 268, 270, 284, 297
Bouquet, 186, 195, 206-214, 261, 297
Bowling Green, 281
Bowman, 115, 281
Bowman, Abraham, 269, 278
Bowman, John, 278, 281-283, 285
Braddock, 137, 159, 186, 187, 191, 198, 206, 210, 211, 261, 286
"Braddock's War" (see War, French and Indian)
Bradford, William, 225
Braintree, 130, 135, 136, 164
Brandywine, 246, 252, 253, 270, 284
Brant, 259, 264
Broad Bay (see Waldoboro)
Brodhead, 291
Brooke, 270
Buffalo Creek, 141
Bullitt's Lick, 286
Bumgardner, 267
Burgoyne, 259, 264
Burnet, Bishop, 67
Burr, 241
Bushy Run, 210, 297
Bussey, 194

Cahokia, 281
Cambridge, 245, 256, 268
Camden, 276
Canada, 205, 209, 245, 259
Canajoharie, 86
Carlisle, 212, 213, 250
Catholics, 14, 19, 62, 70, 71, 92, 106, 107, 110, 131, 143, 150
Charleston, 123, 126, 129, 145, 149, 224, 237, 287

307

Index

Index

Index

310

Index

311

Index

Index

Stoner, 278-280
Stony Point, 272
Stover, 295, 296
Strader, 278
Strasburg (Virginia), 115, 149, 159
Stümpel, 128
Stump family, 280
Sullivan, General, 221, 246
Sunbury, 199
Susquehanna, 86, 87, 114, 115, 118, 188, 193
Swabia, 17
Swift, 70
Switzerland, 25, 27, 93, 94, 121, 138, 238

Taneytown, 118
Tannebergers, the, 233
Tarleton, 257, 280
Tauler, 12, 13, 105
Teedyuscing, 196
Tennessee, 240, 277, 279, 280, 297
Tersteegan, 12, 15, 47
"Theologia Germanica," 12
Thornton, 221
Transylvania, 280
Trenton, 246
Treutlen, 237
Triebner, 237, 238
Tulpehocken, 87, 89, 90, 114, 188, 191, 230
Tuscarawas, 291
Tuscarora Indians, 73, 75
Tyrol, 142, 144

Ulmer, 111, 132-134, 139, 235
Urlsperger, 144
Urlsperger reports, 128

Valley Forge, 246, 271, 272, 274
Van Braght, 164
Van Rensselaer, 264
Van Sommelsdyk family, 37, 38, 41
Vincennes, 281, 282, 297
Virginia, 76, 77, 103, 112, 116, 119, 155, 181, 183-185, 188, 190, 200, 211, 221, 231, 239, 245, 267-270, 284, 288
Virginia, Valley of, 115, 149, 150, 159, 180, 200, 267, 269, 277, 281, 297

Wachovia, 179, 180, 236
Waldenses, 13, 19, 26
Waldo, General, 130-133, 138, 216
Waldo, Samuel, 134

Waldoboro, 111, 130, 135, 138, 140, 141, 235, 236
War Civil, 110
War, French and Indian, 137, 191-207, 211, 230, 236, 247, 258
War of the Spanish Succession, 17, 20, 58, 61
War, Peasant's, 27, 228
War, Seven Years', 17
War, Spanish-American, 138
War, Thirty Years', 11, 14, 17, 106
Washington, Colonel, 257, 280
Washington, George, 112, 190, 246, 247, 249, 250, 253, 254, 268, 271, 276
Wayne, General, 229
Weber heresy, 127
Weedon (von der Wieden), 270
Weiser, Conrad, 6, 84, 87, 101, 152, 186-198, 204, 297
Weiser, the elder, 82, 84, 85, 87, 88, 152, 225
Weissenfels, Catharine (Lady Johnson), 224, 225, 260
Weissenfels, Colonel, 206
Weitzel, 194
Weltner, 255, 256
Wesley, 78, 146, 171
West Camp, 81
Wetterholt, 194
Wetzel, 286, 287
Weyberg, 242
Wheating, 268
White Mountains, 138
Whitefield, 171-173, 179, 192
Whittier, 30, 46, 80
Wilderness Trace, 277
William of Orange, 27
Williamson, 292-295
Willing, Anne, 207
Winchester, 115, 149, 159, 200, 268
Wind Gap, 195
Wissahickon, Hermits of, 54, 103, 296 (see ' 'Woman in the Wilderness")
Witt, Dr., 49, 51
Wittmann, 254
Wolfe, 208
Wolmesdorf, 197
"Woman in the Wilderness," 32, 42-51
Woodstock, 115, 150, 159, 202, 269
"Wreck of the Palatine," 80
Würtemberg, 17, 20, 21, 42-44, 61, 62, 131, 132, 149, 217
Wyoming, 176, 189

313

Index

THE END